D0862524

AUTONOMY, GENDER, POLITICS

STUDIES IN FEMINIST PHILOSOPHY
Cheshire Calhoun, *Series Editor*

Published in the series:

Gender in the Mirror: Confounding Imagery
Diana Tietjens Meyers

Autonomy, Gender, Politics
Marilyn Friedman

AUTONOMY, GENDER, POLITICS

Marilyn Friedman

OXFORD
UNIVERSITY PRESS

2003

OXFORD
UNIVERSITY PRESS

Oxford   New York
Auckland   Bangkok   Buenos Aires   Cape Town   Chennai
Dar es Salaam   Delhi   Hong Kong   Istanbul   Karachi   Kolkata
Kuala Lumpur   Madrid   Melbourne   Mexico City   Mumbai   Nairobi
São Paulo   Shanghai   Taipei   Tokyo   Toronto

Copyright © 2003 by Oxford University Press, Inc.

Published by Oxford University Press, Inc.
198 Madison Avenue, New York, New York 10016

www.oup.com

Oxford is a registered trademark of Oxford University Press

Library of Congress Cataloging-in-Publication Data
Friedman, Marilyn, 1945–
Autonomy, gender, politics / Marilyn Friedman
p. cm.—(Studies in feminist philosophy)
Includes bibliographical references and index.
ISBN 0-19-513850-3; 0-19-513851-1 (pbk.)
1. Autonomy (Philosophy) 2. Feminist theory. I. Title. II. Series
B808.67 .F75 2002
305.42'01—dc21   2002034585

1 2 3 4 5 6 7 8 9

Printed in the United States of America
on acid-free paper

To Elizabeth

Preface

People are everywhere "reinventing" themselves. Social commentaries over-flow with optimistic tales of creative self-reformation and self-renewal. Re-inventing oneself is only the latest of many pop cultural tropes evoking the philosophical concept of personal autonomy. This resilient ideal reaches back to the origins of liberalism and shows no signs of an impending demise.

Traditionally, of course, autonomy has not been idealized for everyone. It has been emphasized much more for certain groups of men than for other groups of men or for any women. In Western liberal societies where the ideal has flourished, white men with middle- or upper-class pedigrees or ambitions have been more able than other social actors to lead autonomous lives. Canonical philosophers doubted that women had the requisite capacities for autonomy. Many social groups were prevented from living autonomously by systematic injustice, subordination, and oppression, conditions that have scarcely disappeared. The lingering force of these practices has prompted many feminists to view autonomy with suspicion and to challenge it as (white) male-biased. There is good reason when theorizing about autonomy to focus especially on a group for whom it has been historically inaccessible. This book focuses on women. If the case for the importance of autonomy can be made out with women in mind, it should be easier to make the case for others not so similarly dogged by past suppression.

Despite, or perhaps because of, those not-so-distant obstacles, autonomy, under various labels and in various guises, has long engrossed my attention. The ideas of living a life of "my own," being "true to my heart," standing up for "what I believe," and doing it "my way," have possessed an alluring plau-sibility. The usual provisos, of course, must apply: one should do others no harm and remain appropriately caring of them. Given those constraints, there is profound value, I believe, in the opportunity and the capacity to live accord-ing to one's own sense of a life worth living. Recent philosophical criticisms of autonomy by detractors who regard it as antithetical to important values have not, in the end, changed my mind. This book is partly a response to objections to autonomy, especially those grounded in sociopolitical, and not metaphysical, considerations.

The first chapter sets out my basic account of personal autonomy as a feature of choices and actions that reflect and are the result of wants, desires, cares, concerns, values, and commitments that the actor has reflectively reaffirmed and that she can sustain even in the face of some minimal opposition from others. The second chapter responds to various objections that have been raised to the coherence and meaningfulness of an ideal of personal autonomy such as this one. The third chapter presents an affirmative defense of autonomy. Taken together, these chapters provide the basic theoretical position of the book.

Each chapter of this book can be read independently of the others, especially the last six chapters. Chapters 4 and 5 investigate in greater depth a topic raised in the first three chapters, the social grounding of autonomy. Chapter 4 shows how feminist and mainstream philosophy have both been converging around this idea for some time. Chapter 5 develops a point made in preceding chapters that autonomy, although socially grounded, has an individualizing dimension, a dimension that I defend against the worries of critics. Chapters 6 and 7 study autonomy in regard to topics pertaining to intimate relationships: romantic love in chapter 6 and domestic violence in chapter 7. Chapters 8 and 9 look at autonomy in the wider realm of liberal theory, considering first John Rawls's recent approach to liberal political legitimacy (chapter 8) and then the policy question of how liberal states should deal with cultural minorities that appear to violate the rights of female members of those communities (chapter 9).

This book gestated for several years before finally emerging as a coherent whole. Over that time, I have talked with people too numerous to recall about the various issues in these pages. In accord with the by-now familiar contention of this book that autonomy is socially grounded, I know well how my own philosophical work has been nurtured by the arguments, insights, and imaginings of others and I am grateful to all of those persons. Alison Jaggar, Sara Buss, and Elizabeth Oljar, for example, each commented on an earlier, shorter version of one or another of these chapters at an American Philosophical Association meeting, and each asked perceptive questions that I hope I have answered. Catriona Mackenzie and Natalie Stoljar offered astute suggestions toward the revision of chapter 5 when I was preparing it for the volume they put together largely from the proceedings of a wonderful conference on autonomy and gender that they hosted at Australian National University in 1996. For several years, fertile ground for thought was provided by the St. Louis Autonomy Discussion Group, usually consisting of Joel Anderson, David Conway, Larry Davis, Sigurdur Kristinsson, Thad Metz, and Eleanor Stump. Thanks also to Joel Anderson for those "autonomy lunches" that helped to launch this project. Audiences at American University, Arizona State University, Australian National University, University of Chicago, University of Colorado, University of Illinois at Chicago, Hendrix College, Virginia Poly-technic Institute and State University, and the University of Western Ontario, as well as at meetings of the American Philosophical Association, the Feminist Ethics and Social Theory group (FEAST), and the Central States Philosophical Association all heard earlier versions of some of these chapters and made sober and discerning comments.

Thanks to Linda LeMoncheck for recruiting me for this exciting Oxford book series which I am proud to join. I am also greatly indebted to Peter Ohlin and Cheshire Calhoun for tolerating with infinite patience and grace my tardy completion of the manuscript and for ensuring its safe metamorphosis into book form.

Finally, and most of all, I thank my family for their essential support, with-out which I couldn't possibly have done it "my way." I am thrilled that Eliza-beth shows every sign of being determined to live an autonomous life, such as I could only dream about at her age, and doing it with zest and imagination. Larry's readiness to talk about anything and everything is a constant source of wit and wisdom. My gratitude is boundless for these and other immeasurable treasures.

Acknowledgments

Four of these chapters have been revised and reprinted from previously pub-lished versions. Chapter 4 first appeared in Diana Tietjens Meyers, ed., *Feminists Rethink the Self* (Boulder, Colo.: Westview, 1997), pp. 40–61. Chapter 5 first appeared in Catriona Mackenzie and Natalie Stoljar, eds., *Relational Autonomy: Feminist Perspectives on Autonomy, Agency, and the Social Self* (New York: Oxford University Press, 2000), pp. 35–51. Chapter 6 first appeared in *Midwest Studies in Philosophy* 22 (1998): 162–81. Chapter 8 first appeared in Victoria Davion and Clark Wolf, eds., *The Idea of a Political Liberalism: Essays on Rawls* (Lanham, Md.: Rowman & Littlefield, 2000), pp. 16–33. For permission to reprint those papers, I am very grateful to the above journal and presses.

Contents

I

THE BASIC ACCOUNT

1

A Conception of Autonomy

Autonomy is a controversial value. Prized by some, scorned by others, it generates ongoing debate. Much of the controversy stems, no doubt, from ambiguity. Not everyone understands autonomy in the same way. What some value as autonomy may not be what others are criticizing. Yet even if all sides could agree on what autonomy meant, disagreement would not simply vanish. This book presents, defends, and applies one conception of the ideal of personal autonomy.

In the first chapter, I set out my basic account of autonomy. In the second and third chapters, I provide a defense of its importance, with special attention to its value for women. As the title of this book indicates, gender concerns permeate many of the discussions. In the fourth and fifth chapters, I explore some social dimensions of autonomy and of the conditions required for its realization. The sixth and seventh chapters deal with issues of autonomy in the context of intimate relationships. The eighth and ninth chapters consider the importance of autonomy in broader political realms involving the state.

In this chapter, after setting out my basic account of autonomy, I consider its social context and dimensions. After that I explore the difference between a substantive and a content-neutral conception of autonomy, opting for the latter. This is followed by some thoughts about the prospects for autonomy under dangerous or oppressive conditions. I conclude this chapter with some remarks about possible counterexamples to my views.

The Basic Account

The term "autonomy" is largely a term of philosophic art, yet it encompasses an array of notions familiar to ordinary people, notions such as being "true to myself," doing it "my way," standing up for "what I believe," thinking "for myself," and, in gender-egalitarian reformulation, being one's "own person."

However unsystematic they might be, these ordinary notions of "folk" understanding provide touchstones for this project. They hint at an ideal that, while scarcely the only or even the supreme moral value, is nevertheless vital and momentous for a great multitude of human lives across many cultural boundaries and other human differences. This ideal of personal autonomy can be a particularly inspirational ideal for those who, in the course of living their lives, must cope with the all-too-familiar human wrongs of abuse, exploitation, domination, and oppression.

Autonomy is, of course, self-determination. Personal autonomy is self-determination by an individual self, a person. My account of autonomy revolves around a conception of what it is for choices and actions in particular to be autonomous. I sometimes refer to choices or actions indifferently as behavior.[1] Other autonomous phenomena may then be defined in terms of autonomous behavior. An autonomous person is someone who behaves autonomously with relative frequency. An autonomous life is one lived by an autonomous person.

Numerous distinctions are necessary when setting out an account of autonomy. One that is worth mentioning at the outset is that between the nature of autonomy itself, its constitutive conditions, and the causal conditions required for autonomy to be realized. The nature of autonomy itself consists of the conditions that choices and actions must meet in order to be autonomous. These conditions constitute autonomy. These are distinct from the causal conditions, both past and present, that must obtain for choices and actions to manifest the constitutive conditions in virtue of which they are autonomous. The distinction between the constitutive and the causal conditions required for autonomy will be particularly important for appreciating the role that social relationships and cultural context play in the realization of autonomy, a topic we shall turn to later in this chapter and again in chapters 4 and 5.

With these preliminaries in mind, we may now turn to the actual account. For choices and actions to be autonomous, the choosing and acting self as the particular self she is must play a role in determining them. The self as a whole, as the particular self she is, must somehow (partly) determine what she chooses and does. This could come about if the particular self that someone is has a distinctive identity and her identity is somehow implicated in her determining of what she does. The features constituting her identity must not simply cause her choices and actions as isolated links in causal chains. Rather, they must be features that are central enough to who someone is so that she herself, as a whole self, becomes somehow thereby a (part) cause of what she does through those centrally distinct features.

In recent decades, the notion of self-determination has been elaborated in terms of a certain sort of self-reflection that involves, one might say, self-monitoring and self-regulation.[2] According to a generic version of this view, to realize autonomy a person must first somehow reflect on her wants, desires, and so on and take up an evaluative stance with respect to them. She can endorse or identify with them in some way or be wholeheartedly committed to them, or she can reject or repudiate them or be only halfheartedly committed to them. If she endorses or identifies with her wants and desires, she makes them more truly hers, more genuinely a part of who she is, and thus, more a part of her very identity as a particular, distinctive self than are the wants and desires that she has not thus self-reflectively reaffirmed. When she chooses or acts in accord with wants or desires that she has self-reflectively endorsed, and her endorsement is somehow a part cause of her behavior, then, according to this familiar generic account, she is behaving autonomously. When wants and desires lead to choice or action without having been self-reflectively endorsed by the person whose wants and desires they are, the resulting choices and actions are not autonomous. They are not self-determined; they have not been determined by the self as the whole distinctive self she is.

This generic conception of autonomy forms the basis of my own account. Self-reflection is the process in which, roughly, a whole self takes a stance toward particular wants and values she finds herself to have. Self-reflective reaffirmation brings the (whole) self into accord with some of those wants or values. A person's self-reflections give a crucial imprimatur to the wants and concerns on which they focus approvingly. Those wants and concerns become more truly a (whole) person's "own."

Autonomous choices and actions, on this account, are self-reflective in two senses. First, they are partly caused by a person's reflections on, or attentive consideration of, wants and desires that already characterize her. This attention need not have occurred closely prior to the occurrence of the choice or action. It may have occurred at some distantly past time. As well, reflective attention need not be conscious or extensive, and it need not be narrowly cognitive in nature. Without an attitude of reflective commitment, someone might still happen to express or promote various of her wants or values in her behavior. She would not be particularly self-determining, however, in regard to that behavior. Behavior on behalf of what one has not ever reconsidered does not, in any special way, involve a self, as the particular self one is, in determining one's behavior or the course of one's life. Only when one reflectively cares in some way about something, thereby reaffirming it and doing so as the distinctive person one is, does it become relevant for one's autonomy.

To realize autonomy, self-reflections must also be partly effective in determining someone's behavior. For self-reflection to be effective in practice, it must not be impeded by interfering conditions. Coercion, deception, and manipulation by others are the paradigm examples of conditions that interfere with the practical effectiveness of someone's self-reflections. They can distort someone's attempts to consider her options in light of what matters to her and to choose what genuinely reflects her own concerns. The choosing person is forced or pressured in those cases to choose other than what she would most want to pursue under the circumstances at hand and is led inappropriately to choose for the sake of values that would not otherwise have been her guiding priorities under those circumstances. Coercive conditions do not entirely preclude autonomy, a point I shall elaborate toward the end of this chapter. However, they typically undermine it to a significant degree. The extent to which they do so depends on how effective they are. What autonomy requires, then, is the absence of *effective* coercion, deception, manipulation, or anything else that interferes significantly with someone's behaving in a way that reflects her wants and values as she would reflect on and reaffirm them under noninterfering conditions.

Autonomous choices and behavior must also be self-reflective in a second sense. They must reflect, or mirror, the wants, desires, cares, concerns, values, and commitments that someone reaffirms when attending to them. To mirror someone's concerns is to accord with them and, especially, to promote them. Choices and actions mirror wants and values by, for example, aiming at the attainment of what is wanted or valued, promoting its well-being, or protecting it from harm.

In this discussion, I use the full gamut of valenced attitude terms interchangeably and ignore subtle differences among them. Wants, desires, cares, concerns, values, commitments, and any other attitudes someone may take up with regard to what she experiences, attitudes that might influence her goals, purposes, aims, and intentions, are thereby relevant to autonomy. In the remainder of the discussion, for stylistic reasons, I generally use only two or three selected attitude terms at a time ("wants and values," for example). These abbreviated lists are always intended, however, as a stylistic convenience that stands in for the full panoply of "pro" or "con" attitudes that someone might hold deeply and that can be part causes of behavior that reflects the content of those attitudes.

Besides being self-reflective in these two senses, autonomous actions and choices also stem from what an agent cares deeply about. They stem from wants and values that are relatively important to the acting person. Relative importance for a particular person is a matter of depth and pervasiveness. Wants and values are "deep" when they are abiding and tend to be chosen over other competing wants and values. Wants and values are also deep when they constitute the overarching rationales that an agent regards as justifying many of her more specific choices. Wants and values are "pervasive" when they are relevant to a great many situations that a person faces. They are frequently salient in someone's life and she chooses in accord with them often. When someone reflectively reaffirms wants or values that are important to her in either sense just described, they become part of the perspective that defines her as the particular person she is. They embody the "nomos" of her self: relatively stable, enduring concerns and values that give her a kind of identity as the person she is. Someone is self-determining when she acts for the sake of what matters to her, what she deeply cares about, and, in that sense, who she "is."

Someone can, of course, reaffirm wants or desires that she regards as trivial in comparison to her other concerns, perhaps a liking for ice cream or a particular television program. However, it seems intuitively appropriate to say that someone lives her life "her way" as "her own person" only when she does so in accord with wants and values that she regards as important to her, and that in fact ground or pervade many of her concerns. Only in that way would they involve her self, as the distinctive self she is, in the choices she makes. It is her deeper concerns, not her shallower concerns, that provide the basis for autonomous behavior. Autonomy is therefore defined here only with reference to someone's deeper concerns.

Wants and values exhibit depth for someone to the extent that she chooses in accord with them frequently or steadfastly. Yet someone's initial choices in accordance with any wants and values are not autonomous. Initially she must simply come to choose somewhat consistently so that certain wants or values guide her choices frequently or steadfastly and thereby become "deepened" aspects of her character or identity. Those deeper wants and values in turn make possible her future autonomy.

Autonomy does not need to be defined in terms of someone's *deepest* concerns. In part, this is because a person's deepest concerns may not be fully clear or delineated until she confronts a wide diversity of types of situations. A person's deeper concerns are always open to changes in meaning and may fluctuate in relative importance as she refines them in response to novel circumstances. Aristotle recognized how our characters may change so long as we still live. So, too, our perspectives and commitments may change, even at their deepest dimensions, so long as we continue to encounter types of situations we have never dealt with before—a difficult colleague, for example, an aging and infirm parent, or the onset of a terminal illness. What to do in response to a novel situation may not be sufficiently determined by someone's prior commitments because those commitments might never have been articulated enough to cope with the sort of novelty in question. In that case, a person may deepen her prior commitments or forge new ones out of her sense of what had already mattered to her and how the choice she makes transforms her priorities and her identity.[3]

Autonomy is a matter of degree. No finite being is thoroughly self-determined. Even self-reflection itself can range along a continuum. The more extensively one reflects on one's wants and commitments, the greater is one's autonomy with respect to them. One rich sort of self-reflection consists in attending to the socialization and other causes lying behind the formation of one's current wants and commitments. If someone goes on to reaffirm her original commitments after recognizing their socialized origin, then, as John Christman argues, she achieves autonomy with respect to them.[4] This level of self-reflection, provided it motivates action, is sufficient for autonomy. On my account, however, it is more than what is necessary. Practically any self-reflective reaffirmation will do.

A self who is at all minimally self-reflective has crossed a threshold. Her actions reflect and issue from the deeper, stable, overarching concerns that constitute who she is. Self-reflection is self-determining when it (partly) shapes behavior that mirrors a person's deeper concerns that she has reflectively reaffirmed. Within the compass of self-reflective selfhood lie capacities not only for choices and actions that reflect superficial or momentary concerns but actions that bear a deeper connection to a perspective that constitutes her distinctive identity as an enduring self. These deeper wants and commitments are the motivating concerns that form who she is and that make the actions that issue from them "her own."

Autonomous behavior is, thus, behavior that is based on the deeper wants and commitments of the behaving person, is partly caused by her reflections on and reaffirmations of them, and mirrors those wants and commitments in the sense of helping her to achieve, promote, or protect them. This account prompts a question about the way autonomy originates. The perspective from which someone reflectively reaffirms what she wants comprises beliefs, values, desires, and so on that may not have yet been subjected to the same self-reflective reaffirmation. How can nonautonomous features of a person's perspective confer autonomy on the wants and values that they lead someone to endorse?[5]

This question echoes the familiar worry about whether someone can be autonomous if her guiding wants and values are the causal products of upbringing and other processes beyond her control, processes that are therefore not autonomous for her. I shall answer that question briefly at the end of this section. To anticipate: human self-determination does not require humanly impossible self-creation. It is a concept about a certain sort of humanly possible causation, one having its own causal antecedents that, in turn, may or may not exhibit self-determination in their own right. Self-determination, or autonomy, occurs so long as a whole self, as someone with a distinctive particular identity as the self she is, plays a role in partly determining her own behavior. So long as the causes of her behavior include her *self* in some significant sense (and so long as behavior mirrors that self by according with its deeper commitments), then her behavior is autonomous.

The self-reflections that make choices and actions autonomous need not be conscious. Someone can be self-determining on particular occasions without representing her deep concerns to herself with conscious awareness at the time. As well, the commitments constituting the standpoint from which someone self-reflects need not be consciously accessible to her. What a person cares about may influence her self-reflection and, from that, her behavior, subconsciously. So long as a person's choices and actions reflect and issue from the self-reflections on her deeper wants and values that she undertakes from her overall perspective at some level of thought, they have at least a minimal degree of autonomy.

Autonomous choice or action also does not need to be highly deliberate or deliberated. It can occur without explicit contemporaneous self-monitoring. It can occur casually, spontaneously, and rapidly. A person must simply have reflected on and endorsed the underlying concerns at some prior time. Once someone reflects on and reaffirms something that matters to her, she takes up a new stance toward that concern. It becomes an "object" of thought or consideration for herself and her choosing. Future actions that accord with that reflection and somehow issue from it constitute her determining of herself.

Autonomy thus requires someone as the self she is to play an active determining role in the choices she makes and the actions she undertakes. This, in turn, requires her to have cares, concerns, and commitments that constitute a perspective or orientation of some sort. This perspective is both (at least partly) definitive of who she is and a (part) determinant of what she does. She has concerns on which she can reflect, and her reflections on her concerns both issue in, and are mirrored in, what she does. Thus, in the last analysis, what matters to someone, what she self-reflectively cares about, when effective in and reflected in her action, makes her behavior autonomous.

Agents are beings who can act from intentions, that is, who can do things because they want to or because of reasons or purposes that are theirs—beings who can engage in doings for which they are, and can be held, responsible. The standard contemporary philosophical account of human agency treats it as distinctively manifested in action done for a reason.[6] Traditional, Kantian-style accounts of autonomy require reflection on one's choices to be a matter of reasoning in a narrower sense.[7] Neither emotions, desires, passions, inclinations, nor sentiments are sources of autonomy on those traditional accounts. This is a standard feature of the Kantian legacy in thinking about autonomy. There is also a romantic conception of autonomy according to which autonomy is a matter of living in accord with the promptings of a true self that lies beneath the dispassionate, impartial veneer of rationality.[8] While they differ in the sides they each champion in the reason-emotion dichotomy, both of these traditions are alike in differentiating reason from emotion, desire, and all variants of these.

Rosalind Hursthouse has plausibly argued in a romantic spirit that action can be intentional even when there are no reasons for it.[9] On Hursthouse's view, action could be intentional simply by virtue of expressing the emotion or character of the agent. Hursthouse is right about the intentionality of emotion- or character-based action but wrong to exclude such action from the category of behavior done for a reason. According to contemporary thinking about rationality, a reason for someone to act in a certain way is either a belief by someone that that action is right or good, or some fact in virtue of which it is right or good. On this approach, there is no reason why features of emotion or character could not constitute reasons, in the sense of facts by virtue of which actions are right or good.

Doings can count as intentional actions if they reflect, or express, what matters to an agent. For something to matter to an agent, as Bennett Helm has argued,[10] it may be sufficient that there are connections among her emotional responses or character traits that manifest a rational pattern of caring about or valuing something. It is not necessary that a person consciously articulate judgments (reasons in the narrow sense) about the value or importance to her of what she cares about. Thus actions that express an agent's emotions and character can reflect what deeply and overall matters to her in case her emotions and character traits show coherent rational patterns amounting to concern. A person shows such coherence when her attitudes over time include, for example, love for a friend, a desire that the friend experience good fortune, and regret over the unkind words one spoke to the friend in an angry moment.

Notice, as an aside, that if these feelings constitute "reasons" for someone to treat a friend in the appropriate ways, then the notion of a "reason" has been widened considerably. Reason would no longer contrast with emotion or desire. Emotions, desires, passions, inclinations, or volitions—in short, any mental state involving any motivation or attitude at all—would all constitute reasons in this sense. This use of "reason" departs substantially from its traditional cognitive sense.

It does not matter ultimately whether the term "reason" is used either in the narrow sense best represented as an articulated statement or in the wider sense that encompasses any mental state from the standpoint of which an action is good or valuable. What matters in this context is that emotions and desires, as well as imagination,[11] can constitute a kind of reflection on or attention to objects or values of concern. They can involve evaluations of those objects. In so doing, they can thereby contribute to the autonomy of a person's choices. Reflection is consideration that can involve an attitude of some valenced sort, either positive or negative. When someone's consideration, of whatever mental sort, involves reaffirming what she wants or values as something important to her, and the reaffirmed commitment motivates her behavior, then (assuming no interfering conditions) she realizes some degree of autonomy.

Autonomous action is action that reflects who someone is. However, someone's personal identity, or "who she is," in a sense relevant to identifying her as a person distinct from others, is an ambiguous notion. It can comprise at least two different sorts of features about a person, only one of which is necessarily relevant to her autonomy. First, "who someone is" can comprise her perspective, outlook, or viewpoint, that is, her deeper, wants, desires, cares, concerns, values, and commitments. Someone can be identified by what she cares about or values. Or, second, "who someone is" can comprise the traits and characteristics that locate her in various classes of identifiable human kinds. Thus, someone's identity can comprise, for example, a particular gender, race, or ethnicity. These human kind categories are not necessarily matters of attitude or concern on the part of a person identified in those ways. They may be, or be thought to be, linked to facts about her birth, biology, or ancestry. The important point to notice is that they are not, as such, attitudes and may be quite distinct from anything a person cares about or values. Thus, a person's identity as the particular person she is can be constituted by her perspective, her deeper beliefs, desires, values, and so on, or it can be constituted by human kind categories used to describe her—or by both of these together.

Call the two sorts of identities constituted by these two sets of features "perspectival identity" and "trait-based identity," respectively. These two sorts of identity may coincide, but they need not. Someone may exemplify socially important human kinds such as a particular gender or race that she simply does not care much about. It is difficult to imagine a human being who is not ascribed an identity of some sort along such axes as gender, race, and citizenship. Yet people do not each care or value their traits in these respects to the same degree. Some care very little about the "kinds" to which they belong or which are ascribed to them. At the same time, someone may obviously have deep concerns and values that are not connected in any way to the human kind categories ascribed to her. The examples are familiar and wide ranging: a passion for justice, a dedication to the arts, and so on.

On my view, what counts for autonomy is someone's perspectival identity, her wants, desires, cares, concerns, values, and commitments. The nonperspectival kinds or traits she instantiates or exemplifies are relevant to her autonomy only if they matter to her, only if they are features of herself she cares deeply about. Otherwise they do not ground her autonomous choices or actions. Thus, when I talk about "who" someone "is" in regard to her autonomy, I shall be referring to someone's identity in the sense of her perspective or outlook, and to what matters to her from her perspective. Behaving or living autonomously is a matter of behaving or living in accord with what matters to someone, not of living in accord with characteristics of hers or categories applied to her that she does not particularly care about. If being white, female, heterosexual, or Jewish are not traits I care about in myself, then I am not being autonomous when I happen to live in ways that accord with those traits. Even if my behavior mirroring those traits is very consistent, it need not realize autonomy for me. The consistency of my behavior might be a thoughtless consequence of living under conditions in which the fact that I am a certain kind—a white person, for example—has simply not been brought to my attention as something important, something I needed to consider or regarding which I needed to make any choices.

Growing up as an American schoolchild, I may have thoughtlessly waved the flag at patriotic ceremonies and cheered the president as he passed in the motorcade, simply because this was what I was expected to do and it never occurred to me, in those early years, to do otherwise. Being an American can ground my autonomy only if it matters to me in one way or another, as manifested in states of cognition, conation, or affect by which I attend to that kind that I am and choose or act in some way that mirrors it. Caring about some kind or trait that I am involves attending to it with some sort of positively valenced attitude toward it that manifests itself in choices and actions that aim to attain, promote, or protect what I care about.

In at least one respect, my position is open to communitarian concerns. The things that matter to someone need not be chosen or voluntary features of herself or her life. They may, for example, be inherited traits or involuntary relationships. Thus, someone can care deeply about her parents, her ethnic group, her race, her community, or her nation. On my view, these concerns could then ground autonomy. It does not matter whether someone's concern is itself the product of her socialization or otherwise the result of circumstances over which she has no control. What cannot ground autonomy are involuntary—or voluntary!—traits or identity categories that a person does not reflectively reconsider or value.

In another respect, my account of autonomy is at odds with communitarianism. Communitarians call upon us to recognize how communal ties shape who we are and impose duties on us. Communal attachments are supposed to be the starting points of our particular identities. Communitarians treat each person's communal attachments as having moral significance for her regardless of whether or not she harbors an attitude of reflective allegiance to them.[12] They portray communal attachments with warmth and fervor, as if to

evoke in readers the very sense of attachment and identification their conceptions of the self posit as constitutive of the self. Thus Alasdair MacIntyre
writes of how "we all approach our own circumstances as bearers of a particular social identity," based on such ties as that of kinship and nation, ties that
impose "rightful expectations and obligations," determine the good for each
person based on the roles she inhabits, and give a life the moral particularity
from which it must start its quest for the good.[13] And Michael Sandel writes
similarly that ties such as those of kinship and nation ground "loyalties and
convictions" having a moral force linked to the fact that they "partly define
the person I am."[14]

If, however, a person feels no allegiance to some community or group to
which she belongs, does not care much about it, does not particularly value it,
and has no special commitment to it, then, on my view, that attachment could
not be the basis of the person's autonomous choices or actions. Communitarians are right to think it implausible that someone would have no concern for
any of the humankind categories ascribed to her, but wrong to ignore how she
might easily be indifferent to *some* of them. Insofar as communal or any other
humankind identity matters to autonomy, it does so to the extent that it constitutes something a person cares about. Matters of perspective, orientation,
outlook, and viewpoint are the aspects of a person that ground autonomy.
And the features of perspective that are particularly important are those
wants, desires, cares, concerns, values, commitments, and the other attractions and repulsions that comprise a person's reflectively reaffirmed concerns.
What matters for autonomy, then, is that someone has a certain distinctive
stance, the stance of cares, concerns, and commitments that comprise a self-
reflective, practical perspective. In this way communitarians are right to sense
that the concept of autonomy is at odds with communal identity. To the extent
that autonomy is, as I argue, based on someone's perspective and not on the
humankind categories that fit or are ascribed to her, community membership
and other humankind traits are inessential to, and may well be occluded by,
the ideal of personal autonomy.

Earlier, I distinguished between, on one hand, conditions that constitute
the autonomy of choices and actions, and, on the other hand, conditions that
are causally necessary for the realization of autonomous choices and actions.
A few words about the latter are in order. They include an adequate array of
available options. Also causally important are the character traits and competencies people bring with them as they face their situations. Whether someone
can have a significant degree of autonomy in the conditions under which she
acts is thus affected both by the conditions she faces and the degree to which
she harbors the competencies for autonomy. An autonomous person has relatively stable and enduring concerns that give her over time a perspective that is
specifically hers, and that shows some continuity in the face of new sorts of
conditions. The wants and desires she reflectively reaffirms cohere to a significant degree. Her perspective must be relatively stable and enduring across a
range of situations and a stretch of time, although it may certainly undergo
change, sometimes suddenly and dramatically. When someone acts from such

a relatively stable, enduring (though revisable over time) orientation of concerns that she tends to carry from one situation to the next and that gives her a perspective that is hers, and when her actions reflect those concerns in the two relevant senses (attentive consideration and mirroring), then (assuming no interfering conditions) a person is self-determining, or autonomous.

Thus, autonomy *competency*[15] is the effective capacity, or set of capacities, to act under some significant range of circumstances in ways that reflect and issue from deeper concerns that one has considered and reaffirmed. The relevant capacities include capacities for having values and commitments, understanding them, taking up valenced attitudes toward them, making choices and undertaking actions that mirror these commitments, and doing the latter with some resilience in the face of at least minimal obstacles. This last capacity is not often emphasized in accounts of autonomy, yet it seems important nonetheless. Someone is more autonomous the more she can succeed in pursuing her concerns despite resistance. Minimally autonomous choice or action requires, then, values or commitments of sufficient depth or strength as to persist somewhat in the face of obstacles and resistance, including those posed by social conditions. An autonomous *person* is one who has these capacities and exercises them at least occasionally. Exactly how often she must exercise her autonomy competency to count as autonomous is, as one might expect, difficult to say, and I shall not try to do so. An autonomous life is one lived by someone who has the capacities for autonomy and is able to exercise them frequently over a substantial stretch of time. She lives her mature and lucid years largely in accord with what matters deeply to her; her life reflects those concerns to a significant degree.

The conception of autonomy presented above is vulnerable to the usual objections. I survey some of them in chapter 2. Here it is useful to consider briefly one common worry about autonomy. Since a person's wants, desires, values, and commitments are the products of socialization, it seems that they are not really the agent's "own," and therefore choices based on them would seem to undermine the possibility of a self genuinely determining itself. This is a question about the ultimate metaphysical ground of personal agency. My goal is a conception of autonomy that does not apply to any and all actions but that differentiates some actions from others. The idea of someone as the agent of her doings is not undermined, on my account, by the fact that those doings had ultimate causal antecedents that were other than the person herself.

My account is thus compatibilist in tenor. It is necessary only that selves emerge somehow with beliefs, desires, values, and so on that constitute their perspectives as the distinctive persons they are, and from which they can reflect on and evaluate particular wants and concerns they find themselves to have. A person is autonomous with respect to what she does so long as her doings reflect and stem from what she reaffirms self-reflectively as important to her. Her reflective reaffirmations of the values and commitments that partly cause her actions must have been key, ineliminable stages in the causal sequences leading from those concerns to her subsequent behavior. Self-reflection can be a kind of causal process in which a person's distinctive perspectival identity plays a role in determining how she behaves. If a person acts simply to get what she wants but has not reflected on what she wants, or has reflected on it but has repudiated it, or has reaffirmed her want but it is not one of her deeper concerns her resulting actions are not autonomous in any significant sense.

This is not to say that "second-order" self-reflection is privileged over "first-order" wants and desires in representing what someone "really" cares about. When someone self-reflectively condemns or repudiates what she nevertheless continues to want in a real sense, then she is ambivalent. Neither attitude has a necessary priority. Action resulting from a condition of ambivalence that persists throughout the course of the behavior is simply not autonomous, and a person is likely to suffer doubts or self-recriminations whatever she does. She has no coherent "nomos" in such a case. Her self does not have a clear perspectival identity about the matter in question. Her behavior is therefore not determined by her *self* in such cases.

To summarize: choices and actions can be autonomous only if they are self-reflective in two senses and meet at least two other conditions. First, they must be self-reflective in being partly caused by the actor's reflective consideration of her own wants and values, where reflective consideration may be cognitive in a narrow sense or also affective or volitional and cognitive in a broad sense. Second, they must be self-reflective in mirroring those of her wants and values that she has reflectively endorsed. Third, the underlying wants or values must be important to the actor. Fourth, her choice or behavior must be relatively unimpeded by conditions, such as coercion, deception, and manipulation, that can prevent self-reflection from leading to behavior that mirrors the values and commitments a person reaffirmed. Thus, autonomous choices and actions are those that mirror wants or values that an acting person has reflectively reaffirmed and that are important to her. In subsequent discussion, I shall abbreviate these four requirements for stylistic reasons by saying simply that someone must act from deeper values she has reaffirmed.

For someone's behavior to be autonomous in this way, various causal conditions must also have been met. A person must confront situations that afford significant alternative options among which she can choose. Also she must have previously developed the competency for choosing or acting in ways that are autonomous. Both of those causal requirements involve substantial social dimensions. To that point I now turn.

Individuality and Sociality

No human competency can be exercised under any set of conditions whatsoever. Each competency must always be understood as presupposing some particular range of conditions under which an agent is able to exercise that competency. People can do things only so long as the necessary enabling conditions are present and the possible disabling conditions are absent. Not all enabling conditions need to be mentioned. A person cannot be autonomous if she cannot breathe, but there is no particular philosophical point to mentioning this requirement. There is good reason to discuss the social relationships that are necessary causal conditions for autonomy. The point of exploring them is to curb an excessive individualism to which statements and paradigms of the ideal of autonomy might otherwise be prone, especially in popular discourse—"self-made man," for example. In recent decades a trend has emerged toward emphasizing the social, relational, interpersonal, or intersubjective dimensions and requirements of autonomy. The notion of autonomy as based on self-reflection is easily amenable to such an understanding.

In a number of ways, autonomy requires a social context for its realization.[16] First, autonomous persons are differentiated selves with identities and commitments. They are products of socialization by other selves into communities of interacting selves within which they are differentiated as distinct particular persons. Second, autonomous persons must have the capacities for autonomy. These capacities include abilities to understand one's own wants and commitments to at least some degree, to recognize alternative options for choice, to act appropriately to achieve what one wants under the circumstances one faces, and to persist in those aims in the face of at least minimal difficulty. These capacities must be acquired through learning from other persons already able to exercise them, in social practices involving discourse and modes of self-representation. Third, autonomous self-reflection requires meaningful options that can be weighed in light of wants, values, or other points of reference. These options are at least partly matters of the social conditions facing someone, and what those conditions permit and prevent. Also, options are comprehensible to persons in virtue of shared cultural practices of representation and interpretation.

There are still other social possibilities regarding autonomy. Thus, fourth, persons in communities or groups may enjoy autonomy as collectivities. Shared or collective autonomy is possible for persons engaged as joint agents who choose and act together as single units. Indeed, the original meaning of autonomy applied to states, governing collectivities, that were free of the political domination of other states. Some philosophers also argue, fifth, that autonomy is a competency the very exercise of which involves certain particular capacities of interpersonal engagement, such as that of being able to give an account to others of oneself and one's choices, itself a mode of discursive interchange.[17] It is particularly the former three of these conditions that my account of personal autonomy emphasizes. Personal autonomy is thus a product of social conditions of various kinds, both those that contribute to socializing someone as a self with autonomy-conferring character traits and behavioral competencies (the first two conditions above) and those conditions that a person subsequently encounters and engages as someone with an already formed, though still revisable, character and set of concerns (the third condition above).

As I noted above, one good reason to stress the social causes required for autonomy is to counteract the excessive individualism to which formulations of the ideal of autonomy might be prone. Social, or interpersonal, reconceptualizations of autonomy are often proposed by those who are highly critical of individualism. Individualism, for many social critics, is the evil demon of modern Western social and political life, the source of much of what is wrong with liberal-capitalist society. There are varieties of individualism, however, and they do not all succumb to the same critical challenges.

Individualism is a problem when it is manifested in norms that promote selfishness and self-aggrandizement through the domination, oppression, and exploitation of others. Individualism is also a problem when it promotes mutual indifference among people by leading its adherents to pursue their own well-being in disregard of the costs they impose on others and to lose the concern for each other that they would otherwise have had, had they accepted different theories about human personality. Not all emphases on individuality have these consequences, however.[18] In the effort to combat individualism critics may shift theoretically too far toward social terms of conceptualization and ignore dimensions of autonomy that are not specifically social. There may be good reasons to emphasize human individuality in an account of autonomy so long as it does not promote mutual indifference or ruthless selfishness.[19]

What are the reasons for thinking that human individuality is important to emphasize in an account of autonomy? For one thing, the social matrix is constituted out of a great number of separately embodied human beings. To take embodiment seriously is to recognize that apart from pregnancy and the rare phenomenon of Siamese twinning, we are each distinct bodies and, therefore, distinct individual entities, however much we interact with each other, depend on each other, and engage in collective endeavors. We each follow our own (separately embodied) trajectory through space and time. Virtually every human being is a named particular—named by other human beings, but a named particular all the same—with a name that distinguishes each one from nearly all of the others. For each human life, a distinct narrative can be written, however much the narrative might resemble or intertwine with the narratives of other persons with whom a person shares traits or fates.

Human beings are thus mutually individuated by embodiment and by ascribed nominal and narrative identities. This separation and distinctness grounds the possibility of attributing to persons a particular identity as well as a degree of separate agency based on her behavior. Autonomy requires individuation to begin with, itself at least partly a product of social practices of differential naming and differential characterizing. At the same time, autonomy is also a mode of (further) individuating. Autonomy involves practices by which physically separate selves, who are already characterized by differentiated nominal identities and spatiotemporal life narratives, may reinforce their distinctness from others and their mutual differentiation by acting on concerns of their own that are distinct from, and may conflict with, those of others.

Doings are the manifestation of the agency of an individual person when they express and issue from intentions that are hers, intentions that arise from the complex of wants, desires, cares, concerns, values, and commitments that characterize the perspective that is hers. A self that is, in some minimal degree, capable of determining herself is, in that respect, capable of action that she partly determines as the particular and distinctive self she is. She has an overall identity that is partly defined by her deep concerns. Although her resources for acting and reflecting are socially grounded, she can act and reflect separately from all other persons. The distinctive set of concerns that partly constitute her perspective further entrenches itself as who she is to the extent that it is at all effective in shaping her actions and her life. Practices of behaving autonomously can thus make us more distinct from each other than we are to begin with. Autonomy further individuates us.

Thus, the capacity for self-determination depends on the nature of selves, the character and perspective of any particular self in question, and on the circumstances in which she has matured and now finds herself. These are not independent sets of conditions. The character and perspective of any particular self is itself a product of the circumstances under which a separately embodied human infant has developed into a person with a selfhood more or less distinct from other persons, other selves, around her. The boundaries of separate selfhood are not always clear-cut for the purposes of agency, responsibility, and other modes of engagement for which autonomy matters, but if a particular human being is not at least partly distinct from all other persons, then she would not be a separate person. She would instead be a mere part of a larger human mass. She would no more have a separate identity than her hand has one, as an integral part of her.

This claim about the individuating tendency of autonomy might prompt some readers to suspect that my account of autonomy resurrects the concept of the atomistic self. That fear is groundless. Atomistic selves, lacking any prior social relationships to other human beings, are not the bearers of autonomy. (Indeed, they are not the bearers of anything. Apart from a few extraordinary cases of feral children, if then, atomistic selves do not exist. Even Robinson Crusoe had to have been raised by others.) Implicit in the idea of acting according to wants, desires, cares, concerns, values, or commitments that are one's own is the idea that one might have acted according to the wants, desires, cares, concerns, values, or commitments of *others* but did not do so. This implicit contrast is a part of what autonomy means; autonomy is *not heteronomy*. In this respect as well, then, autonomy requires a social context as an enabling, or causal, background; it cannot emerge except out of social relationships. Although autonomy is individuating in its effects on persons, it never loses its social rootedness. Socially deracinated, autonomy would be a pointless and meaningless notion.

What is social, however, is not necessarily autonomous. What distinguishes an autonomous self from those who are not autonomous but who are equally the products of social contexts is the degree of individuated distinctness and coherence that an autonomous self achieves by acting in ways that accord with her reaffirmation of certain deeper wants and commitments that characterize her in particular. Autonomy is a matter of degree, which means that selves who are relatively more autonomous come to harbor, within the range of capacities they can exercise separately from others (although they needn't exercise them separately), a greater assortment of the capacities for reflective agency, or harbor them to a more effective degree than do selves who are relatively less autonomous.

Autonomous selves, then, are socially situated selves whose choices or actions tend to intensify their differentiated distinctness from the mass of humanity constituting their social context. Minimally autonomous selves are minimally differentiated and individuated. Highly autonomous selves are highly differentiated and individuated.[20] Yet no person is utterly alone or self-contained over the course of an entire lifetime, nor is any human being with the least capacity for action utterly merged indistinguishably with surrounding humanity as if she were simply a continuous part of seamless human stuff. The crucial social questions about autonomy are matters of degree. How much or how little human interrelationship is necessary for autonomy? What *sorts* of human interrelationship are necessary for autonomy? What sorts of human interrelationship are *hindrances* to autonomy?

To be autonomous, someone should have a significant array of opportunities to act in ways that reflect what deeply matters to her. Conditions should not so limit her options that she cannot choose or act for the sake of any of her deep values or commitments. When widely or deeply obstructed by social conditions that prevent her choices or actions from reflecting her deeper concerns, a person's choices and actions will lack autonomy and she may well be living under conditions of oppression. Unjust or oppressive social conditions are those that prevent some group of people from acting according to what matters to them. An account of autonomy should incorporate a recognition of the impact of social injustice and oppression on autonomy, and to do this it must take particular notice of social conditions that suppress people's options for living in ways that accord with what deeply matters to them.

A disabling social context can obstruct someone's capacity to pursue her goals, ambitions, and dreams.[21] This is another important reason for emphasizing individuality in an account of autonomy. Circumstances can severely limit what a person is capable of doing, and these conditions are not generally something she determines. If someone must struggle constantly to survive or to satisfy basic needs for herself or those she cares for, her ability to exercise autonomy competency will be reduced, although, as I argue below, it is not entirely precluded. An agent must also not be overly subjected to coercive pressures or the controlling power of other persons when she reflects on what matters to her or attempts to act accordingly. The harshness and coerciveness of someone's situation are partly matters of the social context in which she lives and of her relative place within it. Thus someone might have autonomy competency yet not be an autonomous person because she is frequently blocked from exercising that competency by obstacles over which she may have little control. For an agent's choices and actions to reflect her deep concerns, she must be able to persist in promoting those concerns to some extent even in the face of obstacles. She must be able to resist to some minimal degree the efforts by others to obstruct or thwart *her* efforts to act according to her deeper concerns. Whether or not someone can do this is a product of the competencies and character traits she has acquired in her upbringing.

The ideal of autonomy thus gives us a normative standpoint for critically assessing oppressive social conditions that suppress or prevent the emergence of autonomy. Oppression does more than simply limit someone's options at the time of choosing. It also infects the conditions under which growing persons are socialized. Oppression may damage someone's capacity to care about what is worth caring about and it may deform the nature of a person's concern for herself. She may grow to value or seek the very persons or circumstances that keep her in oppressive conditions. She may, that is, end up with "adaptive preferences."[22] In that case, acting according to what someone sincerely cares about may nevertheless undermine her long-term capacity to continue acting according to what she cares about. This is one reason why some autonomy theorists call for a "substantive" account of autonomy, an account that stipulates limits on what a person may care about, as a condition for achieving autonomy. Let us turn to this issue.

Content-Neutral versus Substantive Conceptions of Autonomy

Does autonomy require someone to have commitments of a particular sort or that fall within certain guidelines? Some philosophers have argued that someone is not autonomous unless she chooses in accord with certain values. In particular, she must choose in accord with the value of autonomy itself, or, at least, choose so as not to undermine that value. This is the "substantive" conception of autonomy.[23] The contrast to a substantive conception of autonomy is a "procedural," or, more perspicuously, a "content-neutral," conception. This is a conception that is neutral with regard to the content of what a person must choose in order to be autonomous.

On a content-neutral conception, a person is autonomous so long as the manner in which she reaches and makes her choices, or the relationship between her choices and her substantive concerns accord with certain criteria as specified by the account in question. The substance of her choices and commitments does not matter. She might still be choosing autonomously even if she chooses subservience to others for its own sake, so long as she has made her choice in the right way or it coheres appropriately with her perspective as a whole. Someone can autonomously give up her own future autonomy, for example, by entering a religious order requiring unconditional obedience to church authority. She will become nonautonomous in her behavior after making and adhering to that sort of choice, but this does not mean that she was nonautonomous when first making the choice.

According to substantive accounts of autonomy, by contrast, someone choosing subservience would not be autonomous unless she did so for some higher nonsubordinate purpose which continued to be her own purpose even in the condition of her servitude. Substantive accounts of autonomy are more demanding than content-neutral accounts. Someone must reflect on her choices and actions in certain ways and, in addition, must make choices that, at a minimum, avoid conflicting in their *content* with the ideal of autonomy.

It is important to notice that, on a content-neutral account, substantive autonomy is genuine autonomy; substantive autonomy is thus autonomy on either account. Substantive autonomy is content-neutral autonomy augmented in a certain way. It is content-neutral autonomy "with attitude." It consists of choices that were made in the right way to reflect what the acting person deeply cares about, and it is, in addition, substantively guided by a commitment to autonomy as a value or, at least, devoid of commitments that are inconsistent with a commitment to autonomy. On a content-neutral account, someone who is substantively autonomous is *more* autonomous than someone who is autonomous merely in the content-neutral sense. Substantive autonomy involves more autonomy because with it, autonomy seeking becomes a stable and enduring concern of the agent, one that she aims to pursue in the course of her behavior. She tends to choose intentionally according to that ideal and so helps to secure its ongoing importance as a feature of her character. Her autonomy is not merely the coincident product of sheer persistent determination to pursue her other concerns. The real controversy is thus not between a conception of autonomy as content neutral only and a conception of autonomy as substantive only. The real controversy is over whether the more minimal, content-neutral autonomy counts as genuine autonomy at all.

To think that mere self-reflective activity, even when lacking a commitment to self-reflective activity as a value, is self-determining enough to merit the label of "autonomy" is, in effect, to set a lower standard for autonomy than is set by those who defend a substantive conception. If we think of both of these manifestations of identity and agency as falling along a continuum, we can formulate the debate between defenders of the two views as a question of where along the continuum to "draw the line" that indicates that a minimal threshold for autonomy has been crossed. The substantive autonomy defender sets a higher threshold for minimal autonomy: an agent is not autonomous until she can and does engage in more than mere self-reflection in the right way. She must self-reflect in the right way and, in addition, do so in accord with commitments limited by certain parameters.

Why should we think that so-called content-neutral autonomy is genuine autonomy? Content-neutral autonomy is at least minimally self-determining in that the self has defining concerns that determine how she acts. Her behavior reflects what deeply matters to her. If she acts in a social environment that obstructs her choices or actions, then her actions would only reflect who she is if she were able to persist in her self-reflective behaviors in the face of some minimum of obstacles such as resistance by others. The core idea of autonomy, recall, is expressed by such familiar phrases as "thinking for oneself" or "being true to oneself."

It is indeed a significant threshold for someone with a stable array of deep and persistent concerns to become capable of reflectively reaffirming her deeper concerns and to behave in ways that accord with those concerns partly because of those reflections. A major qualitative difference emerges with be-havior that begins to be self-reflective in this way. That something matters deeply to a person when she attends to it, and that this concern partly directs her choices and actions, imparts a special significance to her behavior that it is appropriate to call determination by herself as the self she is. A self more or less as a whole thereby becomes a part determinant of what she does. Substan-tive accounts of autonomy give no special acknowledgment to this lesser threshold. Content-neutral accounts have the virtue of acknowledging this qualitative difference in agency by counting such behavior as "autonomous."

Another reason for thinking a content-neutral conception of autonomy is preferable to a substantive conception has to do with the exact sort of com-mitment that a substantive conception of autonomy requires of a person. A substantive conception requires someone to be committed to autonomy itself as a value or, at least, to have no values that conflict with this commitment. What exactly should someone be committed to when she is committed to au-tonomy as a value? A person who cares about her own autonomy cares about her own activity of reflecting on her deeper, self-defining concerns without im-pediment and acting accordingly. She cares about her own self-reflectiveness, and the wants and values she reaffirms thereby, as ends to promote. She wants to be able to reflect on and discern her own values and concerns without ma-nipulation or coercion and to be able to act accordingly and with some capac-ity to persist in doing so in the face of opposition from others. This commit-ment is a commitment to nothing other than *content-neutral* autonomy!

Could a substantive account require that a person's commitment be to sub-stantive autonomy instead? To say that I am committed to my own substan-tive autonomy as a value would be to say that I valued *my very valuing* of my own activity of reflecting on my deeper concerns and acting accordingly. Such metalevel self-reflections would certainly be consistent with being au-tonomous. There is, however, no reason to require them, even on a substantive account. They are implausibly cumbersome as reconstructions of what people ordinarily care about. More important, they are more than is needed for someone to care explicitly about her own autonomy and make choices that ac-cord with that concern. Thus a second reason in favor of a content-neutral conception of autonomy is that content-neutral autonomy turns out to be what even a substantive account of autonomy should sensibly hold that peo-ple *need* to care about. The conception of autonomy that someone must care about, even on a substantive account of autonomy, need be no more than au-tonomy in the content-neutral sense. This is sufficient for the autonomy that a substantive account requires anyone to hold as a value. A substantive account would seem to imply, in its very own terms, that content-neutral autonomy is sufficient to count as genuine autonomy.

Other grounds for deciding between substantive and content-neutral con-ceptions of autonomy have to do with the social practices in which the con-ception of autonomy is embedded. Practices of responsibility and accountabil-ity provide important examples to consider. Regularities in behavior that suggest that a person has reflected on her wants and values give evidence of a character sufficiently formed to be amenable to the social character reformation that is part of the aim of practices of responsibility. Practices of responsibility require that a person be able to understand and act on feedback from others about her behavior. A person must be able to understand praise and blame, reward and punishment, and grasp that these responses are directed toward herself. She must be able to direct her behavior in accord with those self-reflective understandings. The degree of autonomy that practices of responsibility require is sufficiently met by the existence of a stable, enduring, defined set of concerns and the capacity to reflect on them and act according to one's reflections. Content-neutral autonomy is sufficient for practices of responsibility; a person is responsible for her self-reflectively chosen behavior even if she is not committed to autonomy as a value.

Practices of interpersonal respect are also important for evaluating the ideal of autonomy. Autonomy has something to do with the respect owed to persons as persons. Many philosophers agree that respect is owed to persons simply by virtue of their potential for being autonomous, whether or not this potential is ever actualized. Nevertheless, someone's actual manifestation of autonomy may warrant yet another form of respect, also connected to sheer personhood. Content-neutral and substantive accounts of autonomy will have very different implications for practices of showing respect to people's actual choices. On a substantive account of autonomy, only choices based on commitments consistent with autonomy would deserve the special respect due to autonomous choices. On a content-neutral view, that respect would be owed more generally to the choices made by anyone with the competency to choose and act self-reflectively; what she chose would not matter.

Both content-neutral and substantive views can direct us to respect people's actual choices as autonomous unless positive evidence shows they are not. For a content-neutral account, however, the sort of positive evidence that might show this is more limited than it is on a substantive account. The substance of what someone chooses is never sufficient by itself to entail that someone has not chosen autonomously. Instead, we must know something about how or why she made the choice she did; this may require knowing something about the conditions she is coping with or under which she was raised. Because these circumstances are often difficult to discern in particular cases, people's choices tend, on a content-neutral approach, to be regarded as respectworthy more often than not. Content neutrality regarding autonomy cautions against overriding someone's presumptively autonomous choices for reasons that are paternalistic, or, as John Kultgen terms it, "parentalistic."[24] Content neutrality cautions against treating someone "for her own good" in a way that conflicts with what she chooses so long as she is content neutrally capable of making up her own mind in accord with what matters to her.[25]

On a substantive conception of autonomy, by contrast, someone's choices cease to be respectworthy as choices if they show undue deference, submissiveness, dependence, or servility. If someone's choices do not accord with the ideal of autonomy, then they would not even prima facie deserve respect as choices. Respect would be limited to choices that manifestly accorded with autonomy.

Note that this dispute is not about the reliability of *expressed* preferences. Both content-neutral and substantive accounts of autonomy are able to take up the same stance toward someone's expressed preferences. Both approaches can warrant treating expressed preferences provisionally as revealing someone's genuine preferences but only so long as no evidence suggests they are insincere, coerced, or otherwise not her genuine preferences. The issue I have been discussing, however, has to do with how others should respond to someone once the question has been settled of just what her genuine preferences are.

The lesser requirements for autonomy on a content-neutral account could have further valuable political implications. Whenever an ideal has more extensive requirements, the risk arises that it will turn out in practice to be attainable, or viewed as attained, by only a privileged minority. The ideal of autonomy is hampered by a history in which it has been associated in Western cultures with a select few, typically, successful white men. A content-neutral conception requires less of a person than does a substantive account as a basis for construing her to be autonomous and showing her the respect that actual autonomy is accorded. A conception of autonomy with fewer requirements is more widely applicable than otherwise. More people can qualify as autonomous.

In practice, someone's failure to manifest recognizable autonomy, or, what is more important for theories of oppression, the failure of others to *recognize* her behavior as autonomous, may well promote the conviction in others that she is not really capable of autonomy and, therefore, does not deserve the respect that is premised on a capacity for it. The more features that people think are required for autonomy, the fewer the number of persons they will judge as measuring up to the ideal. The stumbling blocks to recognizing someone else's behavior as autonomous are increased when people are divided by gender, race, religion, and other major differences in social identity and life experience. Reducing the requirements for autonomy may minimize the number of persons whose autonomy goes publicly unrecognized because of their social marginalization.

To be sure, this last argument is not decisive. It does not give us conceptual reasons pertaining to the nature of autonomy itself for reducing the number of features required for counting choices as autonomous. This argument is meant to tip a scale that is based on conceptual reasons first. If content-neutral and substantive accounts of autonomy are roughly equally convincing on conceptual and intuitive grounds, then a content-neutral account should be preferred for the fact that it will serve better in one of the normative roles that an ideal of autonomy fills, that of motivating people to treat others with an important form of respect. An account of autonomy that is too demanding will prompt persons to regard a greater number of others as failures at personhood and thereby reduce the number of others they will regard as respectworthy. Thus, an account of autonomy with fewer requirements has, independently of other considerations, the advantage of promoting a more inclusive sense of equal worth.[26]

If content-neutral accounts of autonomy are thus preferable to substantive accounts, why do some philosophers reject them? Natalie Stoljar's objection to content-neutral accounts is worth considering in this regard. Stoljar argues that content-neutral accounts of autonomy, in the various forms we know them today, conflict with what she calls the "feminist intuition." This is the intuition that "preferences influenced by oppressive norms of femininity cannot be autonomous."[27]

Stoljar is right about this conceptual conflict, but only if autonomy is understood in a certain way. The conflict arises because what she calls the feminist intuition embodies the assumption that abiding by certain particular substantive norms is indeed not autonomous. In other words, Stoljar's feminist intuition already presupposes a substantive conception of autonomy. It devalues, as nonautonomous, certain preferences in virtue of the normative commitment bound up in them, regardless of whether or not they were reached or affirmed in an autonomy-relevant manner.

Stoljar poses a dilemma. She argues that we cannot retain both a content-neutral account of autonomy and the feminist intuition. We must give up one or the other. This would be true if the substantive notion of autonomy underlying the feminist intuition were inflexible and unyielding. There may, however, be a middle ground. By construing both content-neutral and substantive autonomy as forms of autonomy but treating substantive autonomy as embodying a *greater degree* of autonomy than content-neutral autonomy, we may be able to retain a content-neutral account of autonomy while still giving the feminist intuition important weight.

My view is this. Even if women affirm and choose according to norms of femininity in accord with which they were socialized, and even if these norms divert women from valuing and pursuing autonomy, women could still be content-neutrally autonomous so long as their choices in general accorded with and issued from their deeper wants and commitments. Even if a woman's deeper concerns include subservient roles and relationships and she lacks a commitment to her own autonomy as a value, this would not be all she cares about. Women traditionally cared for family members and friends and had role-related daily activities for which they were responsible. The activities that women were traditionally able to undertake often left women with significant room for discretionary judgment and genuine, although circumscribed, opportunities to pursue what they valued and cared about. Women could still be content-neutrally autonomous in pursuing the deep, traditional concerns other than autonomy they happened to have. That is, when women affirm contra-autonomy norms, such as those of traditional femininity, this diminishes the *degree* of autonomy such women can attain but it does not absolutely preclude it. However traditional or traditionally feminine they are, women can still be autonomous in much of what they do. They can still cross the autonomy threshold.

What about the question of "adaptive preferences" that I asked at the end of the previous section? What if some women accept norms of traditional femininity only because they live under circumstances that penalize contrary choices or preclude them altogether? Women abiding by norms of traditional feminine servility and deference might have narrowed their preferences to what they can obtain without serious harm and given up on what they might otherwise have valued or sought. Does this adaptation of preferences to limiting circumstances make autonomous choice and action impossible?

No. Everyone lives under circumstances that are limited in some way or other. No one has access to every imaginable option. Anyone who is ever content, who is not constantly frustrated by dreaming impossible dreams, has some adaptive preferences or other. This fact alone therefore does not undermine humanly possible autonomy. Even adaptively deformed preferences can be the bases of autonomous behavior if they represent what someone reaffirms as deeply important to her upon reflective consideration and she is able to act effectively on those concerns. If what someone adaptively prefers, and chooses, is behavior so servile that she ceases to act according to her own deeper concerns in any sense and becomes slavishly obedient to others instead, or becomes subject to their coercive interference with whatever subsequent choices she tries to make, then she loses autonomy in a content-neutral sense. Content-neutral accounts of autonomy thus can handle a wide array of the cases in which women seem to lose autonomy when conforming to traditional norms of subordinate femininity. At the same time, content-neutral accounts can accommodate *another* feminist intuition. This is the intuition that, however oppressive their conditions might be and however much change is morally required, traditionally subordinate feminine lives nevertheless can and do often nonslavishly embody and express values worth caring about.

Severely Restricted Options and Autonomy

I mentioned earlier that someone's autonomy is hampered if she faces severely limited options. Joseph Raz[28] and others have argued that someone lacks autonomy if the only choices she faces give her no morally significant alternatives among which to choose. Autonomy is supposed to express an ideal of living, but living is not in any sense ideal when it is devoted to a constant struggle to stay alive or meet basic needs. Raz denies that lives of great struggle and suffering could really be autonomous lives.

Lives of constant suffering are obviously far from ideal; they may be devastatingly tragic. If, in addition, they result from unjust or oppressive social practices, then they are infected by the moral wrongdoings of others. It might seem that autonomy would be impossible under such conditions. There is, however, a useful insight in the idea that lives of suffering, even the suffering that results from human wrongdoing, do not absolutely preclude autonomy. Of course, that such lives might provide opportunities for autonomy does not, in any way, excuse the wrongdoing which infects them. It is furthermore important not to exaggerate the extent to which lives of suffering do afford opportunities for autonomy. It is a crucial moral criticism of the particular social institutions and practices in which oppressed lives are lived that those lives are so circumscribed as to face severely truncated ranges of morally satisfactory options.

Autonomy, however, is not only about choosing a luxurious life from among prosperous options, a life of endless delights. Even the most desperate and tragic circumstances may present someone with different ways to respond. So long as a person has some choice about how to react to the desperate conditions with which she must cope, then the alternatives facing her may differ in ways that have both personal significance for the person facing those options and general moral significance. How to cope with suffering or tragedy may be the most profound problem some people ever face in their lives.

Over the course of history, people have reacted differently to suffering and tragedy, some of them desperately preserving what mattered to them despite grave personal costs. A valiant, noble, inspiring sort of autonomy emerges when someone stubbornly preserves or pursues what she deeply cares about during a time of suffering or tragedy and against hostile opposition. We should not be too quick to accept a conception of autonomy that ignores, as nonautonomous, those lives that are forced to cope with tragic dilemmas. As Hannah Arendt has observed in commenting on the Nazi Holocaust, "under conditions of terror most people will comply but *some people will not*, just as the lesson of the countries to which the Final Solution was proposed is that 'it could happen' in most places but *it did not happen everywhere.*"[29]

What matters to a person, what she deeply cares about in a way that defines her identity and character, is not simply what matters to her under pleasant conditions. In an important sense, we never fully and exhaustively know who we are. We have, at best, working hypotheses that may be highly reliable under familiar conditions but become less reliable under new and different circumstances. (If Aristotle is right, we never fully *are* a particular character until we are dead and then we ourselves will never know for sure who it was that we fully were.) No one ever faces in a single lifetime all the great variety of conditions, prosperous or impoverished, ennobling or tragic, that human beings can face and with which they may have to cope. What one "really" cares about may well become clear only when one must determine how to pursue or preserve it under threatening conditions that make those values realizable, if at all, only at great cost. Someone may enter such a situation not knowing beforehand which of her alternative concerns matters more to her. Someone may well simply *not have had* any pre-ordained priorities among her plurality of deeper concerns. The struggle to decide what to do may be the very process that gives form to what had previously been, as Charles Taylor puts it, inchoate.[30]

It is important to note, however, that autonomous choices, under terrible as well as joyous conditions, need not be the most moral choices someone can make. We tend to think someone is heroic if, under tragic conditions, she makes a choice that gives priority to the wellbeing of others over that of her own wellbeing. Such choices are heroic in part because they are so difficult to make. Whether someone makes that choice autonomously depends on what she finds she really cares about when reflecting on what she wants at a time of danger or suffering.

The selfish choice that forsakes others may well be the choice that best represents what someone most deeply cares about. Autonomy is not, after all, the only moral value. Part of what is tragic about tragic conditions is that they bring out the worst in many ordinarily decent people. Decent people may finally find out, in tragic conditions, how shallow are what they thought were their deeper and nobler commitments. They may find that they do not have the courage or heart to defend what they previously assumed they cared about now that it costs them dearly to do so. Suffering and oppression may corrupt victims as well as oppressors. These conditions may lead us to betray the deeper commitments that seemed secure under light-hearted and plentiful times. This is a large part of what is wrong with oppression. Yet, while tragic or oppressive conditions may well make it much harder to choose rightly or to pursue the good, they do not thereby utterly preclude autonomy.[31]

Autonomy, to reemphasize the point, is not the only moral value. Indeed, autonomy may be less important than other values under conditions of chronic suffering or oppression. What we may culturally prefer to idealize for harsh conditions is not action according to what people find they "really" care about under these conditions, since harsh conditions may pervert our values and bring out the worst in many of us. For harsh conditions, we might be far better off idealizing action according to *genuinely noble* values, whether or not these are what people "really" care about in hard times. Under pervasively harsh conditions, we are more likely each to need the support of others, and may want to inspire each other not merely to follow her own heart, but to struggle to preserve heroic values and mutual concern, values that enable us to do our best for each other just at those times when we are most dependent on each other for survival itself. Autonomy, though still a possible achievement under tragic conditions, may be of far less cultural value at those times than other moral values such as courage and devotion to loved ones. It all depends on what people find out they care deeply about when they are most threatened and endangered.

At the same time, some people do turn out to be autonomously generous or courageous under desperate conditions. Autonomy need not be impossible to achieve or meaningless in hard times. And the precise values that some might choose autonomously to sustain may be exactly those that provide moral goods to others. This result would constitute the best possible response to hardship, a moral triumph over tragic conditions. Incalculable value emerges, with a bittersweet irony, when someone autonomously promotes moral good in the face of tragedy. Autonomy can pull for moral good in bad times so long as people have the real choice of adhering to or forsaking what they really care about, and so long as at least *some* persons care deeply about real moral value to begin with.

In an optimistic spirit, we can hope that most people ordinarily do include some genuine moral goods among their concerns. What they might preserve in harsh times remains an open question before the fact. Idealizing autonomy as one value for harsh and tragic times, so long as it is not the only one, expresses an optimism that the other values to which at least some people will remain steadfast under duress will vindicate the ideal of autonomy after all.

Counterexamples

I have presented a conception of personal autonomy as centering around the notion of choices and actions that effectively accord with deeper wants and values that the acting person has self-reflectively reaffirmed. My conception of autonomy probably allows for counterexamples that fit my core definition of autonomy yet seem intuitively (to some, at any rate) to exemplify the absence of autonomy. If so, this would show that my account of autonomy had not articulated a set of sufficient conditions. As well, there might be counterexamples that seem intuitively to exemplify autonomy yet which do not involve some of the conditions required by my account, such as self-reflective reaffirmation of one's concerns. This would show that my account had not articulated necessary conditions for autonomy.

What if, however, the alleged counterexamples are bizarre and fantastical? Should we care about counterexamples of that sort? Outlandish examples provide jobs and entertainment for legions of analytic philosophers. Yet it is far from clear that they yield insight into the practical or lived significance of everyday concepts. I therefore issue a challenge. On matters of ethical moment, let there be only counterexamples that are empirically plausible and that thereby challenge us to refine our concepts in helpful practical ways. Philosophy is the search for wisdom, not the search for bizarre counterexamples. Ideals and values that are to be relevant to people living everyday lives do not have to be so detailed as to encompass every logically possible, fantastical case. Plausible cases which fall within the fuzzy conceptual border regions surrounding our normative concepts are the only ones we should rely on as grounds for revising our ideals or specifying them more fully.

Granted, there is probably some Smith or Jones in some possible world who makes choices on the basis of what she cares about, yet who seems "intuitively" to be quite nonautonomous, perhaps because her brain is being manipulated in a vat by an evil and bored cognitive scientist locked in a Chinese room. There is no reason, however, to adjust practical ideals to hypothetical examples of this sort. If concepts are indeed understood in terms of paradigm cases, then we should expect there to be shady border regions to such understanding. Philosophical conceptions of autonomy, even without the label, grow out of philosophical traditions dating at least as far back as the Socratic injunction to live an examined life. We can function perfectly well with paradigm-based concepts in common everyday situations even if we have not yet specified how every remotely imaginable or logically possible case would be decided. We thereby loosen the grip of the philosophical obsession with micro-precisifying our moral concepts so as to encompass every bizarre hypothetical case that can be fantasized in the armchair of an ethicist.

Overly precisified concepts represent a style of philosophy suited to technicians. This might be fine for areas of philosophy that do not have much practical relevance in people's everyday lives. Ethics and social philosophy, however, are not only for technicians and intellectual dilettantes. They should also provide meaningful guidelines for people to use in living their everyday lives. They should be comprehensible at levels of detail and specification that still allow sensible application, within real-time parameters, to the sorts of situations that people might actually encounter. Our goal should be to find the best moderately specified conceptions that we can of ideals such as autonomy. Let us abandon the philosophically wasteful strategy of micro-tailoring practical concepts to fit implausible worlds.

This completes my introductory sketch of autonomy. In the chapters that follow, I first defend autonomy against objections (chapter 2) and then defend it more positively as an ideal worth valuing, especially by members of socially subordinated or oppressed groups (chapter 3). In subsequent chapters, I explore further the social dimensions of autonomy and investigate its meaning and importance for women in various social situations and relationships.

2

Autonomy and Its Discontents

The ideal of personal autonomy has not lacked critics. Feminists, communitarians, and other social theorists have raised numerous challenges to its very possibility and its alleged value. Can such charges be answered? Even if the ideal of autonomy survives a general critique, is it an ideal that is relevant to members of historically subordinated groups such as women? Would it be good for women if women's autonomy were given explicit cultural recognition and esteem? This chapter offers a negative defense of autonomy by responding to six critical challenges that have been or may be leveled against it. The next chapter defends the ideal in more positive terms with particular attention to its value for women.

Criticisms of Personal Autonomy

1. Autonomy—self-determination—is impossible because there are no selves

A formidable contemporary challenge looms before us. Various late-twentieth- and early-twenty-first-century theorists deny the existence of selves. There is no such entity as that which the ideal of autonomy presupposes as the determiner of itself. Selves, persons, subjects—these are all fictions, according to this line of thought. What seems to be a self, if actual at all, is actually something else. Perhaps it is merely a narrative construct,[1] or, more specifically and not dissimilarly, a mere repeatable signification in gender-based discourse.[2]

The claim that there are no such things as selves, if true, would undermine the entire autonomy project. Autonomy is self-determination. Obviously, if there were no selves, then there would be no selves who could determine themselves. As self-determination, autonomy requires a being that is a distinct

30

self. Selves must be numerically distinct from others of the same sort and must be separately identifiable as actors, agents, or authors of choice and behavior in the world. Whole social practices of holding responsible, praising and blaming, rewarding and punishing rest on the assumption that there are such distinct selves. Why trust this assumption? Why think there are any such things?

The presumption that there are selves is more specifically a presumption that there are human selves. These are the selves that matter most to metaphysical reflections on selfhood. The features and fates of these selves are the central preoccupations of philosophers reflecting on selfhood. The possibility that nonhuman animals might be selves while human beings are not selves would have limited relevance for philosophical reflections as "we" know them. So the question of whether there are selves is almost immediately the question of whether there are *human* selves, whether human beings are or can be selves.

If the assumption of selves should prove to be misguided, then any study of autonomy would be pointless. I am not, however, going to produce arguments to defend directly the claim that selves exist. Instead I shall argue more obliquely that there are good reasons for having some confidence at the outset that the assumption of selves, and, in particular, human selves, is not entirely misguided. There are good reasons, at least of a provisional sort, for retaining and working with the prevalent assumption that human selves exist.

First of all, let us explore what those in Western cultures tend, in everyday life, to assume about human selves. The framework of this assumption is "folk psychology," the common everyday understanding of selves that is featured in everyday discourse among and about selves. Most philosophical studies of autonomy are explorations of, and attempts to systematize or improve on, folk, or everyday, psychological notions of self-determination. It is in folk psychology that selves are assumed. Many accounts of autonomy, including this one, depend on folk psychological understandings of personhood and would have to be revised or jettisoned if folk psychology were to fall to newer and incompatible understandings of mental processes.

The first reason for retaining the everyday folk psychological assumption that there are selves is that it is bolstered by the nature of human embodiment. According to folk understanding (although not necessarily folk terminology), selves are agents, each one distinct from others of the same kind, who can be the authors of doings and whose doings are to be explained and understood in terms of intentional states that characterize them. Selves are agents who can act, who can reflect on their actions, and who are sometimes responsible as individuals for their actions. Selves are actual, coherent, discrete, relatively unified, behaving systems. Selves are entities whose actions must be explained partly in terms of intentional states that are ascribed to them.

At the same time, one reason for thinking there are no selves is that it seems that the doings of selves are events that can be traced causally back to prior events or conditions that are ultimately external to or other than the selves identified as the authors of the doings to be explained. In particular, what selves do seems traceable back to social conditions in which other selves participate significantly in such a way as to make it seem that they share in the agency seemingly manifested in the doings to be explained. The socially interconnected nature of human community might seem to undermine the discreteness of human selves, their separation from other selves as authors of doings in the world. There seems to be an interpersonal diffusion of agency that, if genuine, would blur the boundaries of seemingly separate selves. Without mutual separation, selfhood would lose its distinct authorship and its differentiated agency. Selfhood itself would seem to collapse.

The socially interconnected nature of human community, however, does not give a sufficient reason for denying the existence of selves. In the midst of social interconnection stands the curious character of embodiment. Human beings are embodied beings and, as I noted in chapter 1, except for pregnancy and the rare condition of Siamese twinning, their bodies are separate physical entities, disconnected from each other. Human beings are not like the organisms that make up a living sponge or a coral reef. Human organisms are not organically interconnected (again, except for pregnancy and Siamese twinning). This feature of separate embodiment has been so important to human communities everywhere that it has universally (among human communities) been marked by the social practice of distinct, "proper" naming. Nearly every human being, once outside her genetic (or, occasionally today, merely gestational) mother's body, is given a proper name of its own by some of the other already-detached human organisms. Human beings are thus separately embodied, nominally distinct, physical particulars who may be more or less uniquely designated in discourse. Proper naming together with pronominal reference enable already discursive human beings to talk separately to and about each new entrant into human community. Separately embodied human beings can thus be separated discursively.[3]

In addition to physical separation from other entities, including other selves, as emphasized by proper-nominal and pronominal discursive practices, a self must also have some degree of coherent unity as a separate entity. What sort of unity? It needn't be a thoroughgoing and unwavering unity of aim or purpose. A self may harbor ambivalences and discontinuities. Continuity of embodiment through space-time supplemented by memory access to some of that body's past and bolstered by distinct intersubjective recognition may provide enough unity for selfhood.

Perhaps, to be a self, a being must also be capable of some degree of self-reflection. This requires the capacity for representing itself to itself, a developed form of the general capacity for representation. Certainly, in order to *determine* herself, a self must be capable of both recognizing alternative options for choice, reflecting on her wants and values, and choosing among her options in a way that reflects what deeply matters to her. It must be plausible to say that the options, the commitments, and the reflections on them are "hers," that is, are attributable to the one particular embodied self-entity that she is.[4]

A second consideration supporting the provisional assumption that there are selves derives from a prior confidence in the moral practices that rest on this assumption. This is a Kantian line of thought. We must accept the existence of selves if we wish to accept certain moral practices that are common in Western cultures, if not other cultures as well. These practices include the usual suspects: holding responsible, praising and blaming, rewarding and punishing. The capacity for some minimum threshold of moral competence must be a feature of any beings who are to deserve to be held morally accountable in these ways. Moral competence requires, among other things, capacities to recognize alternatives for action and to be able to reflect on them in accord with morally significant standards. Moral competence presupposes competence as a person or self; it is a more specific form of general personhood or selfhood. Unless there were human *selves,* there would be no warrant for human moral practices or the evaluations or sanctions inflicted in the name of morality.

Feminists and other social critics might reject this sort of argument on the grounds that moral practices as we have traditionally known them are sometimes oppressive. Because of that oppressiveness, we should not accept any of the presuppositions of our traditional moral practices. This worry, however, would not be reason enough to reject the assumption of selves. The oppressiveness of traditional moral practices does not necessarily undermine any of the presuppositions on which those practices depend. The presuppositions need not contain any of the oppressive content of the practices that presume them.

In addition, the practices I am referring to are general ones of holding persons responsible for their behavior and reacting to them in ways that are warranted by what those persons are believed to have done. Far from rejecting these general sorts of practices, feminists along with other political and social actors have embraced them. To be sure, much feminist analysis is about broadscale social institutions and practices, not individual social actors. Feminist political agency, however, has not dispensed with individual selves as one fundamental unit of analysis and critical reaction. Most feminists on occasion, for example, regard at least some men as individually responsible for sexual violence toward women or children and regard at least some individual employers as individually responsible for economically unjust treatment of female employees. Many feminists have worked for political and legal sanctions against individuals whose actions as individuals have amounted to wrongs of these sorts. Antifemale actions are certainly socially embedded, subject to social construction and often collective in nature. Nevertheless, one of the primary ways in which feminists seek politically to control and suppress wrongful behavior is by sanctioning and regulating individuals for behavior that is traced to them as individual agents, for example, as rapists, sexual harassers, woman batterers, misogynist employers, and so on. So long as these responsibility-based political practices remain important to feminists, then the accompanying presupposition of the existence of selves would seem to have practical warrant, indeed, practical urgency.

A third reason for provisionally assuming the existence of human selves derives from the practical near impossibility of extricating ourselves from modes of thought and language that embody this assumption. A thoroughgoing denial of selfhood is difficult to articulate coherently without contradicting it-self. One form of the denial of selfhood is the claim that selves are social "con-structs" of some sort. On some versions of this view, selves are constructed by linguistic or discursive practices in particular. Yet if selves are the products of linguistic or other sorts of practices, then it is hard to resist the thought that there must be linguistic practitioners, agents who act in those ways. Who or what might those agents be? It seems impossible even to tell the story that selves are constructed by language without at the same time using language that presumes prior existing selves who do the constructing. Daniel Dennett, for example, formulates his denial of selfhood this way: "*Our* fundamental tactic of self-protection, self-control, and self-definition is not spinning webs or building dams, but telling stories, and more particularly concocting and controlling the story we tell *others—and ourselves—*about *who we are.*[5] And: "Thus do *we* build up a defining story *about ourselves*, organized around a sort of basic blip of self-representation. . . . The blip isn't a self, of course; it's a *representation* of a self."[6] "We" tell stories about "who we are"; "we" repre-sent "ourselves" as selves to "ourselves." It is very difficult to tell the story of *how* selves are constructed in narrative or discourse without presupposing the existence of selves as the constructing agents.

On Dennett's view, an individual human organism exists as a biological being that issues "streams of narrative" that "posit a *center of narrative grav-ity*" that is the self of that individual organism.[7] The organisms are real; only the selves are fictional, those mysterious inner entities that are supposed to "control our bodies, think our thoughts, make our decisions."[8] Dennett's ap-proach grants a sort of agency to human organisms, albeit conceptualized bi-ologically and not in terms of what Dennett calls the "intentional stance." The intentional stance is the perspective that posits rational agents with inten-tional mental states who behave in ways that are explicable in terms of those states.[9] Dennett thus uses a conception of individualized, biological, nonin-tentional agency to explain away the seeming contradictoriness of his account of how "we" create "our" selves. His explanatory framework invokes rudi-mentary agents, selfless biological protoagents correlating roughly one to one with each of "us," to explain the origins of the uses of language that construct us as fully fashioned *fictional* centers of gravity.

Judith Butler utilizes a linguistic strategy to dispel the self-contradictory aura that surrounds her story of the discursive construction of selves. She writes, "The substantive 'I' only appears as such through a signifying practice that seeks to conceal its own workings and to naturalize its effects,"[10] and "As a process, signification harbors within itself what the epistemological dis-course refers to as 'agency.'"[11] In Butler's view, agency is located in the re-peated invocation of the rules of signification covering the "intelligible asser-tion of 'I'."[12] This suggests that agency floats freely in uses of discourse, uses that are somehow primordially possible prior to the existence of users of dis-course—that is, selves. Butler finds agency in the uses of language itself and the rules that govern it, all of which somehow preexist language-using selves. Before there were speakers, there was nevertheless somehow speech—self-activating speech. Butler's account of selfhood has a curiously religious dimension to it: in the beginning was the word.

Dennett, too, offers a view of language production similar to Butler's to supplement his story of biological selfless protoagents. He writes: "[W]e . . . do not consciously and deliberately figure out what narratives to tell and how to tell them. Our tales are spun, but for the most part we don't spin them; they spin us. Our human consciousness, and our narrative selfhood, is their product, not their source."[13] In a chapter allusively titled, "How Words Do Things with Us," Dennett all but endorses a theory of language production based on a "Pandemonium model." On this model, language production is viewed as "largely undesigned and opportunistic," a process in which there are "multiple sources for the design 'decisions' that yield" utterances, including "suggestions . . . posed by . . . word-demons."[14] This formulation does eliminate *us* as the agents who construct ourselves through narrative. Still, however, this account features agents of a sort engaged in doings that challenge our understanding if their causes are thought to be mere impersonal forces.

Whether grounded in cognitive science or postmodernism, however, the important point is that the denial of the existence of selves is less plausible (admittedly, perhaps only for a limited historical time) than its affirmation. Although the concept of selves seems outmoded to theorists in certain disciplinary specializations, the discourses that posit or construct selves remain pervasive in most human societies.[15] These discourses are among our most important tools for coping practically with the everyday world.[16] In deference to all of the antiself theoretical movements, we could say that my exploration of autonomy is taking place *within* the discourses that posit or construct selves. Exploring the concept of autonomy is a project undertaken decidedly from within the "intentional stance." While reflecting on autonomy, we inhabit the discursive space in which selves are taken for granted.

This does not mean that we must refrain from challenging the details of conceptions related to selfhood. Indeed, they can be challenged from within selfhood discourses themselves. We can always debate the nature or existence of selves, and nothing prohibits us at any time from exploring the theoretical denial of selves. We are unlikely to linger there long, however, when returning from the ivory tower to the practical exigencies of everyday life. However selfless might be the discourses of contemporary theories at the cutting edge, "we" are far from being able to get along in everyday life without the discourses that do presume the existence of selves. So long as the discursive practices of positing or constructing selves remain widespread, those who use those discourses will continue to gain useful insight by exploring the conceptions related to selfhood, such as autonomy. Any study that investigates how better to navigate those everyday discursive practices thus continues to be of service. Studies of autonomy fall into this camp.

For the remainder of this study, I take up a stance that assumes the existence of selves. I assume that talk of selves makes sense and that selves exist. I do so for the sake of exploring what autonomy, as self-determination, would involve and how it would figure in (human) social life. Selves are agents who can act, who can grow to reflect on their actions and on themselves, and who are sometimes responsible as individuals for their actions. Selves are actual, coherent, discrete, relatively unified, separately embodied, behaving systems, however much their boundaries are blurred by social forces. Selves are entities whose actions must be explained partly in terms of intentional states. Selves have wants, desires, cares, concerns, values, and commitments, and selves are agents who can determine themselves to act in accord with what they want or value.

I assume furthermore that nearly all (discrete) human beings are selves. I do not have to assume that *each* human being is one self. It is no refutation of my view that some human beings suffer from multiple personalities, psychiatric breakdowns, incompetence, or other losses of coherent, unified, discrete selfhood. The wholesale refutation of any conception of selfhood, in other words, cannot be based on psychiatric evidence that some selves are fragmented by personality disorders—unless it is also argued that these "disorders" are pervasive conditions afflicting all selves, in which case the concept of disorder would be virtually vacated of meaning.

The idea of one human being with multiple personalities or who, in some way, lacks one unified coherent self catches our attention only because it is abnormal. Its very conceptualization presupposes that *personalities*, even if not selves, are separate, discrete, relatively coherently unified, and countable. The concept of selfhood has not been eliminated on this view, but rather is merely renamed and untied from its moorings in the metaphysically democratic presumption: one human being, one self.

2. Autonomy is impossible because selves cannot "determine" themselves: human actions are merely links in chains of interpersonal interactions

According to a second critical line of thought, selves exist, but autonomy, or self-*determination*, is a fiction. This argument, in turn, has at least two versions. On one version (discussed in this section), no one is genuinely self-made because no one avoids dependence on others.[17] Human interdependence makes the appearance of genuine autonomy illusory. No human choice, act, or reflection is ever sufficiently disconnected from social relationships or the actions of others so as to be autonomously anyone's own. Everyone begins life in infantile dependency, and most people face significant periods of interpersonal dependency at some times in later life. In addition, anyone's exercise of autonomy competency is dependent on social practices and the contributions of sometimes countless other persons; it is therefore not genuine determination of a self by itself. Thus, citizens and other "autonomous" political agents are actually dependent on the domestic productivity of women and other household members. Economic "self-made men" in market societies are actually dependent on the exploited labor power of workers and the typically socialized nature of modern, income-producing work. Autonomous scientists and experts depend on the efforts of whole knowledge-seeking communities.

And so on. Social interconnections everywhere undergird and constitute autonomous choices and actions. Those choices and behaviors are in reality so dependent on the scaffolding provided by social relationships that they do not amount to self-determination.

In part, this is the argument that whatever we call individual autonomy is actually socially embedded. Autonomy must be reconceptualized in social, relational, or intersubjective terms. This criticism could be carried in two different directions. First, we could conclude that because it is socially embedded, so-called autonomy is not genuinely autonomous. There is no such thing as self-determination. Second, we could conclude that self-determination is possible but it is socially conditioned. On this second approach, we would need to reconceptualize autonomy in terms of its connection with social relationships. As I noted in chapter 1, I adopt the latter alternative. On this approach, autonomy *properly conceptualized* is not impossible at all, and a careful understanding of autonomy shows that social relationships belong somewhere in a complete account. If autonomy could be reconceptualized in social or interpersonal terms, this criticism would not undermine the concept of autonomy at all. It would merely reframe it. That reconceptualization has indeed been going on for some time now.[18]

The objection that selves cannot really determine themselves points also to the familiar metaphysical concern about autonomy. No matter how deeply I reflect on my wants and commitments, they do not ground my autonomy because they are *ultimately* not really "mine." They are traceable, at least in part, to causal conditions outside of and other than myself. These conditions include social, biological, and physical factors. To the extent that these conditions determine a person's wants or commitments, or the choices she makes in light of those wants or commitments, she is not completely self-determining. If self-determination cannot be complete, autonomy is illusory.

This is a traditional worry about autonomy: if the causal chain does not begin with the agent herself, then in what sense is it she who does the determining of herself? A compatibilist answer to this criticism, to which I subscribe, is that autonomy is a matter of degree and requires agents simply to harbor the capacities for certain sorts of reflection and agency, however these were acquired or are interconnected with the agency of others. Those reflective and practical capacities together with wants and desires must constitute a self who, as a self, plays a determining role in the processes leading to her behavior. Self-determination may, ontologically speaking, be merely an intermediate causal process in a causal sequence extending backward and forward to infinity. Such causal embeddedness does not undermine its character as the kind of causal stage in the process that it is: the part determination by a self of her own behavior. All else is history.

Autonomy is clearly a matter of degree. Although obvious, this point may not have been sufficiently emphasized by traditional accounts of autonomy. For Kant, writing about moral autonomy in particular, one either has the capacity to give oneself the moral law and to act for the sake of duty or one does not. If autonomy is a competency, it is tempting to think that one either has it somehow entirely or one does not have it at all. There is no intermediate possibility. Anything less than autonomous moral self-legislation is simply not autonomy. Yet even competencies admit of degrees.

Most theorists of autonomy now note explicitly that autonomy allows for matters of degree. No human being is ever wholly socially independent, so total independence cannot be a requirement of autonomy. Human beings who are autonomous are only relatively autonomous—relatively more so, that is, than others who do less of what autonomy calls for. Someone who is relatively more autonomous than others is someone who harbors within herself the capacities to engage in self-reflection more extensively or more deeply than they. One who reflectively reaffirms her wants or commitments more often than others has, in that respect, more autonomy than those others. As well, someone who notices how her wants or commitments were shaped by social forces and who reconsiders them in light of these reflections has more autonomy in that respect than does someone whose reflections lack that depth.[19] In addition, someone is relatively more autonomous than others if she can engage those capacities alone, without the current input of other persons. And someone is relatively more autonomous than others if she has more of a capacity to persist in behaving according to what matters to her even in the face of some minimal degree of opposition by others. (This, of course, does not mean that autonomous choices, actions, or reflections can be performed without any prior social grounding whatever.)

Thus an agent is autonomous (to some degree) so long as she harbors the capacity to reflectively reaffirm, and persist in acting according to, her own deeper wants and commitments, regardless of how those wants originated and regardless of how she acquired the capacity to reflect on them. Autonomy is a matter of someone as a self, distinguished by a certain perspective of wants and values, reflecting in certain ways on at least some of her choices and actions. So long as someone engages in those reflections to a minimal extent, she crosses the autonomy threshold. It does not matter that those doings, in turn, can be traced to causal ancestors that are "external" to, or other than, the self herself. Socialization and social influences endow human individuals with capacities to carry certain processes out on their own, without further need of input from those social conditions. The concept of autonomy simply requires it to be appropriate to mark off specific choices and actions from the ebb and flow of events and to attribute these to the individuals who carried them out. It does not matter that these actions were caused by prior actions or conditions ad infinitum.

3. Autonomy is impossible because selves cannot determine themselves: they cannot understand themselves accurately

A second version of the criticism that self-determination is impossible challenges the presumption that selves can reliably understand their own wants or values, that they are transparently accessible to themselves. To the extent that autonomy depends on accurate self-understanding, it is vulnerable to the vi-cissitudes of self-knowledge. On the previous autonomy-as-fiction argument, autonomy is made impossible by the reality of interpersonal causal depend-ence. On the present version, the impossibility is due to human inability, whether socially assisted or not, to achieve the degree of self-understanding, and thereby the self-reflection, that the ideal of autonomy requires.

Is self-knowledge in the requisite sense really impossible? Or is it merely difficult to attain or to guarantee? Granted, a good deal of what people claim to know about themselves is faulty; but is it always or nearly always so? There are at least two sources of support for the idea that people know very little about themselves.

Psychoanalysis is one source of misgivings about self-knowledge.[20] Psy-choanalytic accounts of the self theorize that whole dimensions of the self, in-cluding a great deal of memory and desire, are opaque to the self and either subject to radical misinterpretation or simply inaccessible to conscious reflec-tion altogether. The interpretive strategies of psychoanalysis, however, are widely contested. Psychoanalysis is, furthermore, not a tradition known for systematic or controlled data collection. Relying for empirical support mainly on clinical cases, psychoanalysis does not seem to warrant the view that human self-understanding *in general* is always flawed in ways that render au-tonomy impossible.

A second source of misgivings about self-knowledge is the systematic em-pirical data derived from research in social psychology. This research also sup-ports the conclusion that human self-knowledge is deficient, and it does so without relying on contested psychoanalytic theories about psychosexual de-velopment. Is empirical social psychology any more convincing than psycho-analysis in its suggestion that human beings lack the self-knowledge needed for autonomy?

Social psychologists Lee Ross and Richard E. Nisbett survey the empirical research in their field that seems to show that the ordinary ways in which peo-ple understand themselves are flawed. The major flaw is a misguided assump-tion about what best explains human behavior. Ordinary people—"lay" per-sons, in Ross and Nisbett's terms—tend to explain human behavior by reference to underlying, stable, coherent personality traits and dispositions that they regard as the causes of behavior. Ordinary people show a marked ten-dency to posit such personal attributes, thus displaying a "naïve disposition-ism." Social psychological research shows, however, that what are most signif-icant in explaining behavior are the features of the situations that people face. The "principle of situationism" is a hallmark of research in social psychology. On this view, behavior reflects the pressures and constraints to be found in the situations people face much more so than it reflects enduring personality dis-positions or traits. A mistakenly excessive emphasis on personality attributes in explaining behavior combined with a disregard of the explanatory salience of situational conditions constitutes the "fundamental attribution error."[21]

Ordinary people exhibit the same mistakes when reasoning about them-selves as they do when reasoning about others. They mistakenly tend to explain their own behavior in terms of personality traits and dispositions rather than in terms of situational factors.[22] These misunderstandings of behavior and its causes are relevant to autonomy. A person might believe herself to have certain deep wants and values on the basis of past behavior which she has explained by inaccurately attributing those wants and values to herself as stable, enduring personality traits. If a person acted according to wants and values she did not really have, she would obviously not be acting according to her own deep commitments. She would not be autonomous. People's misunderstanding of their own wants and values, if widespread enough, could render autonomy practically impossible.

Ross and Nisbett soften their stark picture of human misunderstanding with some qualifications. They concede that our everyday expectations about the behavior of people well known to us have a great deal of predictive reliability. We can predict behavior reliably, for example, when we have extensive familiarity with actors and their situations. Yet Ross and Nisbett still insist that any accuracy we ordinarily show in predicting behavior derives not so much from knowledge of human personality and character as it does from the ways in which personality and situation are ordinarily confounded; our *accurate* everyday predictions of behavior are based on implicit knowledge of situation rather than knowledge of character attributes.[23]

Thus, Ross and Nisbett's account does not preclude accurate self-understanding. Instead, it requires us to rethink the evidentiary basis for such understanding. On Ross and Nisbett's view, people have no direct access to their own cognitive processes. Even emotional awareness is not based on the feeling of internal physiological states. According to Ross and Nisbett, when someone understands herself accurately, it is because she has correctly attributed her behavior to situational factors, and has probably refrained from attributing personality traits to herself.[24]

Ross and Nisbett argue that an adequate explanation of behavior must take account of the subjective perspective of the actor and, particularly, how she construes the situation she faces. The impact of any situation on an actor depends on the "personal and subjective meaning" attached to the situation by the actor. Her understanding of her situations, in turn, derives in part from her intentions, goals, and preferences.[25] Ross and Nisbett thus allow that people have goals and preferences. These are features of a person's perspective that partly explain why she construes a situation as she does. Goals and preferences sound remarkably like the wants and values that most accounts of autonomy require people to have.[26]

Thus, Ross and Nisbett's account does not actually deny that people have wants and values. What their account requires is that a person come to understand her wants and values not by introspective self-examination but rather by considering her past behavior and the situations in which it occurred and then narrowly tailoring her inferences about herself only to what is clearly supported by that data. She should not extrapolate about her commitments much beyond what she has already shown clearly in past action. None of this is inconsistent with my account of the self-reflection required for autonomy.

Self-reflection needs to be reflection on oneself as an agent, but it does not need to be reflection on a private inner realm. It can equally be reflection on one's past behavior. It can also be cautiously and narrowly linked to clear-cut evidence. As long as accurate self-knowledge is at all possible, even the frequent occurrence of self-misunderstanding would not undermine accounts of autonomy based on reflective self-understanding. Choices and behaviors based on misunderstanding oneself would not themselves constitute autonomous choices or actions but would also not preclude such behavior from occurring.

Indeed, if human beings misunderstood themselves all the time, that would mean that even social psychology and psychoanalysis would both have to be distrusted! Those fields, too, would constitute merely alternative forms of human self-misunderstanding. On the other hand, if psychoanalysis and social psychology were at all reliable in revealing our genuine wants and values, or revealing reliable strategies for us to use in understanding our behavior and ourselves, then reliable self-understanding must therefore sometimes be possible. Thus, rather than undermining the practical significance of conceptions of autonomy by revealing the futility of attempts at self-knowledge, psychoanalysis and empirical social psychology *support* autonomy by enabling us to correct our self-misconceptions and improve our prospects for self-knowledge.

4. Autonomy is possible but not genuinely valuable; indeed, it might be positively harmful, especially to socially subordinated or oppressed groups

Another objection to the ideal of autonomy is that, as traditionally theorized, it is excessively individualistic and, because of this, ultimately harmful.[27] According to some critics, mainstream philosophy conceptualizes autonomy as the achievement of isolated social atoms and promotes independence, self-sufficiency, and disconnection from close interpersonal involvement with others.[28] It also promotes interpersonal distancing and adversariness by leading persons to regard one another as threats, to consider everyone as a merely self-interested, rational utility maximizer.

Any argument that autonomy is harmful must first clarify who exactly is harmed by it. Is it those who possess some degree of it? Or is it those who interact with persons who possess it? Perhaps the autonomy of some imposes burdens on their friends or loved ones. These two charges of harm, harm to the possessor and harm to those with whom she interacts, would be quite distinct and would probably have to be defended differently. It is important to ask of any charge that autonomy is harmful: who exactly is supposed to be harmed by it? And, of course, what exactly is the harm?

Who would be harmed by the cultural idealizing of an individualistic conception of autonomy? Perhaps those who would attain some degree of autonomy, as individualistically conceptualized, would do so by detaching themselves from social relationships that had previously been important in their lives. Misguidedly seeking autonomy through disconnection, they would abandon or destroy the relationships on which they had been depending for identity, survival, and flourishing. How serious a harm this would be for the autonomy seeker would depend on how well she tolerated the disconnection and on the life she managed to live despite the ruined relationships. At the same time, if my earlier argument is right in holding that persons depend on social relationships for the development of autonomy competency, for options for choice, and for cultural resources for making sense of those options, then autonomy need not require disconnection from others. Current interpersonal understandings of autonomy show that autonomy does not require social isolation or self-sufficiency.

Those who seek autonomy might suffer from pursuing self-sufficiency and disconnection from others that were ultimately unattainable and had nothing to do with autonomy. They would therefore have been wasting their time in such pursuits. In those cases, the harm to the autonomy seeker would be the loneliness she might suffer from having severed social ties she didn't need to sever in pursuit of an ideal she misunderstood. In cutting herself off from relational ties, however, she would not have been harmed by autonomy. She would have been harmed, if at all, by the loss of relationships she mistakenly abandoned because of a misconception about what autonomy required.

More significant than harm to someone who seeks autonomy might be the suffering imposed on friends and others close to one who seeks it. Even if autonomy does not require social detachment or personal self-sufficiency, it does not preclude them either. (More on this in chapter 5.) Some who seek autonomy might pull away from relationships on which others depend for survival or for the satisfaction of basic needs. In such cases, those others may well suffer badly from the cultural idealization of an individualistic conception of autonomy, particularly if they have no alternative means of support. The autonomy seeker would have wronged those dependent on her. I shall argue in chapter 5 that these wrongs arise only when the autonomy seeker is someone who has responsibilities to care for or protect others, or to sustain committed relationships with those others on which they rely emotionally. The wrong that an autonomy-seeker commits when seeking individualistic autonomy would consist in the failure to fulfill these responsibilities. Without such responsibilities to particular others, however, a person has no general responsibility simply to remain in just any social relationships in which she finds herself.

Defaulting on responsibilities to others should be distinguished from merely disconnecting from them. Mere social disconnection involving *no* failure to fulfill moral responsibilities to others, to the degree that this is possible, does not involve a moral wrong to anyone else. Indeed, one can default on responsibilities to others even while remaining intimately bound up with them. Disconnection is obviously not a necessary condition for treating others irresponsibly, nor is it, by itself, a sufficient condition. Thus, even if autonomy involved interpersonal detachment, this would not, by itself, make autonomy wrongfully harmful to those who were previously connected to someone now seeking individualistic autonomy.

What about the cultural impact of the idealizing of individualistic autonomy in public life? This ideal is often associated with certain sorts of economic
and political behavior which lead some people to behave in ways that may
have an oppressive impact on others who do not behave in those ways. Rational economic man, one of the models of autonomy in recent theorizing, enters
the capitalist marketplace aiming to maximize his economic gains in competition with others. The epitome of economic achievement is to be a "self-made
man." The drive for competitive success in the world of economic productivity is the force behind some of the ills of capitalism: the economic exploitation
of less competitive and less advantaged workers, the overuse of scarce natural
resources, the creation through advertising of useless as well as harmful con-
sumer demands, a production economy that satisfies the luxury whims of af-
fluent consumers while neglecting the survival needs of the poor, and so on.
Lorraine Code links autonomy to a quest for mastery. "Autonomous man,"
she writes, assumes "he can be master of all he surveys."[29]

The question, once again, is whether the culprit here is autonomy or
whether it is something else. On my view, autonomous choices and actions are
those that accord with the deeper wants and values the acting person has reflectively reaffirmed and that are partly caused by those self-reflections. There
is nothing in this idea of autonomy that necessarily, or even probably, requires
aggressive competitiveness in dealings with others or a quest for mastery over
others. Autonomy requires exploring what one cares deeply about and striving to act accordingly.

If one cares deeply about trouncing one's economic competitors or winning
economic success at any price, then the ideal of autonomy does license the corresponding actions. In no sense, however, does autonomy by itself *call* for
these commitments or actions in their own right. Considering the great variety
of wants, values, and commitments that populate the world of human concerns, it would be surprising if autonomy were only or usually displayed by
competitive, self-aggrandizing behavior. There are cultural supports for economic competition, ruthless aggression, and selfish indifference to others, but
these supports undergird those phenomena directly, and do not seem to operate through the intermediate process of idealizing autonomy. Granted, nothing about the ideal of autonomy *precludes* selfish indifference to others or
ruthless aggression toward them. Since autonomy is not the only morally
valuable ideal, however, such choices, even when made autonomously, are always open to moral criticism in other terms. Thus, autonomous behavior may
sometimes be ruthless, exploitative, and oppressive, but when it is, autonomy
itself is not the moral problem.

Margaret Walker interprets autonomy in a way that suggests a different
harm from that of promoting ruthless individualism. She suggests that autonomy, as defended by various contemporary philosophers,[30] amounts to a
mode of self-superintendence. One becomes accountable for managing oneself. Yet accountability, suggests Walker, is accountability to others. If Walker
is right, it becomes less clear how autonomy would constitute the genuine determination of a self by itself. If the self's determination of itself is subject to

the approval or recognition of others, then the self no longer is the reference point for its own determination; recognition by others becomes the governing standard for what constitutes autonomy. Although proclaimed as something that frees someone from social regulation, autonomy would amount instead to mere internalization of those very regulatory processes. An autonomous person would come to manage or supervise herself very much in accord with the demands of dominant social norms, after all. On Walker's suggestion, "autonomous" persons, as currently conceptualized by philosophers, would in effect be subordinating themselves to others. This prompts the thought that autonomy might function as an "opiate of the masses," leading them to act in ways that they thought were liberating but that in fact merely reinforced their social subordination.

It is not clear that Walker had all the above suggestions in mind; nevertheless, she is right to worry about conceptions of autonomy that depend on accountability to others, especially in regard to women's autonomy. Walker's critique might well apply indirectly to the sort of autonomy that Kant theorized for the moral realm. Everyone's worth, for Kant, consists in a capacity to give themselves the moral law, something that is predetermined by universal reason. On this view, no one's quest for autonomy is successful unless it is done as any rational being would do it. It is predetermined what law one must choose to obey, and one's rational moral nature is not fulfilled unless one gives oneself *just this* law. Giving oneself any other law, or more carefully, any other "law," would be mere heteronomy. On Kant's account of it, an autonomous chooser turns out to be someone who should be able to account for her choices to any other rational nature.

Not all conceptions of autonomy, however, connect autonomy to the capacity for accountable self-superintendence in accord with the normative requirements of others.[31] My own account avoids relying on this notion. Among canonical sources in philosophy, Mill, in *On Liberty,* also defends a different account of autonomy. Mill's ideal is aimed specifically at encouraging public tolerance of unpopular beliefs and unconventional lives that decidedly do not conform to the normative requirements of others. These beliefs and lives might seem quite unjustifiable to others and might, on Mill's view, be in fact unjustifiable because wrong. Yet so long as others are not harmed by the existence of those unconventional lives, Mill calls for the social toleration of individuals who choose them. To be sure, Mill hopes that idiosyncratic individuals will defend their beliefs or behaviors to others, if for no other reason than that the majority is benefited by having to reexamine their own convictions. Mill does not, however, regard the majority as endowed with normative authority and does not think that dissenters who live lives of their own must be able to account for themselves to anyone else.

Walker is right, however, to see in autonomy a kind of self-*superintendence.* This notion alone, however, does not necessitate accountability to others. One superintends oneself for the sake of promoting a life that accords best with a nomos of one's own. On my account, there is no being, rational or otherwise, to whom one must give, or be able to give, an account of that nomos in order to count as autonomous. Autonomy competency might involve such an accounting ability as a coincidental side effect, but it is not constitutively a part of autonomy as such. Autonomy does not require any accounting or accountability to others that would insidiously reduce autonomy to a covert form of intersubjective deference.[32]

5. Autonomy is possible and genuinely valuable, but has been restricted in practice to elite social groups

According to this criticism, the ideal of autonomy has been available for only some people in modern liberal societies, middle- and upper-class white men in particular. Autonomy involves someone acting according to those of her deeper wants or commitments that she has reflectively reaffirmed. For someone's actions to cohere in this way with what she cares about, she has to have options to behave in ways that accord with what she wants or values. The opportunities facing her must be sufficiently diverse to accommodate her concerns. It seems that substantial degrees of autonomy have historically been largely accessible only to those with an array of significant alternative life prospects and the education or training to reflect on such things. In the United States, for example, many young white men could dedicate themselves to the pursuit of financial, political, professional, or business success if that was what they wanted, and have serious hopes of being effective in achieving their goals. Success in the pursuit of such goals is part of the American dream, a founding myth of United States culture. Yet many social groups lag far behind white men in the per capita degree to which they can attain the American dream by dint of their own activities.[33]

There are two aspects to this problem. One is that the good of autonomy has been restricted to a privileged few. The other is that this social good has become available to the privileged few through the exploited labor of many others who are denied access to the fruits of their own labor. Societies constructed around the ideal of autonomy, or around related variations such as the paradigm of the "self-made man," are hierarchical societies in which the autonomy of a few, genuine though it might be, is often sustained by the exploited labor and subordination of the many. Autonomous male citizens, for example, were able to attain political autonomy in the past, and often still today, because they were freed for civic participation by the domestic labor of women and other unacknowledged household workers. Autonomous business tycoons achieved their economic preeminence in virtue of their access to wealth, education, good credit, social connections, college fraternities, cheap labor, or the other social privileges needed to engage in economic risk taking. Autonomous scientists and experts are the credentialed and publicly visible members of whole knowledge-seeking communities. And so on.

Those few members of a society who are able to achieve some significant degree of autonomy in their lives are usually the ones whose lives are not overburdened with the struggle to survive and feed their families. They are the ones who have time to reflect on their deepest convictions and commitments, and they are the ones who have social opportunities for action that accords with such reflections, thus making such reflections significant in and for their practice. They can form rational life-plans and can expect to be able to implement much of what they plan in their familial, occupational, and public lives.[34] They usually face arrays of significantly different, morally acceptable alternatives.

This line of criticism challenges the fairness of social institutions and practices in which autonomy has been embedded as an ideal. In those social contexts, autonomy has been available in practice only to a relative few and unavailable to many. Also according to this criticism, the autonomy of the few is enabled precisely by exploitative social arrangements; some persons labor tediously in subordination and deprivation while others are thereby freed to reflect on their desires and concerns. These are serious issues for anyone concerned about autonomy as a social ideal.

Does this criticism mean that the lived significance of autonomy is irredeemably shaped by the autonomous pursuits of middle-class white men? I believe not. The paradigm cases that flesh out the significance of autonomy during a given era or the historic restrictions on opportunities to attain it can change. Nothing prevents those changes from entering our cultural understanding of autonomy and helping to widen opportunities to achieve it. In particular, the ideal of autonomy can be reformulated so as to make it relevant to subordinated and oppressed lives.

One strategy for making a social ideal relevant to groups that previously lacked or were denied access to opportunities to achieve it is to reconceptualize it in light of the experiences, wants, and commitments of members of those groups. Reconceptualization is at least partly a matter of substituting new exemplars for the old ones that fleshed out people's understanding of autonomy. For a culture to forge new exemplars of autonomy, the people who previously lacked opportunities to be autonomous should become participants in cultural conversations about autonomy.

Autonomy, as I define it, emphasizes a person's behaving according to those of her deeper wants and values that she has reflectively reaffirmed. The wants and values on which such reflection focuses need not be confined to those of privileged elites. They may equally well be desires to triumph over (one's own or others') oppression or they may consist of commitments to end social subordination and hierarchy. Nothing in the core nature of autonomy as self-reflective agency prevents culturally diverse commitments, including goals of social progress and reform, from becoming substantive reference points for autonomous choice and action.

Notice, in addition, how the criticism that autonomy has been hoarded by elite social groups diverges from the other criticisms that I discussed earlier. The criticism of elite hoarding does not imply or presuppose that autonomy is impossible or harmful; far from it. There is no sense in complaining that something has been hoarded by a restricted social group if that something is genuinely possible for others to attain and is a value worth seeking. The objection of elite hoarding is thus in tension with the other objections to autonomy. In the final section of this chapter, I examine this tension more closely.

6. Autonomy is possible and genuinely valuable but can be, and has been, distorted in practice into something harmful

The term "autonomy" is not commonplace in everyday life, and what amounts to autonomy may easily be confused in practice with ideals of character and behavior that seem similar to autonomy but are not identical to it. Some of the substitutes, however, may not be as similar to autonomy as they first appear. In addition, they may be far less valuable than autonomy, perhaps even pernicious altogether. Critics of autonomy may legitimately wonder whether autonomy is tarnished by its practical association with inferior substitutes.[35]

Independence and self-sufficiency are plausible candidates for surrogates for autonomy in popular understanding. Superficially, they seem to have something to do with autonomy. An autonomous person lives by her own "nomos," or laws, and is, in that sense, self-sufficient in ruling her life and being independent of the rule of others. Independence and self-sufficiency have other meanings that also seem relevant to autonomy, for example, taking care of oneself and not depending on the care or support of others. Independence and self-sufficiency seem to be worthwhile ideals. What could be wrong with someone taking care of herself and not needing the assistance of support of others?

The popular worship of independence and self-sufficiency, however, may well have troubling dimensions. One troubling dimension of the ideals of independence and self-sufficiency is that they are often reduced to the activity of earning an income. Income earning has become paradigmatic of what it is to be independent and self-sufficient in U.S. culture today.[36] Lorraine Code notes how an oppressive ethic of independence and self-sufficiency, centered on income earning, has been inflicted on welfare recipients in the name of "welfare reform." Welfare coverage has been cut back in the United States partly on the basis of a popular belief that welfare recipients—a large proportion of whom are women—should become self-sufficient.[37] Thrown off welfare rolls and denied government welfare benefits, women suffer severe material deprivation.[38] There are substantial problems that poor people experience when denied welfare benefits and forced to adhere to standards of independence and self-sufficiency that circumstances may make unattainable, especially while they are trying to raise young children.[39]

If the ideal of autonomy were indeed distorted in practice by association with morally problematic substitutes, how should that situation influence philosophical thinking about autonomy? We would have at least two alternative ways to respond to that state of affairs. One response would be to abandon the ideal of autonomy altogether for practical purposes; perhaps autonomy is simply too difficult to portray accurately in popular discourse. The other response would be to work harder to clarify, in popular discourse, the distinction between autonomy and the other values mistakenly substituted for it, self-sufficiency or independence, for example. Critics of autonomy who worry that the ideal of autonomy is easily distorted in practice seem to me to opt too quickly for the first alternative. Why should philosophers, feminists in particular, give up on a worthy ideal simply because of popular misunderstanding? Part of the philosophical enterprise is to clarify and defend worthy values, whether or not those values are easily and widely grasped.

In addition, there is probably no genuine moral value or worthwhile ideal that is immune to distortion. Sometimes the distortion is a matter of excess or deficiency. Aristotle's Golden Mean is based on the idea that any virtue may be carried to excesses or deficiencies that constitute moral failings rather than moral virtue. Honesty, for example, may lead to the unfortunate Kantian excess of refusing to lie to save innocent life, even when lying is the only means available for resisting the threat to that innocent life. The liability to perverted excess (or deficiency), however, does not render honesty less a virtue. Code acknowledges that the sort of thinking she recommends in place of autonomy-based thinking, and which she calls "ecological thinking," is also susceptible to perversions.[40]

Furthermore, despite superficial resemblance, the ideals of independence and self-sufficiency do not in the end seem to be distorted substitutes for an ideal of personal autonomy. They seem to be distinct notions. Popular Western culture gives much more attention to independence or self-sufficiency, and prizes them more highly, than it does philosophical conceptions of autonomy. If autonomy is indeed understood to be distinct from the other notions, then it should not be judged by their liabilities. Philosophical ideals of personal autonomy center on the notion of a person living by norms and values that are, in some sense, her own. Everyday notions that are relevant to philosophical autonomy include "thinking for oneself," "being true to oneself," "listening to one's heart," "not following orders slavishly," and "not following the crowd." When societies demand that people be independent and self-sufficient, they are not demanding that each person live by her own values. They are not demanding personal autonomy in any typical philosophical sense of this term. They are more likely to be demanding financial independence, in the sense of earning one's own income. Yet financial independence is no constitutive part of autonomy. If the clichés of autonomy ("think for yourself") suggest any sort of independence at all, it is independence of mind or behavior.

Although financial independence and self-sufficiency are not about autonomy in the typical philosophical senses of this term, they are related to autonomy in being conditions that typically promote its realization. Having income or resources of one's own expands one's options in a wide range of situations. An expansion of options increases one's chances of being able to behave in ways that accord with what one deeply wants or values.[41]

To say that financial independence promotes autonomy is still, however, not to say that the ideal of financial independence is a (distorted) version of the ideal of autonomy. Earning an income and paying one's bills are not distortions of what autonomy is about. They may make autonomy more feasible but they are not causally sufficient for it. Even if they were, they would still not necessarily amount to distorted versions of the autonomy ideal itself. Philosophical notions of autonomy tend to be, as with the conception I have set out, about reflecting on one's wants and values and acting on the basis of those reflections. Someone who earns her own income does not necessarily listen to her own heart or avoid following the crowd.

Even in the context of welfare debates, independence and self-sufficiency seem distinct from autonomy. Welfare recipients are not really expected to be autonomous in any common philosophical understanding of the notion. Welfare recipients are not expected, either by welfare bureaucracies or by the public at large, to reflect on their deeper values or to live accordingly. Instead, welfare recipients are asked to become economically "self-reliant": to acquire and hold income-earning jobs.

It is a mistake, thus, to criticize autonomy by trying to link it to the problems of a misguided ethic of financial independence. It is also a mistake to criticize welfare cuts by trying to link them to a misunderstanding of autonomy. The problems with the policies affecting welfare recipients are not that they involve distorted understandings of personal autonomy. In expecting welfare recipients to hold income-earning jobs, the public at large is not making the mistake of misunderstanding the nature of autonomy and then holding welfare recipients to a distorted autonomy standard. The public at large wants welfare recipients to find and hold income-earning jobs *whether or not* this is what autonomy is all about. By contrast, the public at large probably could not care less about whether welfare recipients reflected on their deeper values and acted accordingly. Indeed, the public at large probably thinks that welfare recipients have the wrong values in the first place and need to reorder their priorities.[42]

If the ideals of independence and self-sufficiency are not mere distortions of the ideal of personal autonomy, are there nevertheless distortions of some sort that might arise in a culture that idealizes autonomy? It is certainly possible that autonomy might be carried to excess. Someone might undertake no action until she had reflected substantially on each alternative available to her and each relevant want and value. A person who did this would be rendered inert by her excess caution. Passivity and inaction would be the harmful results in this case for the would-be autonomous agent. Such results, however, are hardly grounds for dismissing the ideal of autonomy for everyone. The remedy for a tendency to excessive self-reflection is to learn how to bring closure to one's reflections and take action in due course when situations call for it.

A more morally disturbing application of autonomy seems to arise when someone reflects on her choices and actions *exclusively* in terms of her own wants and commitments. She thereby ignores other people who are affected by her choices and actions. She acts and lives her life solely by reference to her own wants and commitments. This would be to treat autonomy as a supreme value that overrides other values, including other moral values. Jean Grimshaw found that something like this attitude appeared in the "human potential" movement of a few decades ago, as represented especially in the writings of Abraham Maslow and, to a lesser extent, Carl Rogers.[43] Although that particular movement has faded away, the egoism that underlay it has hardly disappeared from mainstream Western culture.

Does excessive self-concern amount to a distortion of autonomy? Notice that there are two senses in which a person could treat self-concern as overriding: one, a substantive sense, and the other, a procedural sense. While excess *substantive* self-concern is a moral problem, the problem is not that of excessive autonomy. At the same time, excess *procedural* self-concern does exhibit excessive autonomy but it is not necessarily a moral problem. Let us see how this is so.

Someone whose self-concern was substantively excessive would have wants and commitments that were all self-oriented. This is the problem of selfishness. This condition need not, however, involve an excess of autonomy since a selfish person might not reflect much, if at all, on her selfish concerns or check very often to see that her choices and actions accorded with them. By contrast, someone whose self-concern was procedurally excessive would frequently scrutinize her deeper wants, cares, and commitments, and monitor her choices and actions to see that they accorded substantially with her cares and commitments. This sort of self-concern, carried to excess, would amount to an excess of autonomy. Excess autonomy in this case, however, would not necessarily involve a moral problem such as selfishness because a person who scrutinized her wants and commitments excessively might care deeply about the wellbeing of others. Thus, whether excess autonomy leads to a moral problem depends entirely on the substance of what someone wants or values. And in that case, the moral problem lies entirely in the substance of her preferences, and not in any excessive degree to which they are autonomously pursued.

In any case, the ideal of autonomy does not by itself entail that someone's wants and commitments should override those of all other persons, or that the value of autonomy itself should override all other values. How autonomy is to be integrated with other ideals and values is something that requires a comprehensive outlook, and is not determined by the conception of autonomy itself. This takes us to the sixth criticism of autonomy.

7. Autonomy is possible and genuinely valuable, but it is incompatible with other moral goods that are at least as valuable

This is an argument I do not reject. I do not claim that autonomy is a supreme value, that it trumps all other moral concerns. Sometimes—indeed, often—other values will be more worthy of pursuit than autonomy. When people's lives or basic material well-being are in danger, securing those goods is easily more important than striving for personal autonomy, although considerations of autonomy may not be irrelevant. Sometimes the lives or basic material well-being of others take precedence over someone's pursuit of her own autonomy. If I would not sacrifice my own survival to my personal autonomy, I should scarcely sacrifice anyone else's survival to it.[44]

The relationship of moral agency to personal autonomy is relevant here. Personal autonomy calls for using one's own wants and commitments as a touchstone for self-reflection. One makes of one's self, the self of one's cares and concerns, a kind of life project to be promoted and fulfilled. Of course, one's own commitments may well encompass the well-being of at least some others, and the social nature of human beings promotes this orientation in most human beings. However, the conception of personal autonomy itself does not require this sort of commitment, and it seems that some rare human beings are devoid of it. With the exception of egoistic moral theories, morality, by contrast, calls intrinsically for some sort of reflection on the well-being, in some sense, of others. One's own wants and commitments are not the only things that matter to morality. From a moral perspective, personal autonomy may indeed compete with other values in a wide variety of situations. Although my exploration of autonomy leaves open the question of how autonomy should be ranked against other values, I insist that autonomy must be integrated with them and, in practice, may be overridden by them—or may override them.

The Criticisms Taken Together

Thus, setting aside the view that there are no such things as selves, agents, actors, or persons, there are at least six types of arguments against the ideal of autonomy. First, autonomy is impossible because social relationships and interdependencies are so thoroughgoing as to make it impossible for selves to do anything that amounts to determining themselves. Second, autonomy is impossible because persons are simply incapable of the requisite capacities, such as accurate self-understanding. On either of these objections, nothing a self does to itself amounts to (self-)determination. The concept of autonomy would therefore be an impossible fiction.

Third, autonomy is genuinely possible, but it is harmful rather than beneficial. It is a disvalue rather than a value. It might harm those who seek it, and it probably harms those who are connected to those who seek it. Most actual examples of this criticism relate the harm of autonomy to the historic individualistic conception of autonomy. Individualistic autonomy leads its pursuers either to detach themselves from others or to attempt to dominate them. Most of the alleged harms stem from these sorts of interpersonal behaviors. Fourth, autonomy is a value that has been unjustly reserved for members of privileged social elites. Only they have had the socialization that fosters autonomy competency, the social opportunities for exercising that competency, and the social privileges that protect and endorse it. Fifth, autonomy, although possible and valuable, is liable to be perverted in practice into something *else* that harms people rather than helps them. Notice that this does not tell us there is anything wrong with autonomy itself. It merely cautions us to beware of false pretenders. Sixth, autonomy is valuable but not supremely so, and in practice it may conflict with other values that are more important.

Apart from the concerns I raised above about each of these criticisms in its own right, additional problems arise from attempts to combine them into a holistic critique of autonomy. Most important, they do not all cohere with one another. Either of the criticisms that autonomy is an impossible fiction undermines the thrust of all the other criticisms and brings the entire discussion to an end. If autonomy is impossible as defined, then it could not be harmful, could not be something reserved for dominant elites, could not be subject to distortion in practice (there would be nothing to distort), and could not conflict with other values. Of course people might pursue or distort in practice a pseudoautonomy that they idealized under the banner of autonomy. Any problems with this surrogate, however, would not be problems with autonomy as defined if autonomy as defined is impossible. Thus, none of these last four arguments coheres with either of the claims that autonomy is impossible.

The argument that autonomy has been restricted in practice to certain elite groups (argument #4) also does not cohere with the argument that autonomy is valueless or harmful (argument #3). Pointing out that something has been unfairly restricted to certain social groups is a criticism that presupposes the worth of bringing about a fairer distribution of it. The criticism rests on a presupposition that whatever was unfairly restricted is indeed a value and that those who have been denied their share of it were harmed somehow by that denial. If the denial of autonomy is neither a harm nor a deprivation of something good, then why complain about that denial? Unless something valuable is meant by the notion of autonomy, there is no point to the criticism that it has been made the prerogative of privileged social elites. (Analogously, social elites may be the only ones who can afford to spend money on tanning salons, but excessive tanning can cause skin cancer, so the denial of this service should not be the focus of complaints grounded on distributive justice.) In order for there to be moral or political significance in the criticism that a group has been denied access to something, that which was denied must be assumed to have genuine value.

To recap, there are a variety of critical strategies available for challenging the ideal of autonomy, but we cannot, it seems, coherently adopt them all (except to be ironic or provocative). If we argue that autonomy is not possible, then we foreclose the option of arguing that autonomy is a disvalue or that it has been unfairly denied to some social groups. If we consider autonomy to be possible but actually harmful to those who are autonomous, then we foreclose the option of complaining about its denial to anyone. If, on the other hand, we regard it as grievous that autonomy has been denied to certain social groups, then we are committed to assuming that autonomy is both possible and valuable, and we foreclose the option of arguing that it is not either of these.

To decide which critical strategy to adopt toward autonomy, or whether to challenge the ideal of autonomy at all, it is important to be clear about what we mean by autonomy. I have defined autonomous choices and actions as those based on the acting person's deeper wants, desires, cares, concerns, values, or commitments that she has reflectively reaffirmed. On my account, it is of this idea that the above questions should be asked: Is autonomy something genuinely possible for human beings? If possible, is autonomy something genuinely valuable for (any) human beings? If valuable, has autonomy been unfairly denied historically to subordinated or oppressed social groups?

My answers to these questions are: yes, yes, and yes. Yes, autonomy is genuinely possible. Yes, it is genuinely valuable. Yes, it has been unfairly denied historically to some social groups, such as women (in general and overall).

Is liability to distortion in practice a sufficient disvalue to outweigh the value of autonomy? Is the worth of autonomy completely overridden by other values with which it is somehow incompatible? I think not, in both cases. Clarity is always important when defending autonomy, and nothing stops us from pursuing autonomy, with due recognition that it is sometimes misunderstood and sometimes should give way to other values. Those other values and misunderstandings, however, do not require us to jettison the quest for autonomy altogether. (Of course, it is an open question just when autonomy should give way and just which other values should sometimes take precedence over it.)

Let us return to one particular tension noted above between the view that autonomy is harmful and the complaint that it has been reserved for social elites. Although these views do not cohere as a matter of logic, their alliance is not surprising. It is unsurprising that some social critics should both complain about the restricted access of a good and at the same time disparage that good. The ultimate revolutionary act is to repudiate not merely the trappings of power, not merely the lust for power, and not merely the injustices of power. The ultimate revolutionary act is to repudiate the *ideals* in the name of which power claims its legitimacy. Thus, "we reject what you stand for, what you care most about" challenges the founding warrant of socially dominant groups. Yet this repudiation might well be accompanied by a continued covert longing to share in whatever real value those ideals might embody.

Many liberal theorists have construed the ideal of autonomy as the justificatory heart of liberal philosophy.[45] It is therefore tempting for anyone with antiliberal views to try to discredit autonomy. Many feminists are among those who have criticized liberalism as an ideology that has contributed to the subordination and oppression of women. Autonomy has constituted a key liberal value, a cornerstone of liberal philosophy. If autonomy is really part of the justificatory core of liberalism, then such discrediting will undermine the entire intellectual foundation of the liberal enterprise.

An attack on the value of autonomy, however, seems like an inappropriate way to challenge liberalism. The problems with liberalism are not all problems with liberal principles such as autonomy. At least sometimes, they are problems with practices in liberal (or capitalist) societies that are grounded in something other than liberal principles, practices such as racism, sexism, or exploitative labor practices. On some esteemed versions of liberalism, such practices are even antithetical to liberal principles. Societies claiming liberal pedigrees have, in practice, often fallen far short of approximating the best articulations of liberal conceptions of justice, rights—and autonomy.

It is important to beware of the seductive trap of disparaging what Audre Lorde called the "master's tools," or values, just because they are those of the "master."[46] An ideal or value is not necessarily corrupt just because it is admired and sought by dominant groups. People who find themselves in dominant social positions may well believe they have not gained their social status unfairly or oppressively, that it has fallen to them in a natural or social lottery that is not inherently unjust. However erroneous this assumption might be, it nevertheless creates a psychological space in which members of dominant social groups can have sincere commitments to values that happen to be genuinely worthwhile. Positions of social dominance and privilege are not at all inconsistent with a moralistic outlook nor with authentic moral concern. Even Machiavelli realized that power, however oppressively based, can sometimes afford to maintain itself through conformity to genuine moral norms. Only when power faces conditions in which it must rule by fear and moral hypocrisy, rather than through love and moral honesty, argued Machiavelli, does it have to recognize its own moral shortfall.[47] Even then, members of powerful social groups may rationalize their domineering social strategies and avoid facing their self-serving ends.

In addition, dominant elites are neither homogeneous nor monolithic. Numerous dominant groups are rivals to each other and may have to compete for social supremacy. Dominant groups therefore need "tools" or values that will be useful against powerful others. Thus, there is good reason to suppose that the "master's tools," rather than being useless against powerful social groups, might be quite useful indeed against such groups. Even the metaphor of tools suggests a conclusion different from that which Lorde drew from it. Tools can be all-purpose and need not preclude use against those who created them. To think they do in a given case is something that must be argued regarding the particular case at hand. Thus, the tools, or values, that dominant social persons and groups value may be genuinely valuable, and may have real use as means for empowering subordinated groups to fight and overcome their own subordination. I believe the ideal of autonomy to be such a value, and in the next chapter I provide a positive defense of that view.

To be sure, there is a tension among these complex concerns. If oppressors can act oppressively while they espouse certain norms and values, we should wonder whether there is not something wrong with the norms and values by which they live. After all, if people are capable of oppressing others, how could the standards they rely on be legitimate moral guides? Something about their outlook must be seriously misguided. Thus, even while relying on prevalent culturewide standards for criticizing oppressive practices, we should at the same time scrutinize those standards. My scrutiny of autonomy leads me to believe that it is indeed a value for groups, such as women, who have experienced a history of oppression and subordination. It is now time to make good on that claim.

Values of Autonomy

The previous chapter sets out various challenges to the ideal of autonomy and aims to show that they do not succeed, either singly or together, in discrediting the ideal. Those arguments, if successful, are not sufficient, however, to establish that autonomy is an ideal worth pursuing or upholding as a culturewide value. For that we need a positive defense of autonomy. What value is there in reflecting on one's deeper concerns and commitments, acting accordingly, and doing so with the capacity to resist at least a minimum of opposition? What value is there in encouraging people in general to do this?

In this chapter, I bring forward a variety of considerations suggesting that autonomy is a valuable ideal. I focus particularly on its value for (many) women. Most of the reasons I give, if not all of them, may be generalizable to most women and to many, if not most, men, although I do not argue for that generality here. I focus on women for several reasons. First, autonomy has not always been idealized for women. Even though autonomy is more widely encouraged and supported in women than ever before, it is still not regarded as a particularly *feminine* value or virtue. If a case for autonomy can be made out for women in particular against this history, then the case for autonomy in general should prove easier to secure. Second, feminist philosophers have figured prominently among those who have expressed doubts and reservations about the value of autonomy. Focusing on the case of women's autonomy in particular helps to answer those criticisms. It is therefore with diverse women's perspectives in mind that I defend autonomy.

The First Person

An ideal of personal autonomy is based on the presumption that there is value in a life lived in accord with the perspective of the one who lives it. The best way to appreciate that value is to start with a first-person perspective.

I start with my own wants and desires, cares, concerns, values, and commitments. If I want something, that means that I am oriented toward attaining whatever that want is focused on. If I have a certain value, that means that I approve of whatever the value is about. Commitments of these sorts involve me in thinking that certain outcomes I could aim at are better than others. If I also conceive of myself as a being in the world who can act to bring things about, then it is only fitting for me to try to guide my efforts to act so as to attain or realize those things toward which I am positively oriented. There would be something odd about me, given my wants, desires, cares, concerns, values, and commitments, nevertheless setting aside these behavioral guidelines of my own and leaving the direction of my actions to other factors. Those wants and values express how I want to live my life and how I think I ought to live it. My life, after all, is who I am. It is the narrative, space-time trajectory that is me.

This recognition is at least partly appealing to me because all the alternatives are worse. The alternatives involve living in some way that I do not want or think I ought not to live. Aside from the uncontrollable conditions of the nonhuman world, the causes of my living as I do not want to live would stem from control by other persons. If my life is to be lived by me according to someone else's plan or conception, then it somehow ceases to be genuinely *me*. I would become a mere instrument of someone else's intentions. It would be an odd standpoint, to say the least, to be willing to live according to wants and values imposed by others that I could not recognize as worthwhile.

Only someone who has no conception of how she wants or ought to live her life could accept living as others think she ought to live, without any loss to her sense of who she is. When I agree with what others think about how I ought to live my life, I want to live in accord with how others think I ought to live, but not because they think I ought to live it that way. Rather, I want to live as they think I ought to live because I myself think their plan for me is the right plan. That it is the plan of others is entirely incidental to my own interest in it. It is because the plan is right (in my view) that I think I ought to live in accord with what others (happen to) think about how I should live my life. In such cases, I have realized some degree of autonomy.

Wants and values are complex, of course. They can be extended to the long term and combined into more general categories. Sometimes I have to do things I do not enjoy or value to achieve something else, and the value of the goal outweighs my dislike of what I must do to attain it. Living as I want or think I ought overall may thus involve acting in ways I dislike. Suppose that for the foreseeable future, I have to suspend my travel plans and instead return home to care for an ailing family member. To care for my ailing relative, I have to set aside my own immediate wants and desires—my wanderlust, my restless yearning for novelty, the value I place on cross-cultural experience and understanding. Caring for my relative is a thankless task; she is a cranky invalid who needs frequent medical attention. My commitment to taking care of her, however, overrides the importance of the wants and values I temporarily put in abeyance. I am living, for now, as I think I ought to live. It is my overriding wants and values that more deeply define my perspective and shape how I most want to live. If my commitment to my relation is one that I have re-affirmed upon reflection—and choices such as this are likely to be the subject of extensive soul-searching—then I am living autonomously despite having set aside wants and values of great importance to me.

Sometimes we may be glad in retrospect that others pressured us or even forced us to act against our own wishes or better judgment. After the fact, I may be glad a friend pressured me into refusing a certain lucrative job offer that would have involved me in shady schemes to solicit money from poor re-tirees. I may realize only later how my judgment was clouded by the lure of getting rich quick. In general, it is often prudent to leave myself open to argu-ments and even pressure from those who might try to sway me from my in-tended courses of action. I realize I do not always choose what I am later still happy about. Sometimes, I may even accede to the promptings of another with only a vague, semiconscious inkling at the time that her guidance might be better than my own desires or values. I may follow others on the basis of little more than a gut feeling, certainly not a developed want or commitment, per-haps not even a clear reason to trust the one who influences me.

Someone is not diminished as a person, a whole self, by yielding the direction of her life now and then to others. Any of us may at times feel overwhelmed by circumstances or may simply wish to relinquish control for a while. Doing so occasionally may be a useful antidote to living in a cul-ture obsessed with control.[1] In addition, we always rely on others for many of the concepts and content of what we think about our world, our selves, and our responsibilities. The narrow range of actions that comprise what anyone "does" through the course of her life are sustained and made mean-ingful by conditions and events she did *not* do and by a world of information and understandings she has derived often unquestioningly from others. It is only against such a background that we make sense of some actions as the doings of a particular person. Only an infinitesimally small fraction of all that happens, obviously, are any one person's doings, for which she is re-sponsible and which are more distinctly *her actions* than they are mere events or anyone else's doings. It is only for those happenings against the background of the person's socially derived understandings and circum-stances that the question of who acted and who was responsible for it could even arise.

Yet arise it does. For the small range of events constituting the activities of a person, the questions do arise of who acted and who determined that they would take the course they took rather than some available alternative. It is for this tiny range of all that happens, as made understandable by social means of comprehension, that a person would want control. Unless someone is facing entirely new, unpredictable, or extreme conditions there is something odd in a person's allowing others, simply and for no good reason at any level of gener-ality, to determine the direction of a great deal of her life. Such attitudes might be symptomatic of either psychiatric problems or a moral breakdown.

From a first-person perspective, there would be something amiss if I did not presume that my intentions for my life have value as the intentions for my life simply because they are my own intentions. Granted, I may know about my weaknesses, obsessions, and addictions. I may know that in certain situations I cannot count on myself to resist the attractions of certain substances, persons, or malicious acts. Knowing this about myself is a matter of evaluating my desires and behavioral tendencies. I cannot, at the same time, utterly discount the evaluative attitude toward my wants and values I thereby take up. Sometimes I might try to repudiate all my attitudes at once. We can imagine a convoluted psychological narrative: I desire to have such-and-such, but I know it would be wrong to have such-and-such, yet I cannot get rid of the urge for it, and I hate myself for still wanting it, but I am also appalled at the depth of my self-hatred over still desiring it, and so on. Yet unless I am utterly overwhelmed by ambivalence and indecision of this sort when I think about what I want or value, I normally do take up a stance of some sort carrying implications for what I should do in regard to my concerns and how I should live my life accordingly. It would be incomprehensible of me to harbor concerned attitudes yet not care to act in ways that accorded with what I most cared about. To have wants and desires, cares, concerns, values, and commitments is, conceptually speaking, to have a practical orientation. It is to intend to act in ways that best promote what one, in the most general sense, wants.

Even if I were to rely on others to help me negotiate such convoluted attitudes—by joining Alcoholics Anonymous, for example—and could not resolve them without help from others, nevertheless, if that help is leading me to act as I retroactively approve, and if seeking that help is something I do, why would I give up being able to choose the help on which I rely? If I can choose it, if I am not overwhelmed by fatigue or illness, why would I give up being the one who determines whose guidance I follow? From the first-person perspective of being capable of acting and of deciding how to act, it makes no sense to yield the determination of those capacities at all levels of generality and commitment, for no good reason apparent to myself, to other persons. Someone's doing so is a puzzle in need of an explanation.

There would also be something odd in my not wanting others to respect my intentions as guides for my own behavior. Others who care about me may advise, caution, or beg me to act in certain ways and not in others. If, however, we are peers in normal adult competence, then I want them to refrain from unduly interfering with my attempts to do so (assuming I do not violate my moral responsibilities to others). I realize that these modes of regard need not be strict or absolute. They may be unwarranted in case I were to embark on wild or crazy schemes that threaten to destroy me. (These modes of respect would always be unwarranted on the face of it if I were to embark on wild or crazy schemes that threatened harm to others.) Absent such countervailing considerations, however, respect by others for my own intentions for my life is something I want and need in order to be able to live my life according to my own wants, values, and conception of how I ought to live.

Once one recognizes, in the first person, what value lies in living a life with some measure of autonomy, it is a short step (and a familiar sort of philosophical argument) to recognizing how autonomy is a value for people in general. I simply ask: Why should others show me the respect and freedom I want from them and need in order to live my life as I think I ought? Doing so might involve their curtailing their own impulses or motives about how to behave toward me. In order that I may deserve the respect and freedom I need from others to live my life as I think I ought to live it, I grasp that I *should* show to others the same sort of respect. This is a normative point. As well, in order to have any hope of actually *getting* them to show their respect for my capacity for personal autonomy, I have to treat them in the same way. This is a point about actual motivation. Reciprocity then is both the principle and the motivation that prompts me to grasp that I should show respect to others' wants and values regarding their lives, the same respect I value from them in return for living my life as I care to do.

Thus, my interest in living my own life autonomously gives intrinsic value to the ideal of autonomy from my point of view. From that thought, I am led to recognize at least an instrumental value in autonomy as a general ideal. Do I also recognize an intrinsic value in the autonomous behavior and lives of other persons? I can certainly find direct and immediate value in the autonomous life of someone I care about. I feel wonder (and nervousness!) as my child grows in the knowledge of what she deeply cares about and the capacity to pursue it; I feel joy when sharing my best friend's retrospective satisfaction at having lived life "her way"; I feel pride in the aunt who overcame tough odds to follow her dream. These sorts of reactions extend the apprehension of the intrinsic value of autonomy beyond the circle of self-concern. I can go on from there to recognize that anyone can find intrinsic value in both her own autonomy and that of those she cares about. This recognition lays the groundwork for grasping an intrinsic general value in autonomy.

Breaking with Tradition

People's values and commitments are often grounded in social norms and conventional practices. Most people assimilate to some extent the norms of their cultural milieus. People who reflect on their values and commitments are often thereby reflecting on norms they have assimilated from the culture(s) in which they were raised or currently live. Such reflections may, of course, result in the personal (re)affirmations of those norms. Yet critical reflection on norms also harbors the undeniable potential for personal repudiation of assimilated norms.

A traditional source of autonomy's appeal is the potential it offers for breaking with tradition and convention, for social nonconformity. An emphasis on personal autonomy certainly does nothing to reinforce tradition. If autonomous persons are sometimes rebels against tradition, then a social matrix that idealizes autonomy will occasionally foster personalities that challenge at least some of the social practices in which they live. When traditional practices are oppressive to a group, the opportunity to challenge those practices is crucial to the group's betterment.[2]

Ironically, this promise of potential social nonconformity was part of the allure of personal autonomy even when autonomy in Western cultures was esteemed as a value only for (white) men. In *On Liberty*, John Stuart Mill calls for the tolerance of unconventional, and even subversive, forms of expression and idiosyncratic living.[3] Society would benefit, argued Mill, from the tolerance of what we might call social marginality and ideological contest. Mill's plea should alert us to the need to give a sufficiently nuanced account of autonomy's historic appeal to white men. It may seem that socially elite, privileged white men act harmoniously and in concert to exercise extensive control over social norms and do so to serve their own interests. On that view, however, it is hard to explain why an ideal with socially nonconformist potential should have been made available to *anyone*, let alone to white men. It is not obvious how the social nonconformity of members of privileged elite groups would work to the advantage of those groups. Would they not be challenging their own privileges?

Of course, what passes for social nonconformity among elites might not be genuinely revolutionary. Perhaps social nonconformity among elites themselves will never be so thoroughgoing as to subvert elite power wholesale. Perhaps it will always be confined within elite, self-serving limits. This view, however, presupposes a degree of solidarity and uniformity of outlook among privileged white men that is historically unsubstantiated. Elite groups of men clearly challenge each other's norms and often fight with each other, sometimes to the death.

The nonconformist possibilities that the ideal of autonomy promises seem genuine, even when exercised by one elite social group against another. Social criticism and rebellion against dominant powers are themselves elite options. Largely excluded from the public domain for most of human history, women may underestimate the depth and virulence of hostilities among men. The differences among men, however, are hardly minor. Feudal aristocracies have challenged the power and traditions of churches, bourgeoisies have challenged the power and traditions of feudal aristocracies, and churches have challenged the power and traditions of bourgeoisies. In fighting against each other, men have devised weapons with the power to annihilate all life on earth including, obviously, all male life. Even if autonomy has been an ideal available largely only to socially privileged men, there is no reason to underrate its subversive potential as an ideal that invites people to challenge dominant norms and values.

Of course, a weapon devised by men for combat against other men might be a weapon women would want to abjure. The nature of the tool has to be considered carefully.[4] The point here, however, is a simple one. Autonomy is a competency that enables men to take up a perspective potentially critical of

tradition, and there is no reason to think that this feature of autonomy is limited to white men. To understand the revolutionary potential of autonomy for
all people, we would do well to explore those literatures of revolt that specifically call upon readers (admittedly, presumed male) to reflect on their lives,
values, and commitments, and that uphold those sorts of reflections as the key
to social protest and rebellion.

Henry David Thoreau's "On Civil Disobedience," for example, glorifies
what amounts to autonomy, both personal and moral. Thoreau urges his
readers to reflect in what is effectively an autonomous manner on the norms,
values, and commitments by which they live, which he thinks they have absorbed uncritically from their social environments. Thoreau's appeals are
frankly masculinist: "Oh for a man who is a *man,* and . . . has a bone in his
back you cannot pass your hand through!" Yet the message of "On Civil Disobedience" can be vindicated despite the masculinist garb in which its ideals
are cloaked. This is obvious from a glimpse at the conventional practices that
Thoreau regarded as requiring the gravest moral criticism in the United States
of his day: imperialism and slavery.[5]

Women, too, can be conquered, colonized, and enslaved. And women can
hold slaves, and in various other ways participate as agents in the social practices and institutions that permit or protect slavery, imperialism, oppression,
and injustice. Women benefit from autonomous, critical reflection on social
norms and practices both as potential subjects or victims of those practices
and as potential agents engaged in perpetrating or sustaining those practices.
As victims or subjects of customary wrongs, women would be more likely, if
autonomous, to recognize the injustices perpetrated against them by wrongful
norms. Such a recognition might inspire women to summon the courage and
wherewithal to resist and subvert those oppressive practices. As agents of customary wrongdoing, women, if autonomous, would increase their chances of
recognizing their own immoral complicities and dissociating themselves from
the wrongful practices they had helped to sustain.

Mere nonconformity to conventional norms, of course, is not necessarily a
good. It does not necessarily manifest itself in desirable social movements or
moral attitudes. This is a crucial qualification of my thesis. Nonconformism is
a purely formal notion. In the twentieth century, fascist and Nazi movements
challenged and temporarily overpowered more humane governments and cultures. Nonconformist autonomy is not restricted to progressive social movements or thinkers. It can be implemented by factions that crush the autonomy
or well-being of others.

Nevertheless, purely formal nonconformity to convention *can* be relevant
to subordinated and oppressed groups struggling against the customary
wrongdoing inflicted on them. It can be exercised in progressive ways that
promote social justice and future individual autonomy. Social nonconformity
is merely a necessary, not a sufficient, condition of resistance to oppressive
customs and practices—but necessary it is. Toward promoting critical reflection in general, the ideal of autonomy thus invokes as a paradigm case the critical repudiation of wrongful practices.

Self-Governance and Morality

Determination, in the sense of governance, involves the locus of "control." Control of individual persons is part of what is at issue in regard to autonomy. Control of a particular person is a matter of whose understandings, wants, values, and choices are most immediately responsible for her behavior. Self-determination is the person's own control over herself. In self-determination, the understandings, wants, values, and choices that are most immediately responsible for a person's behavior are states or features of that person herself. This is a necessary condition for self-determination. In addition, the wants and values most immediately causing someone's behavior must have some deep relation to the self in question. They must be deeply important to her and she must have reflected on them and reaffirmed them.

The alternatives to self-determination include governance by other persons, or heteronomy. In those cases, the understandings, wants, values, and choices that are most immediately responsible for a person's behavior are states or features of *other* persons who are somehow effective in getting her to behave as they choose, want, or think she ought to behave. Alternatives to self-determination also include behavior that results from an actor's wants or values that are not important to her or that she has not reflectively reaffirmed.

Autonomy is desirable despite its drawbacks in part because heteronomy is worse. To see what is wrong with personal heteronomy (the contrast to personal autonomy), let us proceed by way of a not irrelevant digression into the notion of *moral* heteronomy. There is an important analogy between the two. Personal autonomy links choices to states of oneself, namely, one's own wants, values, or commitments. Moral autonomy, on my non-Kantian view of it, also links choices (about moral matters) to states of oneself, namely one's own conceptions of what morality requires. Both sorts of autonomy require the competences of situational awareness, commitment, and self-understanding.

The ways in which people are prepared for personal autonomy resemble the ways in which people are prepared for moral autonomy. In both cases, persons must be able to conceptualize themselves as selves among other selves, understand their own attitudes and motivations, grasp the nature of situations they face, reflect on and compare alternatives for choice, and make choices that accord with their own relevant attitudes. We might thus learn something about the value of personal autonomy by considering how moral autonomy has been regarded in the Western tradition. Unfortunately, in this matter, Western culture has made serious mistakes.

In his recent study, *The Invention of Autonomy,* Jerome Schneewind traces the modern evolution of the concept of moral autonomy.[6] On Schneewind's account, Kant's conception of moral autonomy was the revolutionary culmination of modern moral philosophy's developing view of morality as self-governance, an idea that gradually replaced an earlier Western view of morality as obedience. Moralities of obedience hold that most people are not individually capable of discerning what morality requires or of motivating themselves to live morally. In order for them to live moral lives, on this older view, most people must obey those few persons who do possess moral competence. Societies should be organized hierarchically and those with the greatest moral expertise should rule the rest. Of course, there are different traditional views about who has moral competence and about where they get it, whether, for example, through divine revelation or rational insight into the nature of the Good. Whatever the exact source of moral competence is supposed to be on the view of morality as obedience, the crucial point of that view is that human moral competence is limited. Only some human beings have the requisite insight and motivation to be moral on their own. The rest need to be guided and regulated both to their own good and toward behaving for the good of others.

In contrast to this historical view, on Schneewind's account, modern moral philosophy gradually evolved the view that all persons are *equally* capable of understanding what morality calls for and of being motivated to act accordingly. We can see the practical significance of this ideological shift in a gradual movement throughout the modern period toward social institutions and practices that became increasingly democratic, both politically and morally. This movement, however, was gradual indeed. *Pace* Schneewind, what evolved throughout most of the modern period was often merely the *view* that persons are equally morally competent. Most of the time, that view was implemented only in part.

Thus, for most of the modern period, as we all know, only some men benefited from the theoretical view that all persons are equally capable of morality. Over recent centuries, more and more men did come to be respected as competent moral (and political) agents, and gained formal privileges of participating in social institutions and practices predicated on the basis of this assumed moral competence. Meanwhile, however, adult women—of whatever class, race, or group—remained morally (and politically) subordinated to male power and authority. It was not until the twentieth century that women in substantial numbers in Western societies were gradually allowed by men to exercise their moral agency across a great variety of social contexts. Even so, major religions and most human societies today still fall short to some degree in both acknowledging women's full moral equality with men as moral agents and recognizing women's individual moral competence for the whole range of human activities and social institutions.

To be sure, in some historical periods, the public rationale for excluding women from participating in various social or political institutions, such as full citizenship and elective office, was not stated as the view that women lacked moral competence. Women were sometimes instead portrayed as morally superior beings, angels in the house, but who would be easily corrupted by the rough-and-tumble of the public realm. This view, however, covertly presumes that women are not fully morally competent after all. Either women's moral judgment or their moral motivation would, on this view, be susceptible to easy impairment by political participation. Women's alleged moral superiority, even on this view, was thus implicitly treated as a fragile flower easily destroyed, unlike the moral capacity of men, and thus hardly a case of genuine moral competence.

One important strand of feminist thought is a reaction to this attitude that women lack moral competence. Feminism challenges the globally common presumption that women are not competent moral agents and must be subordinated ultimately to male power and authority. Challenging this presumption requires, in turn, defending the contradictory presumption that women *are* competent moral agents, or, at least, defending the notion that women should no more have to prove their moral competence than do men, that women should be *presumed* to be at least as capable as men of grasping what morality requires and of being motivated to act accordingly. Putting the case this way allows us to remain (for the time) agnostic about just what morality requires and what the source of moral motivation is. Whatever morality requires in the way of understanding and motivation, there is no reason to suppose that women lag behind men in their general ability to achieve it.

It is crucial to realize that the moral practices that depend on the presumption of moral competence usually focus on individuals as the locus of that competence. The paradigms of moral competence are individual human persons. This paradigm does not preclude holding groups of persons responsible for joint actions. Collective agency and collective moral responsibility are comprehensible under existing moral practices. Nor does this paradigm preclude recognizing that individuals gain their moral understanding and motivation in part from socialization and from sustained social contact with others. No one becomes a competent moral agent alone, in lifelong isolation. As I argued in chapter 1, however, any of the practices that support moral agency—practices such as assigning responsibility, rewarding and punishing—rely heavily on the individuation of moral selves. It is as individuals that human beings tend most often (in Western cultures, at least) to be the subjects of moral practices involving social accountability. Even in Eastern societies that are communally oriented, people are often punished or rewarded one at a time for their doings. Individual human beings are thus widely treated around the world as paradigms of moral agency.

To make the case for women's moral competence in an individualistic framework requires making clear that it is *as individuals* that women harbor the capacities to become competent moral agents—at least to the same degree that men can do this as individuals. Women's moral agency, like that of men, is both socially grounded and individuated. Ordinary adult women, as much as men, are morally competent individual persons who must be nurtured and trained for that competency by other persons in social interrelationships shaped by cultural resources. A social conception of moral competence tells us that a morally competent person must first acquire from others a distinct selfhood and capacities to reflect on herself and to choose among alternatives in light of those reflections. Each person must acquire from her social milieu the meanings and norms in terms of which to reflect on her commitments and her circumstances. The concepts and values that shape moral understanding, responsiveness to others' wants and needs, and sensitivity to moral saliencies in various sorts of situations are all nurtured and sustained in dialogical communities. It is crucial not to forget the social context that alone enables moral competence to emerge.

Socialization alone, however, does not explain how anyone emerges from her social background able to make individual moral choices. A socialized and socially interconnected person might simply be an extension of those who socialized her. She might be *incapable* of exercising moral agency as an individual or of resisting the sway of morally misguided partners or communities. A merely social conception of moral competence does not by itself help to vindicate the moral agency of each woman in her own right. It does not warrant a society in allowing women to make moral decisions and take moral action as individuals—no more than would be the case with men if they were not individually morally competent. For that sort of warrant regarding women, we need an account of women's individual moral competence.

What is at stake in having individual moral competence is the entitlement to act on one's own with some significant range of freedom—freedom from the domination and control of others. One might not actually be accorded that freedom by others in practice, but the entitlement to it is a crucial basis for various moral and political claims someone might make. The entitlement to act with a significant range of freedom seems so obviously a value that it would be difficult to contest it. Who would *not* want to be entitled (and also able) to act freely without domination by others?[7] Who would want to be dominated by others with no good reason for thinking the dominator's wants or values were morally superior?[8]

Schneewind's historical survey makes abundantly clear that when a culture fails to perceive moral competency in certain sorts of persons, the culture is likely to incorporate, into major social institutions, mechanisms for the subordination of those persons. Those persons will be substantially denied the freedom to act individually according to their own wants and values and will be subordinated to the dictates of others who are regarded as having the requisite moral competence. Plato and Aristotle, we recall, who both famously reject the idea that most ordinary people are capable of (successfully) governing themselves morally, each imagine a political elite with the requisite rationality and wisdom to regulate the moral lives of all their inferior others.

As long as we continue to operate in our everyday lives within a moral accountability framework that takes human individuals to be the primary or paradigmatic moral agents, then women benefit by being regarded as individually capable of autonomous moral competence.[9] A certain sort of status accompanies the social recognition of someone's individual moral competence. She is more likely to be regarded as a reliable (though not infallible) witness to moral events and circumstances. Her perspective on morality is likely to receive relatively greater interest and trust from others. She is less likely to be morally dominated by others. If individual moral competence entitles someone to greater freedom of action, then those who cannot exercise moral competence individually—young children, for example—have to be nurtured, socialized, or governed by those who have the requisite competence. Within such a general framework, women benefit by the assumption that, however much human selves depend on socialization, women are full moral agents as *individuals* and should therefore no more be individually dominated or subordinated over the course of their adult lives than are men.

How does this view of moral autonomy bear on personal autonomy? One way of connecting moral to personal autonomy is to compare the sorts of values or commitments on which each is based. Moral autonomy, on my view, involves choosing and acting on the basis of moral norms and values which someone has made more truly her own through reflective reaffirmation. Personal autonomy involves doing so on the basis of nonmoral norms and values. Either sort of autonomy requires someone to reaffirm her deeper (relevant) commitments self-reflectively and to act accordingly as a result. There may, however, be a deeper interconnection between the two.

Suppose that personal autonomy is a generic term for acting in accord with any and all commitments one has self-reflectively reaffirmed. Some of those commitments and values would be moral commitments, while others would not be. Moral autonomy is thus one variety of personal autonomy. If personal and moral autonomy are interrelated in this manner, or if they are on a par but so intimately intertwined that moral autonomy is not possible without personal autonomy, then one additional value of personal autonomy would be that it is necessary for moral autonomy. One could not have moral autonomy without having at least a degree of personal autonomy. As the preceding discussion clarifies, moral autonomy, as a key component of moral competence, entitles someone to live freely without domination by others. It seems, then, that personal autonomy may be a necessary condition for the entitlement to live freely from domination. Thus, if personal autonomy is, or is regarded as, necessary for moral autonomy, then people who fail to be personally autonomous may be, or may be regarded as, incapable of moral autonomy and may accordingly be subject to social domination as a result.

To be sure, moral autonomy is not all that is required for moral competence. Moral autonomy has to do with reflecting on one's morally relevant commitments and values and deciding accordingly how to behave in the situations one faces. Moral competence also includes, for example, the ability to discern the moral saliencies of the situations one faces, responsiveness to the needs and attitudes of others involved in those situations, and the capacity to engage dialogically with others in order to learn how it is with them and how best to understand the moral situations they all share. The capacity to make decisions about how to conduct oneself at times when individualized conduct is required is only one aspect of overall moral competence.[10] It is not, however, an eliminable capacity. Moral competence is not complete in an individual unless she is able to make those individualized decisions. Doing so with moral autonomy involves deciding on the basis of her deeper commitments regarding what morality requires, commitments that she has reflectively affirmed and that result in concordant behavior.

Interpersonal subordination and domination are not, in and of themselves, morally acceptable. They require justification. The reasons for subordinating someone must be either for the good of others or for her own good. If people in general have the moral competence as individuals to fulfill their moral requirements, then they do not have to be constantly monitored toward this end by those with moral "expertise." They do not have to be subordinated for the good of others. If people have the personal competence to live satisfying lives without supervision by "superiors," then there is no justification for subordinating them to the will of others for their own good.

My argument, to repeat, is this: Personal autonomy seems to be a necessary condition for moral autonomy; moral autonomy is a necessary condition for full moral competence; moral competence is a necessary condition for being entitled to live free of domination by others; therefore, personal autonomy seems to be a necessary condition for being entitled to live free of domination by others. To the extent that women are regarded as incapable of personal autonomy (a necessarily individualized trait), a culture is likely either to regulate their lives excessively or subordinate them to other persons close to them who are regarded as capable of directing women's lives for them, as English common law subsumed women into the legal personalities of their husbands, who were thereby authorized to direct the course of their wives' lives. Another possible value of personal autonomy is thus its contribution to moral autonomy and, therefore, to the entitlement of its bearers to live lives free of the domination of others.

More about Individuation

I have argued that moral and personal autonomy, although socially grounded and sustained, are also individualized and individuating competencies. They involve persons harboring as individuals the capacities for moral discernment, responsiveness, judgment, and choice. I have suggested that individuals who cannot do any of these things alone might not be trusted individually, by others, with the direction of their moral or personal lives. They might end up being socialized, governed, or dominated by others. The moral communities of which they are a part might institutionalize practices ensuring their subordination.

The idea that morally incompetent people should be governed morally by others should not be entertained lightly due to its potential abuses. Any conception of moral competence can be the basis of subordinating whole groups of people who are seen in terms of distorted cultural stereotypes. The remedy for potential abuses is to make the concept of moral competence as clear, decisive, and absolute as possible and place the burden of proof on those who *deny* anyone's moral competence. Also, no one should be treated as morally incompetent simply because of her membership in particular groups. The proof of anyone's moral incompetence must be based on individual cases only. Individualized proofs of moral incompetence could involve the same sorts of legal procedings now required to show that individuals are legally incompetent for, say, the purposes of medical decision making.[11] The relevant practical principle, then, is that every individual adult be presumed morally competent unless a strong positive individualized case can be made to the contrary.

This approach emphasizes individuation. It accepts and works with the Western paradigm of individual human persons as the standard case of moral agents. Some may think an individualist approach constitutes a relapse into misguided forms of moral theory of the past. Feminists have made great strides in reconceptualizing autonomy in interpersonal terms.[12] Surely reintroducing individuation is a retrograde step, a backsliding into revisionist individualism. I argued in earlier chapters, however, that the problems that seem to arise from individualism derive instead from selfish egoism and other values that become commingled with individualism. They are not as such problems inherent to a focus on individuals or individuality. Thus, while an emphasis on individuality allows for selfish egoism, it does not entail it.

One reason for emphasizing women as individuals is that progressive change in women's lives needs to be interpreted partly in terms of what happens to individual women. Women's lives are diverse; justice and an end to oppression and subordination do not require the same ameliorating conditions for all women's lives. One size does not fit all. A focus on individual women acknowledges the differences among women and their needs and commitments. Some women lack access to material necessities of life for themselves and their children; other women need opportunities within their communities to fulfill their spiritual callings; still other women need racism to end, and so on.[13] Many nontraditional improvements in women's lives, such as increased job opportunities or diminished vulnerability to sexual assault, happen to them as individuals, even if as individual members of a certain group. Autonomy as a revolutionary or evolutionary ideal calls upon people to reflect on their own needs and commitments in order to determine what to choose or how to act. Each woman is better able to discern for herself what to do to improve her life the more capable she is of making choices and acting in ways that cohere with her own wants and commitments, and the less she is dominated by the conventions and traditions upheld by others with power and influence over her.

Differences among women are not merely a matter of differentiation by subgroups within the larger group, women. Just as black women should not be assumed in advance to have the same views or concerns as white women, so, too, no single black woman should be stereotyped as having a viewpoint that defines black women in general. The differences among women that feminists emphasize and celebrate point to individuality as their limiting manifestation. Differences among women go all the way down to the level of individual female persons. If there is reason to avoid blurring differences at the level of groupings among women, then there is just as much reason to avoid blurring differences among women at any subgroup level of identification. Progress in women's lives must be measured by its impact on the diversity of women's lives, and diversity goes all the way down. Diversity is a matter of both group differentiation among women and discrete human individuality.

One value of an emphasis on individuation is thus that it completes the recognition of diversity among women.

A second reason why individuation is a valuable aspect of autonomy stems from the fact that women should not understand ourselves so collectively as agents of social change that we are unable to protect ourselves against danger or oppressive conditions when physically separated from our support networks. We nearly always move through the world physically separated from each other no matter how close we are in solidarity, love, or other relational ties. Often, when we face abusive persons or oppressive conditions, there are no supportive others nearby to whom we can turn for help. We must sometimes rely on ourselves—even if the capacities for such "self-reliance" had to have developed out of nurturant social relationships.

Some situations are, of course, so threatening that we will be overwhelmed and defeated individually, no matter how well prepared we are for self-defense. Often the best strategy for coping with danger or oppressive conditions is to seek supportive others, close family members and friends, or support groups of those who have faced similar problems. The advantages to women of collective strategies to resist injustice and oppression cannot be overstated.

Yet some situations make it difficult or impossible for us to rely on collective support. We may find ourselves facing danger alone, or may be rebuffed by those to whom we turn for support. At the same time, those same situations may allow us scope for effective, individualized self-defense. The point is to supplement collective forms of struggle with individual capacities for recognizing domination and for responding to it. To be motivated to act self-defensively as individuals, however, we have to be ready to recognize situations as threatening to what we want or value. To be ready for these situations, women need to harbor, each within herself, the capacities for questioning norms and practices that might subordinate or oppress her, and to do so in terms of what she wants and values. Using one's own wants and values as a touchstone for that recognition and for the corresponding behavioral reaction is the contribution autonomy makes to the overall project of being able to defend oneself as an individual.

What about the apparent tension between group solidarity and cohesiveness, on the one hand, and the individualism of autonomy, on the other? Cohesiveness is important to all social groups, but it can be particularly significant to groups struggling to overcome injustice or oppression. I argued earlier that autonomy promotes in individuals a greater degree of critical reflection on traditional norms and customary practices, and that this reflection gives individuals greater opportunity to recognize norms that are harmful to them. These insights by themselves, however, may not bring about changes in social norms. Individuals acting alone are seldom able to bring about substantial social change. Members of social groups seeking to overcome subordination or oppression need to work together to accomplish that aim.

Even if isolated women can defend themselves against threats and oppressive conditions, they can hardly hope to overthrow whole social practices that oppress, abuse, exploit, or subordinate women. To change social practices is a major effort, generally requiring a lot of cooperation, joint efforts, solidarity, and mutual support among a large number of people.[14] Resisting women's subordination on a culturewide scale requires collective action and solidarity, or community, among women. The mutual empowerment of a sufficient number of women engaged in collective action seems necessary in order for any number of women to attain the critical political mass necessary to bring about, for example, culturewide economic or legal change. Indeed, the enhanced personal autonomy that is possible for many of today's young women who decline to call themselves feminists might not have been possible were it not for the collective action of yesterday's feminists who worked in solidarity to break barriers to women's participation in all major social institutions. As Claudia Card has noted, Mary Wollstonecraft, who wrote an eminently reasonable critique of the misogynist views and practices of her day, had no perceptible public impact for many years to come, undoubtedly because no community of women was able to rally together in her time to advance the goals she set out.[15]

The effectiveness of collective effort may require individuals to subordinate their particular wants and concerns when those concerns undermine collective effort. Collective action may require some suppression of the individual autonomy of at least some of its participants. Group solidarity can sometimes be antithetical to autonomy. Part of my argument for the value of personal autonomy is its emancipatory potential for victims of injustice and oppression. It is therefore crucial to consider the ways in which personal autonomy might undermine the collective struggles those groups need to undertake in their fight against oppression.

Collective action can manifest or promote collective autonomy, the autonomy of a group. A group realizes collective autonomy by living according to its own group wants and values, free of domination by outsiders. Collective autonomy is a possibility for groups that cohere well enough to have internal practices that establish and reaffirm group wants and values and that constitute group decision making about how to act based on those concerns. Oppressed groups can benefit enormously from collective autonomy. Collective autonomy, however, is not something fully realized within any single individual's own choices or actions. An individual realizes collective autonomy only as a member of a group, in concert with others. Collective autonomy is the achievement of a plural subject. Collective autonomy may not translate into individual improvements in the lives of every individual person in a group.

So long as the choices and values of a group acting as a whole cohere with the personally autonomous choices of individual group members, there is no conflict between the collective autonomy of a group and the personal autonomy of its members. An individual member of the group who wants or values what her group as a whole decides to pursue or promote will be at one with the aims of her collective. There is no guarantee, however, that the two forms of autonomy will always cohere or will cohere for all group members. The group's own wants and values may have been determined by a process in which some group members did not participate. Individuals in a group differ in their degrees of influence over the collective values and choices of the group. Group wants and values may also subordinate some group members to others. When the two forms of autonomy conflict, then an individual group member is put in the unenviable position of having to choose between, on the one hand, acting or living as she thinks she ought and, on the other hand, acting or living as her group has somehow collectively resolved to do to advance the cause of the whole group.

The problem from the standpoint of the group is that allowing group members latitude for individual autonomy runs the continuing risk that individuals will deviate from the collective aims and values of the group and undermine the group's revolutionary efforts. The problem from the standpoint of an individual group member is that she may not participate equally in forging or endorsing the values and choices that define "the standpoint" of the group, and the group's activities reflecting that standpoint may undermine her efforts to live an individually good life.

Individuals in an oppressed group may be required by the pressures of group solidarity to act in ways that violate their own deep convictions. The alternatives to personal autonomy include uncritical deference to the wants or values of others, sometimes even to members of one's own group. One alternative to the personal autonomy of members of a group fighting oppression is solidarity around movement values and goals. But which values? Whose goals?

This problem is particularly acute for feminists. To reject personal autonomy is, by implication, to reject the personal autonomy of individual women and thereby to give implicit support to the alternative to autonomy for women which is women's heteronomy—that is, women's deferential submissiveness to others in the living of their own lives. This is precisely the behavior called for by the feminine role that feminism has explicitly repudiated.

There is probably no general principle that would cover all such conflicts. Sometimes it is good that people subordinate their own wants and values to collective aims and actions. At other times, it is better for individuals to refrain from participating in collective social action and to follow their own hearts or minds—sometimes better for all concerned, as the examples of fascist and Nazi social movements suggest. The important point to insist on here is that the individuated dimension of personal autonomy sometimes has a social value that cannot be ruled out a priori.

One final complication in the debate over individuation. Culturally idealizing autonomy for women would signal that women's beliefs, choices, actions, and lives were important as such to the culture and not simply for their value in serving the needs and interests of others. Women's individuality would come to take on an importance of its own. Yet this development might have undesirable consequences. It might, for example, lead to egoistic, Nietzschean excesses in which women indulged themselves at the expense of others and neglected all the innocent others who depended on them. Would an emphasis on women's individuality lead women to become selfishly egoistic and to neglect their (genuine) responsibilities to treat others morally? This is frequently what the public fears about feminists.

In this regard, there are both optimistic and pessimistic possibilities. Optimistically, we might anticipate that support for women's individuality would no more lead them to selfish egoism than it has led men to selfish egoism and, therefore, women should receive the same degree of support for individuality that men have received. Pessimistically, it might seem that support for men's individuality has indeed led many men to selfish egoism, so that men's individuality should be culturally restrained to the same degree as has women's individuality. Either alternative supports the conclusion of promoting the individuality of women and men to the same degree, that which allows them to be both morally responsible agents and moral equals.

It should be repeatedly stressed that personal autonomy by itself does not constitute a complete set of character ideals. A complete set of character ideals would include personal autonomy supplemented by other ideals, values, and virtues having to do with how to treat others. It is important that the ideal of autonomy allows scope for the crucial debates about just what those values and virtues should be. So long as people can make mistakes about their responsibilities to others, people will need to keep open the options for reconsidering moral norms. Their own wants and deepest commitments remain a relevant basis for those reflections.

Respect

Autonomy is an ideal that invites persons to act and live their lives in a certain manner. The ideal of autonomy also makes interpersonal normative demands on us. It calls upon us to treat others in certain ways. This feature of autonomy is a social dimension of the practices that support autonomy. The ideal of autonomy enjoins respect for others and carries implications regarding the sort of "respect" that is relevant. When a culture idealizes autonomy, it not only encourages individuals to seek autonomy; it also calls upon them to respect each other's capacity for and exercise of autonomy and to respect each other in virtue of that capacity. By lacking social access to the means of autonomy, women and other subordinated groups have also received less of the respect due to persons in virtue of their capacity for and exercise of autonomy.

What is involved in respect for autonomy? Respecting someone's autonomy means not interfering unduly with her choices or behavior (assuming she is not harming others). It means giving her the freedom to choose and act unimpeded by such hindrances as deception, manipulation, and coercion. In case someone's autonomy competency has not yet matured, respecting her autonomy calls for treating her in ways that promote the development of autonomy competency, for example, encouraging her to explore what she wants and supporting her initiatives.

To respect someone's autonomy does not require supporting or conforming to the contents of the choices she makes. She may choose foolishly or badly. To respect her autonomy is to take her perspective seriously, to regard it as the stance she chooses to take up in the world, to hold her responsible for it,

and to treat her appropriately in virtue of what she wants and values. The reactions of praise and blame, reward and punishment, are part of the repertoire
of potentially appropriate reactions by others to the perspective of someone
who deserves respect in virtue of her autonomy.

Respect is not, of course, the only sort of moral response that people owe
each other. Care and protection are two other possible moral responses.
Whether or not care or protection is owed is not contingent on someone having the actual or potential capacity for autonomy. Someone does not need to
be autonomous in order to deserve care and protection from other human beings; nonautonomous human individuals are not bereft of moral entitlements.
Respect is, however, the distinctive reaction owed to those who have perspectives comprising important wants and values they can reflect on and evaluate
and who can act accordingly.

As I argued in the previous section, in an autonomy-idealizing culture, it is
crucial that manifest autonomy not become a credential determining who
"deserves" respect and who does not. Everyone, whether known to be autonomous or not, should be treated presumptively in accord with the requirements of respect. First, it is never fully clear that any particular person or
choice falls short of the requirements of autonomy, whether defined as I have
defined it or in some other way. People do not usually reflect aloud on the
choices they are making. Second, respecting someone as if she were at least
minimally autonomous is one way to promote someone's autonomy. It gives
her the social space in which to make idiosyncratic choices with less opposition than she would have otherwise received. Being able to make idiosyncratic
choices—or even conventional choices—with lessened opposition allows
someone greater opportunity to experience firsthand the results of those
choices and thereby to grasp more fully the wider significance of what she
chose to do. This behavioral experimentalism, supposing it does not risk life
or health, is one source of knowledge about available alternatives that promotes the actor's future, more well-informed autonomous decision making.

Respect for someone's autonomy competency can take at least two different forms that are quite distinct from each other. One form of respect for autonomy is to treat a person as she prefers to be treated (assuming that this
does not involve acting immorally). On this approach, an individual's own
choices would be considered first when deciding how to treat her, for example, when providing her with health care. A second form of respect for autonomy is to treat someone in accord with one's own best considered judgment
about what autonomy calls for, whether or not this coincides with how she
wants to be treated. Of course, one may think that what autonomy calls for is
precisely to treat her as she wants to be treated; in that case, the two approaches would coincide. One may think instead, however, that respecting
someone's autonomy calls for treating her in some way she dislikes, rejects,
even abhors—for her own good, of course. This form of respect involves overriding a person's preferences.

In chapter 1, I argued that a content-neutral account of autonomy supports
the form of respect for autonomy that involves treating someone in accord

with her own wants and values on the presumption that these are autonomous unless proved otherwise. By contrast, substantive accounts of autonomy support the form of respect that favors treating people in ways that promote their autonomy, whether or not this accords with their own wants and values. As I argued in chapter 1, there are advantages to the content-neutral approach of respecting the choices someone makes based on her reflectively reaffirmed wants and values.

Although there may be exceptional cases, in general and overall, women seem better served by being treated as they want to be treated. The history of cultural disregard of women's perspectives shows the horrors that arise in the absence of respect for women's actual choices. In the realm of heterosexual relations, when a woman's "no" is treated as a "yes" and women's own views are routinely disregarded, the result is women's widespread vulnerability to sexual harassment, sexual assault, and rape. The importance to women of having their perspectives, their wants and values, treated with cultural respect is thus crucial to women's well-being. The assumption that there is value in women living their lives in accord with what they want and value, with women living personally autonomous lives, seems to be the surest and most plausible basis on which to ground that respect. Justifying cultural respect for women's perspectives is thus another value afforded by the (content-neutral) ideal of personal autonomy.[16]

Liberalism and Autonomy

Liberalism and liberal societies have long celebrated autonomy. The liberal tradition views autonomy not simply as an ideal for a satisfying life but also as a value that properly grounds the nature and purposes of political power. I end my discussion of the value of individual autonomy by highlighting one aspect of the liberal emphasis on autonomy, namely the importance of personal autonomy to political legitimacy.

One foundational liberal principle, if not *the* foundational liberal principle, is the requirement that the exercise of the coercive power of government is justified only if it is considered legitimate from the standpoints of those over whom it is exercised.[17] Of course, this ideal has never been even closely approximated in practice. Granted, for it to have any claim to plausibility, it would have to be qualified in ways that would raise serious concerns about whether question-begging formulations of it could ever be avoided. For example, endorsement of political power would probably have to be limited to those human beings with certain sorts of commitments, such as a commitment to viewing society as a cooperative endeavor among free and equal persons.[18] This is itself a liberal commitment. Thus, the liberal principle of legitimacy appears to need protoliberal citizens in order for anything approaching widespread endorsement of a liberal government to be a serious possibility. Once the appropriate standpoint for endorsement is thus circumscribed, it appears that not everyone's viewpoint gets to count from the perspective of liberal legitimacy. The way is thereby opened for arbitrary historical contingencies to determine what legitimacy requires.[19]

Despite this problem, however, many theorists continue to think there is great merit in the familiar core liberal idea that legitimate political power is rooted in something like the consent or endorsement of those adults who have to live under the exercise of that power and that this ideal can be specified in some coherent and plausible manner.[20] The point is not to jettison the liberal ideal of political legitimacy but rather to alter it so as to make it as inclusive as possible without undermining itself. On this view, then, the endorsement of the governed, when that endorsement is suitably qualified, plays a crucial role of some sort in establishing the legitimacy of the coercive power that may be exercised over the governed by other persons organized as the agents of large-scale social and political institutions. After all, the alternative is that the perspective of the governed is irrelevant to the legitimacy of political power exercised over them. Some other source of legitimacy must replace the perspective of the governed. What could that be? Divine will? The Form of Justice? The options all seem even less plausible than the consent of the governed.

Any account of legitimacy other than one based on the consent of the governed seems to require two assumptions: (a) the governed in general cannot be trusted to evaluate the form of political power under which they ought to be governed, and (b) the form of political power under which they ought to be governed need have no connection to what the governed together would endorse. On the first assumption, the governed cannot tell what is politically good for them. On the second assumption, they are not even entitled to live under the sort of (presumably inferior) system they happen to want. In contrast to this view, the foundational liberal legitimacy principle seems to depend on the assumption that either the governed can manage to evaluate adequately enough the form of political power under which they ought to be governed, or, even if they are not capable of doing so, at least they are entitled to live under the sort of political system under which they happen to want to live.

Liberalism is generous with autonomy in theory, seeing its value at the foundations of justification for political order. In practice, as we know all too well, actual societies claiming liberal principles and pedigrees have disregarded the viewpoints of many groups among the governed, thereby suppressing the personal autonomy of the members of those groups. This shameful history might prompt us to jettison liberal principles altogether. This is not, however, the only response open to us. We can instead revise liberal principles specifically to counteract wholesale historical exclusion of certain groups from the liberal legitimation project.

My proposal is that we revise the liberal legitimacy principle so that it takes specific account of previously politically excluded groups, blacks and women, for example. Accordingly, we liberals may say that a government is not legitimate unless it is acceptable specifically from the perspective(s) of members of previously excluded groups who now live under it. A transformed version of the foundational liberal principle, relevant to women, would read this way:

The exercise of the coercive power of government is justified only if it is considered legitimate from the standpoints of the women—all the women—over whom it is exercised. Other versions would substitute a reference to different groups that are also combating historic subordination, oppression, or injustice within a theoretically liberal society.

By singling out particular groups for emphasis, these particularized liberal legitimation principles do several things. First, they amplify and clarify what is already implicit in the general formulation of the liberal legitimation principle. They add nothing new to what the general version already specifies. Thus, they follow trivially from the general version and logically should not be rejected by anyone who accepts the general version. Second, the particularized legitimacy principles focus attention on the full breadth of what is required for legitimation in liberalism, making it much more difficult in practice for this full breadth to be ignored. In practice, it has been all too easy for, say, the endorsement of governmental power by the white men who participated in public dialogue and public affairs to be regarded culturally as a sufficient basis for a social contract that binds everyone. The particularized legitimacy principle(s) I am proposing makes this narrowed focus more difficult to sustain.

Third, the particularized formulations bring attention to the typical conditions under which live the various groups that have to consent to the political power of a given society. Some groups may live largely under impoverished or oppressive conditions that make it implausible to think those group members would endorse the political power that governs them. Perhaps the existing political system contributes to those oppressive conditions or, at least, does too little of what it should do to alleviate them. Given those conditions for various social groups, liberal theorists must face up to what would be needed for political power to lessen the injustice or oppression facing oppressed group in order to make it plausible that those group members would consider that power to be legitimate.

A fuller statement of the liberal legitimacy principle would thus consist of a list of particular statements such as these:

1. The exercise of the coercive power of a particular government is justified only if it is considered legitimate from the standpoints of the women (of all races, ethnicities, sexualities, etc.) over whom it is exercised.
2. The exercise of the coercive power of a particular government is justified only if it is considered legitimate from the standpoints of the men (of all races, ethnicities, sexualities, etc.) over whom it is exercised.
3. The exercise of the coercive power of a particular government is justified only if it is considered legitimate from the standpoints of the blacks (of all genders) over whom it is exercised. (This formulation is redundant with the first two statements, but the point is precisely to highlight each socially significant humankind category separately.)
4. The exercise of the coercive power of a particular government is justified only if it is considered legitimate from the standpoints of the people of Asian ancestry (of all genders) over whom it is exercised.

And so on.

With this revised statement, or, rather, list of statements, of the foundational liberal principle of political legitimacy in hand, we are in a better position to grasp how the autonomy involved in liberal legitimacy is a value for all members of a liberally legitimate social order. Those who are governed by a form of political power they regard as legitimate enjoy the benefit of living under a government they would voluntarily choose. Of course, choices can be manipulated and people might be deceived into thinking they benefit from living under a particular form of political power when they do not benefit. For this reason, the liberal principle needs further adjustment, perhaps in the direction of requiring that consent be based on good reasons and careful consideration. However, it is not possible to say exactly how much consideration is enough. No such qualifications are foolproof, and they introduce complications of their own; for example, the more it is necessary for consent to be undergirded by extensive information and rational reflection, the less plausible it is as a reconstruction of the reasoning of ordinary members of a liberal society.

The simple, core idea of legitimacy as based on the consent of the governed is, for all its flaws and limitations, intuitively more appealing to many of us than conceptions of legitimacy that disregard altogether the consent of the governed. In accord with the more precise formulations of the liberal legitimacy principle stated above, we may say accordingly that women, as one group in particular, are better off for living under political power they regard as legitimate, especially if they do so for good reasons based on careful reflection, than they would be living under political power they did not regard as legitimate and would not choose. To live under a political system one would choose as according with one's reflectively reaffirmed wants and values is to be politically autonomous. This modified liberal position represents yet another facet of the value to women of personal autonomy.

In this chapter, I defended the ideal of personal autonomy on several interrelated grounds. I argued that autonomy (1) has intuitive plausibility from a first-person perspective; (2) encourages critical reflection on conventions that may be oppressive; (3) entitles someone to live free of domination by others; (4) involves aspects of individuality that can contribute to the fight against oppression and injustice; (5) entitles people to cultural respect for their normative perspectives and behavior based on those; and (6) grounds the invaluable liberal conception of political legitimacy. In the next chapter, I integrate into my account the contemporary social reconceptualization of autonomy, showing how this trend of thought has roots that extend back to philosophical writings on autonomy from the 1970s.

II

THE SOCIAL CONTEXT

4

Autonomy and Social Relationships:
Rethinking the Feminist Critique

Recent feminist philosophy has engaged in a love-hate relationship with autonomy. In the 1970s, feminists praised the ideal of autonomy and extolled its liberatory potential for women. They lamented only that this character trait had traditionally been idealized as a masculine achievement and unfairly repressed in females.[1]

In the 1980s and early 1990s, this view was challenged by other feminists who rejected the ideal of autonomy as it had traditionally been conceived. The mainstream conception, so they argued, is overly individualistic. It presupposes that selves are asocial atoms, ignores the importance of social relationships, and promotes the sort of independence that involves disconnection from close interpersonal involvement with others.[2] The traditional concept of autonomy, feminists argued, is biased toward male social roles and reflects male conceits and delusions.

As an alternative, some feminists in the 1980s began recommending a relational concept of autonomy, one that treats social relationships and human community as central to the realization of autonomy. The 1990s, accordingly, witnessed a renewed feminist interest in autonomy—but as relationally conceived.[3]

In this chapter, I first survey prominent feminist writings that call for a relational conception of autonomy and that criticize the philosophical mainstream for lacking such an account. Second, I show that prominent mainstream accounts of autonomy do acknowledge the importance of social relationships, thus tending to converge on this point with the prevalent feminist view. Third, I raise four related feminist concerns that will, I hope, advance the discussion beyond this simple acknowledgment.

Feminists have raised a number of objections to mainstream conceptions of autonomy. In this chapter, although I summarize other objections briefly, I deal only with the charge that mainstream accounts do not take account of social relationships. It is also worth noting that the mainstream philosophical discussions of autonomy to which I refer belong to what is now loosely called the analytic tradition and are often explicitly linked to defenses of liberalism.

The Feminist Critique

Feminist philosophers have criticized mainstream conceptions of autonomy on at least four different grounds, all of which were discussed in chapter 2. Before turning to the criticism based on social context, I summarize three other feminist criticisms here. One feminist criticism of mainstream theories of autonomy is that they presume a coherent, unified subject with a stable identity who endures over time and who can "own" its choices. This presumption is challenged by postmodern notions of the subject as an unstable, fragmented, incoherent assortment of positions in discourse.[4]

A second feminist criticism of mainstream theories of autonomy is that they treat the self as being transparently self-aware, able both to grasp what it wants and subject those wants to critical self-reflection. This view is challenged by psychoanalytic theories which construe the self as having significant dimensions that are opaque to its own conscious self-reflection. The psychoanalytic self harbors repressed desires that are not evident to the self, and is capable of mistaking that which *is* accessible to its self-consciousness.[5]

A third feminist criticism of mainstream theories of autonomy is that they elevate reason over emotion, desire, and embodiment as the source of autonomy, sometimes construing reason as the self's authentic or true self. Such theories make reason normatively hegemonic in the structure of the self and deprecate the moral role of emotion, desire, and embodiment.[6] (For my response to these three criticisms, see chapter 2.)

The feminist criticism that I explore in this chapter is that mainstream conceptions of autonomy ignore the social nature of the self and the importance of social relationships to the projects and attributes of the self. Mainstream conceptions construe individuals as social atoms who realize autonomy through independent self-sufficiency and self-creation in selfish detachment from human connection. Mainstream autonomy theories assume that we should each be as independent and self-sufficient as possible. This ideal, however, ignores the great importance of interpersonal relationships in sustaining everyone's life. It also promotes interpersonal distancing and adversariness by leading persons to regard one another as threats.[7]

Mainstream autonomy, according to this criticism, is allied with liberalism, and in particular with liberal abstract individualism. The self of abstract individualism, according to many feminist critics, is atomistic, asocial, ahistorical, emotionally detached, thoroughly and transparently self-conscious, coherent, unified, rational, and universalistic in its reasonings. This liberal grounding leads mainstream conceptions of autonomy to promote such unwelcome traits as atomistic self-definition, denial of the self's own development out of and ongoing dependence on intimate personal ties, a disregard for nonvoluntaristic relational responsibilities, detachment from others, and an impartial, universalistic mode of reasoning that ignores the self's own particularity.[8]

This charge derives much of its plausibility from the gender-linked manner in which mainstream conceptions of autonomy are often deployed. Popular culture as well as psychological personality studies associate autonomy with men more than with women. Popular gender stereotypes, for example, treat autonomy and independence as male but not female character ideals. Ideals for women, by contrast, emphasize nurturance and relationality. Gender stereotypes thus reinforce an autonomy/relationality split. Psychological research has supported this dichotomy by telling us that men more than women exhibit the strong ego boundaries and relative independence from others required for autonomy.[9] Since autonomy has also functioned as a general human ideal, the combined effect of popular gender stereotyping and psychological research has been to imply that women are deficient as persons when compared to men.

In the 1970s, feminist psychologists began to challenge these gender biases.[10] This 1970s research contributed importantly to the 1980s feminist philosophical critique of autonomy. The most prominent psychologists who contributed to this development are, of course, Nancy Chodorow and Carol Gilligan.[11]

Chodorow argued famously that gendered selfhood as we know it is due to childrearing practices in which the primary caretakers of all children are women. For girls, the sense of self and of being gendered female develops from learning that they are *like* the female caretaker from whom they separate. Hence females' separation and differentiation are less radical, and their sense of self remains ever more enmeshed in relationality than it does for males. For boys, by contrast, a masculine core gender identity calls for a radical differentiation from the female caretaker. Their achievement of a sense of gendered selfhood is uncertain and insecure, for it is always threatened by the primordial sense of oneness with femaleness. As a result, males are more driven than females throughout their lives to shore up their ego boundaries through separating and disconnecting from others, and through differentiation, especially from that which is female. Hence, men are more likely than women to fear intimate relationships and to see other persons as threats.[12]

Carol Gilligan carried Chodorow's insights into the realm of cognitive moral development. In particular, Gilligan challenged Lawrence Kohlberg's influential theoretical framework for understanding the developmental of moral reasoning. This framework idealized as the highest stage of moral reasoning the autonomous moral reasoner choosing for herself according to a rational moral law that is abstract and universal, beyond mere custom and tradition. When first used to measure the cognitive moral development of real people, this scale showed women scoring on average lower than men and thus ranking as less morally autonomous or cognitively mature than men.[13]

Gilligan, as is now well known, argued that Kohlberg's framework was biased in favor of male moral values and ignored the different moral concerns that women were more likely to exhibit. Women's alternative moral concerns center on caring for others and maintaining interpersonal relationships. This moral orientation sets its own distinctive developmental path. Whereas men fear intimacy and attachment because it threatens their autonomy, wrote Gilligan, "women [instead] portray autonomy rather than attachment as the illusory and dangerous quest."[14]

The impact of this work in feminist psychology has been to suggest that autonomy is a masculine but not a feminine preoccupation and that, for men, it is regrettably associated with individuation, independence, disconnection from others, and a tendency to see other persons and close relationships as threatening to the self. Some feminist philosophers have echoed that sentiment. Sarah Hoagland, for example, writes that individual autonomy seems to be "a thoroughly noxious concept," suggesting separation, independence, self-sufficiency, and isolation. She recommends replacing it with a notion of "self in community." The self in community has a sense of herself as a moral agent connected to others who are also self-conscious moral agents in a communal web of relationships which permits the separateness of selves without undermining mutual concern and interaction.[15]

Other feminist philosophers, however, have not utterly rejected the concept of autonomy. Instead they construe the individualistic emphasis on independence and emotional detachment from others as merely one way to conceptualize autonomy: it is the traditional, mainstream, or masculine way. These feminists recommend that we develop a new and female, or feminist, conception of autonomy, one that presupposes the relational nature of human beings and emphasizes the social context required for the realization of autonomy. These feminists achieve the same conceptual end as Hoagland, but without actually rejecting the concept of autonomy.

Thus, for example, Evelyn Fox Keller writes that the notion of autonomy admits of a range of possible meanings only one of which is "radical independence from others." Our culture's tendency to "confuse autonomy with separation and independence from others," she writes, "is itself part of what we need to explain." Labeling that view "static" autonomy, Keller offers her alternative conception of "dynamic autonomy" which, she says, acknowledges the human interrelatedness that produces autonomy, recognizes that the self is influenced by and needs others, and allows for a recognition of other selves as subjects in their own right.[16]

Keller does admit that there is probably an unresolvable tension between "autonomy and intimacy, separation and connection, aggression and love." She argues, however, that "tension is not the same as bifurcation" and urges against thinking of autonomy and intimacy as mutually exclusive.[17] Keller's admission is noteworthy. It exemplifies a common tension in feminist writings on autonomy throughout the 1980s. On the one hand, many feminists argue that interpersonal relationships contribute to personal autonomy, and, indeed, are necessary for its realization. On the other hand, many of these same feminists also suggest that the value of autonomy should not be emphasized at the expense of the values of interpersonal relationships—as if the two were really mutually exclusive. I will return to this problem in the final section of this chapter.

Jennifer Nedelsky recommends that feminists develop a new conception of autonomy that will "combine the claim of the constitutiveness of social relations with the value of self-determination." She charges that the prevailing conception of autonomy is saturated with liberal atomistic individualism, a perspective that fails to "recognize the inherently social nature of human beings." Autonomous liberal individuals, Nedelsky writes, are "self-made . . . men." We must instead recognize, first, that social relationships and practices are necessary to foster our capacities for self-government, and, second, that the content of the laws that someone takes to be her "own" is "comprehensible only with reference to shared social norms, values, and concepts."[18]

The contemporary liberal conception of autonomy, according to Nedelsky, is incapable of incorporating the role of the social because it presupposes a "dichotomy between autonomy and the collectivity." On the mainstream account, autonomy is to be achieved "by erecting a wall (of rights) between the individual and those around him. . . . The most perfectly autonomous man is thus the most perfectly isolated." This "pathological conception of autonomy as boundaries against others" has led us to equate personal autonomy with individual security from collective power.[19]

Interestingly, Nedelsky displays the same tension as does Keller when connecting autonomy to social relationships. Nedelsky concedes that "there is a real and enduring tension between the individual and the collective" so that the collective is both a source of and a potential obstacle to autonomy.[20] More particularly, Nedelsky regards democratic processes as a "necessary component of autonomy," yet autonomy "can be threatened by democratic outcomes." A "democratically organized collective" can "do violence" to its members.[21] Mindful that this concession moves her view closer to the mainstream conception of autonomy, Nedelsky takes pains to differentiate the two. The distinction, she claims, lies in her belief that individuality is inconceivable apart from the social context in which it arises. There is thus "a social component built into the meaning of autonomy."[22]

Lorraine Code argues against what she calls the "autonomy-obsession" of mainstream philosophy. She defends instead a reconceptualization of autonomy that integrates it with the notions of interdependence and solidarity.[23] She writes that the contemporary mainstream conception of "autonomous man" is of a person who is supposed to be

> self-sufficient, independent, and self-reliant, a self-realizing individual who directs his efforts toward maximizing his personal gains. His independence is under constant threat from other (equally self-serving) individuals: hence he devises rules to protect himself from intrusion. Talk of rights, rational self-interest, expediency, and efficiency permeate his moral, social, and political discourse.[24]

Code charges that mainstream autonomy treats "self-making" and "separate self-sufficiency" as key traits whereas relational and communal values "are frequently represented as intrusions on or threats to autonomy."[25] "Autonomy-oriented theories" posit self-sufficiency and individuality as the *telos* of a human life, treating individuals as separate, alien, threatening, and "other" to each other. Interdependence and cooperation are seen as diminishing autonomy.[26]

Code further proposes that moral theory start from the recognition that persons are "essentially" what Annette Baier has called "second persons." They begin in interrelationship with and dependence on other persons from whom they "acquire the essential arts of personhood," and with whom they remain in relationships of interdependence and "reciprocal influence" throughout their lives. Writes Code: "Autonomy and self-sufficiency define themselves against a background of second personhood."[27]

It is noteworthy that Code does not simply want to substitute a care obsession for an autonomy obsession; she writes that an ideal of care and connectedness has as much potential to oppress women as do autonomy-centered theories.[28] She even suggests that "autonomy-promoting values" might, in some situations, be worthier guides to practical deliberation than "traditionally female" values such as trust, kindness, responsiveness, and care.[29] This caution reiterates the tension in feminist thinking about autonomy that I noted in my discussion of Keller and Nedelsky, and to which I will return shortly—namely, a tension between thinking that personal relationships are necessary to the realization of autonomy, on the one hand, and thinking that they can be definite hindrances to its realization, on the other.

Seyla Benhabib censures the social contract tradition for presupposing a "disembedded and disembodied" self. The backdrop of this tradition's conception of the self is the metaphor of the state of nature, a metaphor whose profound message is that "in the beginning man was alone."[30] She cites Hobbes's recommendation that we consider men as "mushrooms, come to full maturity, without all kind of engagement to each other."[31]

Benhabib finds this tradition of thought alive and well in John Rawls's assumption, in *A Theory of Justice*, that when establishing the social contract, individuals are to be considered mutually disinterested. In other words, they should be thought of as indifferent to each other's interests, and (to quote Rawls) "not bound by prior moral ties to each other."[32] For Hobbes, of course, peace and social cooperation are to be found *only* according to the terms of the social contract that establishes a "common power" to keep all persons subdued. Apart from that condition, human beings are relentless mortal threats to each other, and human life is not merely "poor, nasty, brutish, and short," it is also "solitary."[33] "The vision of men as mushrooms," writes Benhabib, "is an ultimate picture of autonomy."[34]

The Hobbesian social contract, writes Benhabib, is to be established voluntarily in light of its eminent rationality—but only by men, in whom alone reason, volition, and autonomy coalesce. Women do not engage in early modern political contracting; instead they are invisible in the domestic realm where, among other things, they nurture the men who sally forth into the public world, some of them privileged to conduct the business of governing themselves (and everyone else). In Benhabib's view, the dichotomy between autonomy, independence, and the male governmental sphere, on the one hand, and nurturance, bonding, and the female domestic sphere, on the other, is a legacy of early modern social contractianism that still pervades contemporary moral and political theory.[35]

Thus, the predominant tendency for feminist philosophers writing about autonomy in the 1980s and early 1990s was both to criticize mainstream theorists of autonomy for their male-oriented neglect of interpersonal relationships and to propose the development of an alternative, relational conception.

The Convergence of Feminist and Mainstream Conceptions of Autonomy

Mainstream conceptions of autonomy by leading contemporary philosophers tend to display a common core notion of autonomy. They tend to regard autonomy as involving two main features: first, reflection of some sort on relevant aspect(s) of the self's own motivational structure and available choices; and, second, procedural requirements having to do with the nature and quality of that reflection (for example, it is usually required to be sufficiently rational as well as uncoerced and unmanipulated).

Mainstream discussions devote considerable attention to the conditions that hinder or obstruct autonomy. Anxieties about paternalism, governmental decrees, indoctrination, brainwashing, and a host of other social horrors crop up with surprising frequency. Feminist critiques of such literature are no doubt partly a reaction to this obsession. Nevertheless, some prominent contemporary mainstream autonomy theorists do explicitly acknowledge the importance of the social to the realization of autonomy, and have done so for some time.[36] Mainstream philosophical theorizing about autonomy is not a monolithic enterprise.

Gerald Dworkin, for example, suggests that there are a variety of traditional notions of autonomy. He himself calls explicitly for a conception of autonomy that can be endorsed from nonindividualistic perspectives.[37] Dworkin notes that autonomy would be impossible if defined as an overly stringent sort of self-determination. The concept of autonomy should be compatible with the slow social development and maturation that human beings undergo, a development permitting the heavy influence of "parents, peers, and culture." Also, autonomy should encompass the making of reasonable choices. To make a reasonable choice, argues Dworkin, one must be governed by standards of reasoning that one could not have chosen but has probably acquired from the teachings or examples of other persons.[38]

Dworkin is especially concerned to develop an account of autonomy that is compatible with other values that we cherish, particularly such values as "loyalty, . . . commitment, benevolence, and love." He tries to accomplish this compatibility by placing no constraints on the *content* of what someone can autonomously choose to be or do. In Dworkin's view, autonomy does not require that people's choices be substantively independent; they need only be procedurally independent, that is, they must be arrived at in a way that is free of coercion and manipulation. On Dworkin's view, one can autonomously choose to act in a substantively independent manner, for example, selfishly, or one can choose to act in a substantively dependent manner, for example, benevolently, accepting "the needs of others as being reasons for altering [one's] own plans and projects."[39] Either sort of choice can be autonomous provided that it is uncoerced and unmanipulated and that the agent is able to consider whether or not to identify with the reasons for the choice.[40]

Most important for our purposes, Dworkin's conception of autonomy does not require disconnection from other persons. He claims: "To be committed to a friend or cause is to accept the fact that one's actions, and even desires, are to some extent determined by the desires and needs of others. . . . To be devoted to a cause is to be governed by what needs to be done, or by what the group decides. It is no longer to be self-sufficient."[41] In addition, Dworkin notes that "the self-sufficient, independent, person relying on his own resources and intellect is a familiar hero presented in novels by Ayn Rand and westerns by John Ford." Yet, Dworkin makes it clear that he is not defending this notion of substantive independence. In Dworkin's view, autonomy is about giving meaning to one's life, something that one can do "in all kinds of ways: from stamp collecting to taking care of one's invalid parents."[42]

Dworkin further argues that moral autonomy in particular, contrary to the Kantian tradition lying behind this notion, could not be about creating or inventing our own moral principles. Such creation, argues Dworkin, is impossible; it is a view that "denies our *history*" [italics in original] and the profound influence on us of our families and other social groupings and institutions in which we participate. "It makes no more sense," he urges, "to suppose we invent the moral law for ourselves than to suppose that we invent the language we speak for ourselves." Moral principles have a "social character." The nature of our duties to others, and the precise others to whom these duties are owed "are to some extent relative to the understandings of a given society."[43]

Thomas E. Hill Jr. defends a modified Kantian account of moral autonomy that, he claims, "does not imply that self-sufficiency is better than dependence, or that the emotional detachment of a judge is better than the compassion of a lover." To respect someone's autonomy, argues Hill, is to grant her the right to make important decisions about her life without being controlled or manipulated by others. We can grant this right, Hill urges, without endorsing such goals as "self-sufficiency, independence, [or] separation from others." One can respect personal autonomy, on Hill's view, and still accept advice from others, sacrifice for their interests, and acknowledge one's dependence on them. Although Hill does note that "self-sufficiency, independence, [and] 'making it on one's own'" have been associated with autonomy, his view is that these goals are not obviously morally desirable and so are no part of an ideal of autonomy.[44]

Lawrence Haworth similarly stresses procedural but not substantive independence as part of his notion of autonomy. No "logical or conceptual conflict" prevents someone from aspiring to be both autonomous and communally related to other persons. Thus, for instance, a group of people might well "independently" decide on a life of deeply shared "goals, values, principles, and tastes." Haworth notes that too much procedural independence by its members might be disruptive to a community; but rather than giving up on either autonomy or community, he calls for social institutions that integrate the two, urging that "in principle the most extensive autonomy is achievable within the most intensive community."[45]

Joel Feinberg's writings about autonomy seem at first glance to express the excessive individualism that many feminists see in the mainstream conception of autonomy. For example, the virtues that Feinberg associates with autonomy include self-possession, distinct self-identity, self-creation, self-legislation, moral independence, self-control, and self-reliance.[46] In explicating these notions, however, Feinberg asserts clearly that no one can *literally* be a "self-made man," and that the habit of self-reflection must be "implanted" in a child by others if she is to play any part in directing the course of her own life.[47]

For Feinberg, the "most significant truth about ourselves" is that "we are social animals." As he puts it, none of us select our early upbringing, country, language, community, or traditions, "yet to *be* a human being is to be a part of a community, to speak a language, to take one's place in an already functioning group way of life. We come into awareness of ourselves as part of ongoing social processes." Feinberg refers to these claims as "truisms" that "place *limits* on what the constituent virtues of autonomy can be." The literal atomistic separation of independent "sovereign" selves is impossible. Liberal autonomy, Feinberg contends, is the ideal of "an authentic individual whose self-determination is as complete as is consistent with the requirement that he is, of course, a member of a community."[48]

In a 1982 essay, S. I. Benn tries to modify classical liberalism so as to accommodate communitarian conceptions of the social nature of human beings and the "moral claims of 'community.'" Benn makes it clear that he wants to retain "the core liberal values of individuality and autonomy."[49] Benn argues that although classical liberal individualism took little account of people's concerns for one another or the collective enterprises in which they engage, nevertheless liberal theories can be extended to cover those practices without distorting core liberal values.

Autonomy does not, on Benn's view, preclude participation in collaborative enterprises. Indeed, individual autonomy requires the "conceptual resources" of *traditions* of rationality inasmuch as such traditions enable a person to accomplish the sort of reasoning about rules that Benn sees as the nature of autonomous choice. Those conceptual resources are made available to an individual "by the particular cluster of sub-cultures that combined to make" her the person she is.[50]

Benn does not believe that every sort of communal relationship is compatible with autonomy. Communities that demand unconditional commitment to their standards and that withdraw their concern from those persons who show "independence of judgment" actually hinder the realization of autonomy. By contrast, argues Benn, relationships of "mutuality" require autonomy of their participants. Each partner of a mutuality actively participates in

creating and developing the relationship. Mutual concern for the other partners is an "ineliminable element of the mutuality enterprise." Friendships,
marriages, and "sometimes families" constitute what Benn regards as the
locus for mutualities. Granted, Benn thinks that mutualities are limited to
small numbers of people in intimate relationships since the partners have to
know a great deal about each other and be able to monitor the relationship
rather continuously.[51] Nevertheless, Benn recognizes that autonomy is compatible with social relationships and to some extent requires them.

Benn makes the same acknowledgment in a 1976 paper on autonomy,
even though he was not then trying to reconcile liberal individualism with
communitarian critiques. In that earlier paper, Benn mentions the role relationships of father and friend as two examples of activities in the course of
which agents could achieve autonomy. They would do so by identifying with
the roles in question and monitoring their performance and achievements according to relevant standards.[52] Benn also admits that the autonomous person is just as socialized as a heteronomous person, just as influenced by her
society's conceptual framework for understanding the world, its traditions
and its role demands. The autonomous person, furthermore, is social in needing to derive, from the people around her, criteria for rational choice and conceptual schemes for grasping relevant issues. The notion of an autonomous
person, he urges, must be made clear *within* the "conception of a socialized
individual."[53]

For Benn in 1976, autonomy is a matter of "criticism internal to a tradition." More specifically, it is "an ideal available only to a plural tradition" in
which there are alternative critical standpoints that can be adopted by each
person for reflecting on the principles and values that she has internalized.[54]
Like Dworkin and Feinberg after him, Benn denies that autonomy depends on
substantive independence. Pointedly noting that his account omits discussion
about the content of the autonomous person's "principles and ideals," Benn
states that he finds no reason why an autonomous person "should not be
deeply concerned about social justice and community."[55]

In a 1973 essay, R. S. Peters explores the means by which the institutions
and practices of formal education can foster the development of autonomy.
Along the way, he touches on the importance of relationships in home environments. In Peters's view, socialization is crucial to the development of the
capacity to be a chooser, which he considers to lie at the core of autonomy.
The best home environment for encouraging this capacity, recommends Peters, is one in which "there is a warm attitude of acceptance towards children,
together with a firm and consistent insistence on rules of behaviour without
much in the way of punishment."[56]

For Peters, autonomy requires authenticity, which he explicates in terms of
an individual's tendency to be moved by considerations "intrinsic" to a mode
of conduct rather than by extrinsic considerations such as reward and punishment; his example of an intrinsic consideration is "the sufferings of others."
The school environment can contribute to the development of autonomy by
providing "a general atmosphere of discussion" about rules and the reasons

for them, and *not* by "an authoritarian system of control in which anything of importance is decided by the fiat of the headmaster."[57]

Advancing the Discussion

As shown in the previous section, mainstream philosophical work on autonomy, at least as far back as 1973, has included prominent theorists who acknowledge the contribution that social relationships make to the realization of autonomy. Feminist philosophy and mainstream philosophy have thus been converging around this theme. This is not to say, however, that feminist critiques of mainstream conceptions of autonomy are now obsolete. A number of still-relevant feminist concerns can be raised both about how philosophy contributes to a culturewide understanding of autonomy and about the exact details of relational conceptions of autonomy. In the remainder of this chapter, I will present four such concerns.[58]

First, although *some* leading mainstream philosophers acknowledge that social relationships contribute to the realization of autonomy, not all mainstream philosophers do so. Harry Frankfurt's varying and widely influential accounts of autonomy, spanning more than three decades of work on this topic, are devoid of any reference to social dimensions or conditions of autonomy. Frankfurt generally grounds autonomy in some form of volitional commitment or endorsement, processes that he depicts as solitary enterprises.[59]

Thus there are philosophical examples of solipsistic accounts of autonomy that do ignore social aspects of autonomy. Nevertheless philosophical accounts may not be the best targets of this feminist criticism. The feminist critique of autonomy seems much more appropriate for many of the male images and role models in popular culture than they are for the theories of philosopher-scholars laboring over intricate explications of authenticity and procedural independence. It is popular culture, and not philosophical culture, that seems to be the real culprit in presupposing an overly individualistic conception of autonomy.

Popular culture has long lionized the self-made man, the ruthlessly aggressive entrepreneur who climbs over the backs of his competitors to become a "captain of industry"; the rugged individualist, the loner, the "Marlboro man" fighting cattle rustlers out on the open range; and the he-man, the muscle-bound "superhero" avenging his way to vigilante "justice." These male figures tend to be independent, self-reliant, aggressive, and overpowering. Often they defy established authorities and institutions to accomplish their goals. Usually they have no dependents or family responsibilities, but on the rare occasions when they do, those relationships either support their aggressive efforts or become merely additional obstacles to be overcome. Male figures tend to be heroes or protagonists struggling against the forces set against them, whether business competitors, mob bosses, cattle ranchers, escaped criminals, or the women who want to marry them and settle down. What we have here is a cultural glorification of men (but seldom of women) who are independent, self-reliant, aggressive individuals who defy and defeat the social actors who try to control them or make them settle down to conventional lives. At a minimum, feminists are critical of the cultural glorification of male figures such as these.

If the feminist critique of autonomy is really a critique of those images of Marlboro men in culture at large, then how is it relevant to academic philosophy? One possibility is that mainstream philosophical theories of autonomy are unwittingly supporting popular masculine ideals. Perhaps the philosophical notion of autonomy actually serves to bolster the popular masculine ideal of the aggressive, independent, wholly "self-made" man.

The suggestion that contemporary analytic philosophers have a significant impact on popular culture is, admittedly, far-fetched. Few works of serious philosophical scholarship become popular best-sellers. Nevertheless, it does seem reasonable to ask philosophers to articulate our theories in ways that ensure that, should we be read by a wider audience, our words will not be misunderstood as supporting questionable values and ideals. Feinberg, for example, warns against a literal interpretation of the common expression "self-made man" and carefully reconstrues it as entailing *extensive* participation in shaping oneself.[60] Would an unwary audience, however, remember his careful reconstruction? In one refreshing passage, Feinberg juxtaposes the notion of someone being "her own woman" alongside the more familiar "his own man."[61] Yet masculine nouns and pronouns predominate throughout his discussion. "Her own woman" is eclipsed by this outmoded pronominal style.

It is important to note, however, that these concerns do not indict mainstream conceptions of autonomy for their internal particulars. Marlboro men are not necessarily autonomous according to the substantively neutral conceptions of most mainstream philosophers. Indeed, mainstream philosophical autonomy requires that men choose and live in accordance with relevant self-reflections about their motivations and values, not merely in accordance with conventional ideals of masculinity. Thus, men who each thoughtlessly strive to be independent and aggressive just for the sake of being what society considers a "real man" are not acting autonomously at all. The really autonomous man, on a *careful* reading of mainstream philosophy, is more likely to be the one at home changing his baby's diapers than the one riding off into the sunset on his Harley.

A second concern raised by the feminist critique has precisely to do with this substantive neutrality of mainstream accounts of autonomy. Many mainstream accounts of autonomy do not specify the substantive choices that someone must make in order to be autonomous.[62] As I discussed in chapter 1, they are content neutral. On this view, autonomy can be realized through voluntary commitments to, say, authoritarian religious orders, and through fulfillment of nonvoluntary moral role duties such as caring for one's aged parents. A content-neutral conception of personal autonomy requires only that a self be capable of the right sort of self-reflection and sufficiently determinate so as to find within herself reference points for directing such self-reflection.[63]

A content-neutral conception of autonomy, by itself, does not rank available alternative choices nor does it rank the widely varied types of selves we might each become. In particular, it does not provide a critique of substantively *independent* behavior, such as isolation, narcissistic self-absorption, and indifference to the needs and desires of those to whom one is closely related. A content-neutral concept of autonomy provides no basis for a general *analysis* or *critique* of such substantive independence. It neither condones nor condemns such behavior.

Many feminists are not neutral, however, about substantive independence. As Diana Meyers has carefully documented,[64] males in our culture are socialized for greater degrees of independence, aggressive self-assertion, and emotional distancing from others than are females. This means that when men engage in self-reflection about what they "really" want, they tend to find, lo and behold, that they really do want to be independent, aggressively self-assertive, and emotionally distant from others. These attitudes, in turn, might well foster male tendencies toward evading the responsibilities of close personal relationships and exhibiting aggressive and violent self-assertion, including sexual aggression, against others.

If autonomy is indeed best conceptualized as substantively neutral, then a critique of substantively independent behavior will have to be based on something other than the ideal of autonomy. We cannot fault autonomy theories for failing to do what might lie beyond their proper scope. Nevertheless, feminists may well worry that by approving procedural independence and neglecting to criticize substantive independence, mainstream autonomy theories might seem to be endorsing independence in general, thereby distracting us from the task of exploring what is wrong with overly individualistic, substantively independent behavior.

Thus, one concern implicit in the feminist critique of mainstream conceptions of what happens to be content-neutral autonomy might be that it is the wrong ideal to emphasize for our culture. Before encouraging people simply to be more fully and coherently what they already are, we should first think about what it is that they already are. At this historical juncture, rather than promoting autonomy, we might be better off urging that some of us change what we "really" are, specifically so as to avoid the patterns of socialization that lead males to focus obsessively on asserting themselves apart from or against others.

Notice that, like the first concern raised earlier, this line of thought is not an internal criticism of mainstream conceptions of autonomy. Rather, the argument is that substantively neutral ideals of autonomy should be subordinated to cultural critiques of the substantively independent selves that males are socialized and pressured to be. Mainstream (content-neutral) autonomy is not about the *radical* reconstruction of selves. It is, more modestly, about the nonradical ownership or reconstruction of aspects of the self. Feminists who discuss autonomy are concerned instead with the need for a more thoroughgoing reconstruction of our gendered selves. A content-neutral conception of autonomy is not useful for this task and might tend to distract us from it.

As I suggested in chapter 2, I myself am skeptical about the prospects of developing a feminist critique of overly individualistic, substantively independent selves or behavior as such. It is important to distinguish between individualistic behaviors and traits that harm other persons from those that do not. A father who abandons his dependent family for the sake of personal gratification exhibits the sort of disconnection that is morally culpable because he has harmed those who rely on him and toward whom he has special responsibilities. In general, to focus only on our own needs and interests while ignoring our legitimate responsibilities to others arising out of the relationships in which we find ourselves embedded and on which those others depend is to exhibit an excessive individualism that is morally culpable.

Consider, by contrast, a person who currently lacks any special responsibilities of care, support, or companionship toward anyone else. There would seem to be nothing morally wrong with such a person, say, spending long periods of solitude living in the backwoods. Of course such a person may harbor delusions about just how self-reliant he really is. He might, for example, not recognize how indebted he is to those who taught him how to feed and shelter himself and otherwise survive off the land. Apart from this minor conceit, however, there does not seem to be anything wrong with living such a markedly individualistic life.

Thus, individualistic behaviors or styles of living do not seem intrinsically wrong. When they are wrong, I maintain, they are so because the person living in isolation has ignored her or his special responsibilities to care for certain other persons. It is noteworthy that our culture more readily tolerates or forgives men who abandon their dependents than it does women, in part precisely because individualism and substantive independence are prized in men but not in women. A critique of this cultural double standard around substantive independence is long overdue. The problem, then, is not substantive independence as such but rather a culturewide glorification of *irresponsible* substantive independence on the part of men alone, to the misfortune of those who are harmed by it.

A third issue that emerges from feminist discussions of autonomy is the feminist ambivalence noted earlier between thinking that autonomy should sometimes give way to relational values and thinking that autonomy is relational in itself. One of the ideas underlying the feminist call for a relational conception of autonomy is the now-familiar social conception of the self. Feminists tend to share with communitarians the view that selves are inherently social. On this view, even the most independent, self-reliant, and emotionally self-contained among us are nevertheless social beings who are connected to and dependent on a great many others for material and emotional support, for the development of our capacities, for the sources of meaning in our lives, and for our very identities. This perspective on the self leads easily to the view, discussed in chapter 1, that autonomy should also be conceptualized relationally.

At the same time, a little reflection on everyday life reveals that autonomy sometimes results in *severing* relational ties, that it does sometimes disconnect us from others, including those who are closely related to us. Adolescents often find, for example, that giving up the religious or moral views learned from their parents will lead to a deep rift in their family lives. Many people are ostracized by their peers for questioning the norms and conventions those peers hold dear. (This point is developed more extensively in chapters 2 and 5.)

Can we reconcile the idea that autonomy is relational with the idea that it can also *conflict* with the maintenance and values of relationships? I think that we can. Doing so, however, will require us to give up the *unqualified* assumption that social relationships are necessary to the realization of autonomy. The conclusion has to be that relationships of certain sorts are necessary for the realization of autonomy whereas relationships of certain other sorts can be irrelevant or positively detrimental to it. The connection between autonomy and the "social," in other words, is manifold and diverse.

Social relationships are, after all, a highly varied lot. This point should come as no surprise. Social relationships can either promote or hinder the development of autonomy competency (e.g., through the right or wrong kinds of socialization), and they can either permit or obstruct its exercise (e.g., by enlarging or constricting the range of someone's choices). Not only might relationships differ from each other in their contributions to personal autonomy, but any one relationship might vary over time in terms of the bearing it has on the personal autonomy of its participants. One relationship might, furthermore, foster the personal autonomy of only *some* of its participants while at the same time hindering the personal autonomy of other participants. In relationships of domination, for example, someone asserts his or her will and someone else is subordinated to it.

In light of the variety of relationships, practices, and traditions that characterize the social sphere, it is implausible to specify one uniform sort of connection between that sphere and autonomy. Specifically, we need an account that explores how social relationships both promote and hinder the realization of autonomy. Representing these two sorts of effects with roughly accurate proportionality is, however, a formidable project. Matters of degree are notoriously difficult to specify philosophically.

One distinctive feminist contribution to the positive side of the ledger is see how relationality contributes to autonomy in social roles that have fallen predominantly to women. As noted earlier in this chapter, mainstream autonomy theorists consider role relationships such as those of parent and teacher to be mainly conditions of socialization that can promote or hinder the autonomy of others—children, in particular. This one-sided appraisal fails to consider how such caregiving practices affect caregivers themselves.

Feminists, by contrast, have explored the resources available to caregivers, especially female caregivers, for realizing their own autonomy. Sarah Hoagland, for example, has identified subtle and covert practices of resistance to male domination that women have exhibited as caregivers.[65] Sara Ruddick has investigated the ideals that constitute mothering practices and the forms of thinking that arise rooted in those practice.[66] By ignoring the possibilities for women's own autonomy within their traditional relationships, mainstream autonomy theorists, who are for the most part men, have unbalanced their accounts considerably.

A fourth concern raised by feminist calls for a relational account of autonomy has to do with the theoretical nature of the connection between autonomy and social relationships. I have emphasized that mainstream autonomy theorists acknowledge that social relationships are necessary to the realization of autonomy. Marina Oshana has charged, however, that mainstream conceptions of autonomy treat social relationships merely as causal conditions that are required for autonomy but are no part of what autonomy specifically *is*.[67] Mainstream theorists admit that people must be socialized for self-reflection and the other capacities required for the achievement of autonomy (could anyone really doubt this?), but mainstream theories do not generally define autonomy as *intrinsically* social. Oshana is thus objecting to the sort of social conception of autonomy that I present in chapter 1.

Are social relationships merely causal conditions that are necessary to bring autonomy about but are external to autonomy proper, rather like sunshine causing plants to grow? Or are they somehow partly "constitutive" of autonomy? Put differently, is autonomy merely the (nonsocial) result of certain other social conditions or is it inherently social in its very nature? In Nedelsky's view, as noted earlier, there is "a social component built into the *meaning* of autonomy."[68] This unresolved issue, I suggest, is one major philosophical concern that continues to divide, on the one hand, feminists who advocate a relational account of autonomy from, on the other hand, mainstream theorists who acknowledge that social relationships contribute to autonomy.

This issue raises a number of questions. If autonomy is indeed intrinsically social, is this simply because human selves and self-identity are intrinsically social? Or is autonomy itself, as a trait or competency of human selves, intrinsically social? In other words, is the inherent relationality of autonomy fully explained by the social nature of the selves who realize it, or is autonomy, apart from the social nature of the persons who realize it, also a social trait or process? For that matter, what could it mean to say that autonomy per se is intrinsically or constitutively social?

Charles Taylor argues that autonomy requires a certain kind of self-understanding that one cannot sustain on one's own but must always define partly in conversation with interlocutors or through the shared meanings that underlie certain sorts of cultural practices.[69] In Jürgen Habermas's view, self-interpretation is the performative dialogical assertion and reason-based justification of one's identity to a potentially unlimited audience.[70] Joel Anderson conceptualizes personal autonomy as the capacity to give an account to others of those commitments that are essential to who one is, in the sense of one's "practical identity."[71] Marina Oshana regards autonomy in part as a function of social states of affairs that are independent of someone's psychological properties, states of affairs such as security against reprisals for unconventional goals or values.[72]

Relational, or constitutively social, accounts of autonomy such as these, I believe, set the stage for the next round of feminist explorations of autonomy.

A crucial aim of those explorations should be to determine, as I suggested above, what it could mean to say that autonomy is intrinsically or constitutively social. Another crucial aim should be to determine whether feminism really needs to regard autonomy as intrinsically or constitutively social. Perhaps it is enough for feminist purposes simply to recognize how relationships constitute personal identity and provide the causal conditions that socialize individuals for autonomy competency. These, at any rate, are questions for another occasion.

To conclude: I have argued that mainstream philosophers of autonomy are not guilty of the feminist charge that they simply ignore social relationships in their accounts of autonomy. Indeed, they explicitly acknowledge the role of social relationships. There are, however, other concerns that feminists can raise about mainstream accounts. First, culture at large treats autonomy asocially and mainstream philosophers might be unwittingly contributing to this culturewide perspective. Second, content neutrality, while acceptable in a philosophical account of autonomy, may distract us from recognizing the need for radical critiques of gendered personalities and might thereby reinforce those personalities. Third, social relationships both promote and hinder autonomy, and mainstream accounts have not provided an adequate account of this balance—in part because they have neglected the possibilities for autonomy available in women's traditional relational practices. And fourth, mainstream accounts of autonomy are not *sufficiently* relational because they tend to regard social relationships merely as causal conditions promoting autonomy but do not construe autonomy as inherently social.[73]

Having thus endorsed a social conception of autonomy, I turn in the next chapter to some complications in this account of autonomy.

Autonomy, Social Disruption, and Women

Of Autonomy and Men

Are women in Western societies alienated by the ideal of autonomy? Many feminist philosophers have recently suggested that women find autonomy to be a notion inhospitable to women, one that represents a masculine-style preoccupation with self-sufficiency and self-realization at the expense of human connection.

Paul Gauguin's life epitomizes what many feminists take to be the masculine ideal of autonomy. Gauguin abandoned his family and middle-class life as a stockbroker in Paris to travel to Mediterranean France, Tahiti, and Martinique in search of artistic subjects and inspiration. He deserted his wife and four children, one might say, to paint pictures in sunny locales. The historic records show that Gauguin agonized for some time over the decision to leave his family. Gauguin once wrote: "One man's faculties can't cope with two things at once, and I for one can do *one thing only*: paint. Everything else leaves me stupefied."[1]

Gauguin's self-reflective agonies qualify as autonomous according to many contemporary definitions, including my own. Gauguin reflected on his deeper wants, values, and commitments, and, in his middle thirties, altered the course of his life so as to live more closely in accordance with those concerns, even in the face of resistance and opposition by others.

How has Western culture assessed Gauguin's life and work? Gauguin was *canonized* by Western art history. Of course, he had the moral good luck to have painted important pictures, something that Bernard Williams might call a "good for the world."[2] While Gauguin's fame is certainly based on his paintings and not his familial desertion, nevertheless the fact of his having left behind a wife and four children to pursue his dream has done nothing to tarnish his stature. If anything, it has added a romantic allure to his biography.[3]

Narratives of this sort suggest that autonomy in practice is antithetical to women's interests because it prompts men to desert the social relationships on which many women depend for their own survival and well-being and that of their children. In the past, because of women's restricted opportunities, the loss of support suffered by abandoned women has often been worse than the heterosexual relationships on which they depended.

Men are supposed to "stand up like a man" for what they believe or value, including the simple assertion of their self-interests. Women instead are supposed to "*stand by* your man." The maxim "stand up like a *woman!*" has no serious meaning. It conjures up imagery that is, at best, merely humorous. There is no doubt which model of behavior as exhibited by which gender receives the highest honors in Western public culture.

Still today, women in general define themselves more readily than men in terms of personal relationships. In addition, women's moral concerns tend to focus more intensely than those of men on sustaining and enhancing personal ties.[4] As well, popular culture still presumes that women are more concerned than men to create and preserve just the sorts of relationships, such as marriage, that autonomy-seeking men sometimes want to abandon.[5] Feminist analysis has uncovered ways in which close personal involvement and identification with others have been culturally devalued, in tandem with the devaluation of women, by comparison with the public world of impersonal relationships that men have traditionally monopolized.[6] Focusing on the importance of the social is one feminist strategy for combating these traditions of thought and for elevating social esteem for women. Many feminist philosophers have thus emerged as champions of social relationships and of relational approaches to diverse philosophical concepts.[7]

The cultural understanding of autonomy needs to change if the concept is to be relevant for women. Autonomy, to reiterate, involves reflecting on one's deeper wants, values, and commitments, reaffirming them, and behaving and living in accordance with them even in the face of at least minimal resistance from others. This philosophical formulation of autonomy, however, is abstract and may not provide enough flesh for popular understanding. As I suggested in chapter 4, philosophers should pay more attention to how our cherished notions that pertain to people's everyday lives are in fact understood in the culture at large. Popular understanding is more likely to proceed by way of paradigm cases and narratives than by abstract formulas.

In order to make my female-friendly conception of autonomy more widely accessible, I therefore suggest in this chapter two changes to the presentation of the concept that should promote the popular understanding that autonomy is relevant to women: first, new paradigms of autonomy that involve female protagonists, and second, narratives of autonomy that avoid stereotypically masculine traits. To reinforce the female-friendly nature of autonomy, it is also important to make explicit the social nature of autonomy, as discussed in the preceding chapter. Thus, I develop further the notion that autonomy involves social relationships or is at least not antithetical to them. This reconceptualization of autonomy has been under development for some time now in philosophical literature and my suggestions on these points are not new.

Of course, nothing guarantees a priori that we will find an account of autonomy that synthesizes these elements consistently with the core notion of self-determination that sets limits to our understanding of autonomy. I am optimistic, however, that a female-friendly account of autonomy can be, and has in part already been, developed.

At any rate, I mention these points merely to set the stage for my final, and primary, thesis of this chapter, which is this: At the same time that we embrace relational accounts of autonomy, we should also be cautious about them. Autonomy increases the risk of disruption in interpersonal relationships. While this is an empirical and not a conceptual claim about autonomy, nevertheless, the risk is significant and its bearing on the value of autonomy is therefore empirically significant. It makes a difference in particular to whether the ideal of autonomy is genuinely hospitable to women.

Of Autonomy and Women

First: the historic association of autonomy with men. Autonomy, its constituent traits, and the actions and lives that seem to manifest it are publicly esteemed much more often in men than in women. To be sure, women are more prominent as public agents today than they used to be and in a greater variety of social roles. Yet men still seem to predominate in fact and fiction as the protagonists of stories about heroes who pursued their values and dreams even in the face of militant opposition, whether as war heroes, civil rights activists, entrepreneurs, or adventurers. As I noted earlier, the preponderance of men in narratives of autonomy could easily cast a masculine shadow over the concept.

Does a concept become irrevocably shaped by the paradigms that initially configure its usage? I believe that it does not and that autonomy can accordingly be freed of its historically near-exclusive association with male biographies and male-identified traits. Doing so will require systematic rethinking. In part, we need new paradigms of autonomy featuring female protagonists.[8]

A particularly *feminist* appropriation of the concept of autonomy requires narratives of women who strive in paradigmatically or distinctively female situations against patriarchal constraints to express and refashion their deepest commitments and senses of self. Such narratives are already widely available. Susan Brison, for example, writes of regaining autonomous control over her life after she was raped and almost murdered.[9] Patricia Hill Collins explains the power and importance of self-definition to African-American women, who fight dominating cultural images of them as mammies, matriarchs, and welfare mothers.[10] Minnie Bruce Pratt tells of how she struggled to live as a lesbian while at the same time renouncing the racism and anti-Semitism which she had derived from her family and community of origin.[11]

In addition, there are women's autonomy narratives that are not particularly about overcoming patriarchal constraints. Sara Ruddick's account of maternal thinking, for example, draws heavily on stories of women who reflected deeply on how to care well for their children, an otherwise conventional female task.[12] In short, there is already available a large variety of narratives that exemplify women's autonomous struggles, both feminist and nonfeminist.

It is, in addition, helpful to remember that autonomy is not always valued in men. For one thing, whole groups of minority men have had their autonomous aspirations crushed by white Western societies. For another thing, white men do not always tolerate autonomy among each other. In traditional, patriarchal hierarchies such as military or corporate structures, even many white men are routinely punished for being autonomous, for challenging accepted norms and authoritive dictates, for not being a "team player."[13]

Some male philosophers, in addition, criticize the ideal of autonomy in at least some of its versions. Male communitarians challenge what they take to be the overly individualistic and ungrounded autonomy of the liberal tradition.[14] Sounding a different note, Loren Lomasky regards autonomy as a source of "massive dislocation" and "widespread human misery." He criticizes autonomy as a rallying cry of the "Red Guards" and of proponents of the welfare state who reject the "traditional ways" of family life.[15]

Thus, the historical link between autonomy and men is not uniform. It is being further challenged today by the growing diversity of women's lives. Autonomy is now available to, and sometimes celebrated in, women, and it is not always celebrated in men. The gender paradigms of autonomy are shifting. On the basis of paradigms alone, autonomy is no longer straightforwardly male oriented or alien to women.

Autonomy and Gender-Stereotypical Traits

Second, we should articulate our conceptions of autonomy in terms of narratives that avoid stereotypically masculine traits.

Autonomy has often been conceptualized in terms of traits that suggest an antifemale bias. Traditional ideals of autonomy, for example, have been grounded on reason. Genevieve Lloyd and others have argued that traditional conceptions of reason have excluded anything deemed "feminine," such as emotion.[16] The exclusion of emotion from the concept of reason, however, is less prominent a view today than it once was. Some recent accounts of rationality by both feminists and mainstream philosophers blur the boundary between reason and emotion and thus promise to undermine this traditional dichotomy.[17] In case those accounts prove well grounded, this particular philosophical basis for thinking that autonomy is an antifemale ideal will have been eliminated.[18]

Besides connecting autonomy to reason, popular Western culture has also associated autonomy with other masculine-defined character and behavioral traits. Independence and outspokenness are two such examples.[19] Traits popularly regarded as feminine, by contrast, have no distinctive connection to

autonomy—social interactivity, for example.[20] Thus popular gender stereotypes have associated autonomy traits coded as masculine but not with traits
coded as feminine; these stereotypes may invidiously infect philosophical
thinking about autonomy.

To be sure, because of gender differences in socialization, autonomy may
actually *occur* less often in women than in men. As Diana Meyers has documented, male socialization still promotes autonomy competency more effectively than does female socialization.[21] Overall, men have had far greater opportunities than women to act and live autonomously.[22] Such modes of action
and living have, in the past, been closed to most women because they required
unavailable (to women) resources such as political power, financial independence, or the freedom to travel unmolested in public space—to jog safely, for
example, through Central Park.

The more frequent appearance of autonomy in men than in women combined with the association of stereotypically masculine but not feminine traits
with autonomy may bias philosophical investigations of autonomy. Together
with their nonphilosophical peers, philosophers may fail to recognize manifestations of autonomy by women. Philosophers who try to conceptualize autonomy may do so with autonomous males in mind as paradigm cases. They
may go on to mistake what are merely masculine traits for the traits that comprise autonomy competency as such. Thus contemporary philosophical accounts of autonomy should be scrutinized particularly with a view to eliminating any covert masculine paradigms that may lie behind those accounts.

In addition to creating a male bias that might influence philosophical reflections on autonomy, male stereotypes are also easy to exaggerate in ways
that may further distort the conception of autonomy. The male-stereotyped
traits of independence and self-sufficiency have often been interpreted, both in
general culture and in philosophical traditions, in asocial, atomistic terms that
seemed to sanction detachment from close personal relationships with others.[23] Many feminists have argued that this illusory goal of atomistic self-
sufficiency has indeed structured male development and male perspectives in
those cultures that require men to repudiate the feminine in order to consoli-
date their own masculine gender identity.[24] Some feminists worry that the
very concept of autonomy has been irremediably contaminated by this atomistic approach. An atomistic approach neglects the social relationships that
are vital for developing the character traits that are required for mature autonomy competency.[25] Much of that socialization consists of women's traditional child-care labor.

Philosophical accounts may err in this regard more by omission than by
commission. Some contemporary accounts, for example, fail to mention how
the human capacity for autonomy develops in the course of socialization.[26] By
neglecting to mention the role of socialization in the development of mature
autonomy competency, accounts of autonomy ignore one crucial way in
which autonomous persons are ultimately dependent persons, after all, and in
particular, dependent on women's nurturing. This philosophical omission

does nothing to undermine the conceited cultural illusion of the "self-made man" as a paradigm of autonomy.

As shown in chapter 4, however, many contemporary accounts of autonomy explicitly acknowledge that a social upbringing and ongoing personal interaction are necessary in order to become autonomous. These conditions impart the self-concept and resources for critical reflection that autonomy requires. As well, no respectable philosopher would deny that women's labors still comprise the lion's share of child care, especially in its crucial years of early formative socialization. Careful philosophical thought on these issues should correct the pop-cultural view of some men as self-made, a view that denies women their proper share of credit for nurturing or supporting the autonomy competency found in those men—and in women as well. The point is that philosophers should actively take pains to weed out inappropriate male paradigms that contaminate their own or a wider cultural understanding of key philosophical notions.

In virtue of disregarding the fundamentally social nature of autonomy and autonomous persons, the myth of the self-made man rests on a mistake. The fact that mistaken conceptions of autonomy are male biased, however, does not show that autonomy *properly understood* is male biased or antifemale.

Social Reconceptualizations of Autonomy

My third point is to reiterate the by-now-familiar idea that we need an account of autonomy that brings out its relational character. Fortunately, a relational approach to autonomy has been emerging for some time now. Two developments are relevant to this issue. One is the content-neutral conception of autonomy that I defended in chapter 1; the other is the relational or intersubjective approach to autonomy that I discussed in chapter 4.[27]

According to a content-neutral account, personal autonomy is realized by the right sort of reflective self-understanding or internal coherence along with an absence of undue coercion or manipulation by others. Autonomy, on this sort of view, is not a matter of living substantively in any particular way.[28] While this sort of account can be debated,[29] it is nevertheless common in philosophy today. On a content-neutral conception, avoiding or abandoning close personal relationships is in no sense required by autonomy. Nor is it for any reason inherently a better way for any individual to strive for autonomy.

While the language of autonomy in popular culture might still suggest asocial atomistic images of the self-made man, academic philosophers now seldom share this view. The atomistic, self-made conception of autonomy is a substantive conception of a particular sort of life or mode of behaving that someone must choose in order to realize autonomy. Such an ideal is not properly a part of content-neutral accounts of autonomy. On a content-neutral account, if someone does not care about trying to raise herself up "by her bootstraps," does not value being able to supply her own needs through her own labors, does not want to achieve professional success "on her own," then there is no particular reason for her to live according to those aims.

In addition to characterizing autonomy in content-neutral terms, many contemporary philosophers of autonomy have also tended to gravitate toward social, relational, interpersonal, or intersubjective accounts of autonomy. This is true of both feminist and mainstream philosophers, as I showed in chapter 4.[30] According to the relational approach, persons are fundamentally social beings who develop the competency for autonomy through social interaction with other persons. These developments take place in a context of values, meanings, and modes of self-reflection that cannot exist except as constituted by social practices.

Recent reconceptualizations of autonomy thus do not require someone to be a social atom: radically socially unencumbered, defined merely by the capacity to choose, or able to exercise reason prior to any of her contingent ends or social engagements.[31] Our reflective capacities and our very identities are always partly constituted by communal traditions and norms that we cannot put entirely into question without at the same time voiding our very capacities to reflect.

We are each reared in a social context of some sort—typically, although not always, that of a family—itself located in wider social networks such as those of community and nation. Nearly all of us remain, throughout our lives, involved in social relationships and communities, at least some of which partly define our identities and ground our highest values. These relationships and communities are fostered and sustained by varied sorts of ties that we share with others, such as languages, activities, practices, projects, traditions, histories, goals, views, values, and mutual attractions, not to mention common enemies and shared injustices and disasters.

Someone who becomes more autonomous regarding some tradition, authority, view or value in her life does not stop depending on other persons or relationships, nor does she evade her own necessarily social history of personal development. Her initial detached questioning does not arise in a social vaccuum but is likely to be prompted by commitments reflecting still other relationships that, for the present time, remain unquestioned and perhaps heteronomous. A shift in social relationships or commitments is not equivalent to, nor need it betoken, wholesale social detachment.

Autonomy does not require self-creation or the creation of law ex nihilo, a limitation that we need not join Richard Rorty in lamenting.[32] Becoming more autonomous, in a content-neutral sense, regarding particular standards, norms, or dictates involves reflecting on them in a language that one did not create, according to further norms and standards that one has almost surely taken over from others, in light of what is of deep concern to that product of social development that is oneself.[33] As well, autonomy is always a matter of degree, of more or less. Reflective consideration still counts as a gain in autonomy even if done in the light of other standards and relationships not simultaneously subjected to the same scrutiny.

How Autonomy Disrupts Personal Relationships

I come now to the main thesis of this chapter, namely, that despite its relational grounding, autonomy is potentially socially disruptive.

Feminists have sought a relational account of autonomy in order to render it relevant to women. Philosophers in general have sought such an account in order to make good on a widely shared intuition that autonomy is not antithetical to other social values and virtues that concern us all, such as love, friendship, care, loyalty, and devotion.[34] Many philosophers seem to expect that most of what we want or value in interpersonal relationships will prove to be consistent with the ideal of autonomy, once we develop an appropriately social conception of it.

That conviction, however, may be unfounded. It underestimates, I believe, the disruption that autonomy can promote in close personal relationships and in communities. Although autonomy is not inherently antithetical to social relationships, nevertheless in practice, autonomy may contingently disrupt particular social bonds. In chapter 3, I linked that tendency to a potential for promoting social nonconformity and, thereby, resistance to possibly oppressive social norms and practices. Let us now explore further how autonomy sometimes interferes with social relationships and what this implies regarding the value of autonomy for women.

Human relationships and communities, as noted above, are held together by a variety of ties that persons share, including languages, practices, traditions, histories, goals, views, and values. Any of these elements in someone's life can become the focus of her critical scrutiny. Whenever someone questions or evaluates any tie or commitment that binds her to others, the possibility arises that she may find that bond unwarranted and begin to reject it. Rejecting values that tie someone to others may lead her to try to change the relationships in question or simply to detach herself from them. Someone might also reflect on the very nature of her relationships to particular others and come to believe that those ties are neglecting or smothering important dimensions of herself. In order to liberate those aspects of herself, she might have to distance herself from the problematic relationships.

Most personal and communal relationships are multifaceted and based on more than one sort of tie. Kinship, for example, keeps many people in touch with relatives whose values repel them. Childhood friends who travel disparate paths in life may retain shared memories that keep them ever fondly in touch with each other. A shared ethnic identity may link economically diverse people in the pursuit of collective political ends or cultural self-affirmation. Thus, friends, relatives, or other associates who diverge over important values may still remain related to each other in virtue of other shared ties.

The resilience of social relationships is, of course, not always a blessing. Relationships in which one partner exploits or abuses the other can also last for years.[35] Sometimes, however, a person becomes so disenchanted with her relationships or their underlying values as to find them no longer bearable. At that level of discontent, and assuming viable alternatives, she may begin to withdraw from those relationships. If she does so because of and in accordance with deep value changes that she has reflectively reaffirmed, then the relational disconnection she causes stems from her autonomous dissatisfaction with her prior commitments.

Alternatively, someone's increasing autonomy may result in the breakup of a relationship not because she rejects it but rather because other parties to the relationship reject *her*. They may despise the changes in her behavior that they are witnessing. Some parents, for example, disown children who rebel too strongly against deeply held parental values. Peer groups often ostracize their members for disregarding important norms that prevail in their own subcultures.

Strictly speaking, to say that autonomy unqualified (sometimes) disrupts social relationships is misleading. The mere capacity for autonomy is not intrinsically socially disruptive. What disrupts a social relationship in a particular case is the actual exercise of the capacity. More strictly still, the differences that arise between people as a result of one person's autonomous rejection of values or commitments that another affiliated person still holds may lead the first person to draw away from or reject the other. Thus, it is not *autonomy* (as a dispositional capacity) that disrupts social relationships; it is *people* who disrupt social relationships.

The exercise of autonomy, it should be emphasized, is neither necessary nor sufficient as such to disrupt particular relationships. The connection between autonomy and social disruption is merely contingent. Someone's autonomous reflections increase the chances of disruption in her social relationships because of the divergence in wants and values that can result, but do not make social disruption a necessary consequence. Under certain sorts of circumstances, autonomy may not even make social disruption more likely than it already is. Someone's reflective consideration might lead her to appreciate in a new light the worth of her relationships or the people to whom she is socially attached and to enrich her commitment to them. In such cases, autonomy would strengthen rather than weaken relational ties. Even if someone began to disagree with significant others about important matters, their relationship might still not suffer. People use many interpersonal strategies to keep differing commitments from disrupting social harmony—"never discuss religion or politics," for example.[36]

Thus, someone's autonomy is not a *sufficient* condition for the disruption of her social relationships. Nor is it a *necessary* condition. A person might end a relationship because of new commitments that she has reached heteronomously. Peer pressure, for example, can promote knee-jerk rebelliousness that disrupts personal relationships as much as the greatest soul-searching and critical self-reflection. Someone's attitudes can also change as the result of traumatic experiences over which she had no control. These changes may occasion deep rifts in her relationships with close others.[37] Someone's increasing autonomy is thus neither a sufficient nor a necessary cause of disruption in social relationships.

Nevertheless the contingent connection between autonomy and social disruption is of noteworthy importance. When a culture places great value on autonomy, members of that culture are thereby encouraged to question their prior allegiances and the standards that impinge on them. Autonomy as a cultural ideal creates a supportive climate for personal scrutiny of traditions, standards, and authoritative commands.[38] Public discourse in such a culture will tend to promote open dialogue and debate over values and traditions. Autonomy-idealizing societies may protect such discourse, and the normative critiques it can foster, with legal guarantees of a substantial degree of freedom of expression.

Thus, other things being equal, in a culture that prizes autonomy, all traditions, authorities, norms, views, and values become more vulnerable to rejection by at least some members of the society than they would be in a society that devalued autonomy. No commitment in such a culture remains entirely immune to critical scrutiny, whether the commitment be about religion, sex, family, government, economy, art, education, race, ethnicity, gender, or anything else.

Once such scrutiny takes place, the likelihood increases that people who are socially linked to each other will begin to diverge over views or values they previously shared including the value of their social ties. Once people begin to diverge over important matters, they are more likely than they were before to disagree and quarrel with each other or to lose mutual interest and drift apart. In this way (other things being equal), an autonomy-idealizing culture increases the risk of (though it certainly does not guarantee) ruptures in social relationships.

To be sure, cultures that idealize autonomy do not always extend this ideal to all social groups. Sometimes certain sorts of people, white men for example, receive the lion's share of the social protections and rewards for being autonomous. As well, even an autonomy-idealizing culture may shield certain norms or values from critical scrutiny. In such a society, values that protect dominant social groups, those privileged to enjoy the value of autonomy, might not get as much critical attention as they deserve. While limitations on rampant autonomy might be necessary to prevent wholesale social breakdown, they can also create bastions of unquestioned autonomous privilege. In such a culture, autonomy might well be a restricted, domesticated, socially nonthreatening luxury.

Nevertheless, so long as autonomy is culturally valued even for only some groups and with respect to only certain issues, its very cultural availability opens up the possibility of wide social transformation. Even if idealized for only a privileged few, it can always fall into the "wrong" hands. New groups might coincidentally acquire autonomy competency in virtue of social changes such as the spread of literacy and formal education. They might then go on to contest norms and values previously left unscrutinized. As I argued in chapter 3, this possibility has been historically crucial for women and other subordinated groups. The ideal of autonomy is thus always a *potential* catalyst for social disruption in interpersonal relationships.

Notice also that the rupture that autonomy can promote in any one particular social relationship does not necessarily amount to an overall decline in the societal quantity of relationality, to put the point inelegantly. Typically, when someone questions some prior commitment of hers, such as a religious commitment, which cemented certain relationships in her life, she is probably doing so in company with other skeptics whose reflections prompt and reinforce her own rising doubts. When she turns away from her prior religious community, she is likely to be turning toward a different community, perhaps a religiously neutral secular community or a new religious group. Those with whom someone shares her new commitments may have provided her with a vocabulary or perspective for reflecting on her central concerns. Without any empirical backing for this claim, I nevertheless estimate that in most cases in which autonomous reflection does lead people to reject the commitments that bound them to particular others, they are at the same time taking up new commitments that link them through newly shared conviction to *different* particular others. This is one important additional reason for thinking of autonomy as social in character.

Although people in an autonomy-valuing society might have as many interpersonal relationships as those in a society that devalued autonomy, it is reasonable to speculate that the nature of people's relationships would differ in the two cases. Where people were permitted with relative ease to leave relationships that had become dissatisfying to them, we should expect attachments to be less stable, to shift and change with greater frequency, than in societies in which personal autonomy (or relational mobility) was discouraged. The types and qualities of relationships in an autonomy-promoting culture would also likely differ from those of an autonomy-discouraging culture. Relationships into which people are born and in which they are first socialized—relationships of family, church, neighborhood friendships, and local communities—would likely be disrupted first by widespread individually autonomous reflections on basic values and commitments. A culture that values autonomy is more likely than one that devalues it to foster people who gravitate toward voluntary relationships formed in adult life around shared values and attitudes.[39]

Women and the Social Disruptiveness of Autonomy

What difference should it make to our theory of autonomy that autonomy, however social its nature or origin, might promote the disruption of social relationships? More precisely in the present context, what difference does this possibility make *to women*? If autonomy is sometimes socially disruptive, does that make it inimical to the relational orientation that many feminists celebrate in women and display in their own moral concerns?

Some people exhibit what I call "autonomophobia," or fear of autonomy. What they usually fear is not their own autonomy; it is the autonomy of *others* that scares them. Their concern is that autonomous people will disrupt or desert the relationships the autonomophobes regard as valuable and on which they may depend. Traditional female roles make relationships and dependence on others a standard and (contingently) necessary feature of many women's lives, for the purposes of material as well as emotional sustenance and, even more so, for the sustenance of their children. Feminists, and many women in general, may worry that the cultural idealization of autonomy will threaten precisely these relationships on which many women depend in crucial ways.

Whether any particular woman benefits or suffers in virtue of the exercise of autonomy, however, depends on how she is socially positioned in relation to it. When a woman is connected to someone else whose autonomous pursuits disrupt their relationship, then the immediate affect on her is likely to be simply a loss—of whatever benefits she derived from their relationship. Autonomophobia is thus a legitimate concern. It arises from the ways in which our lives are intertwined with those of other persons. When others who are close to us reflect on their own deeper commitments, they might well find grounds for challenging or abandoning the relationships and communities that we share with them. We might find ourselves helpless as a result. Social relationships and communities are collective projects. They function best when sustained jointly by people with important values or norms in common. In a culture that idealizes autonomy, each individual faces the insecurity of investing herself in relationships and communities that the other participants might, on critical reflection, come to reject.

Historically the disruption of personal relationships has had a different impact on men than on women. Because women usually depended on men for financial support while men had no comparable limitation, women doubtless suffered more than they benefited from the cultural idealization of autonomy. Men have been historically better situated than women to forsake personal relationships dissatisfying to them. Unlike most women, many men have had the material and cultural resources by which to support themselves, as well as greater opportunities to seek more satisfying relationships elsewhere. Men were able to abandon their responsibilities to women and children in order to pursue forms of personal fulfillment unavailable to women.

Men who, like Gauguin, produced good enough subsequent works have sometimes been celebrated for autonomous pursuits that involved neglecting or abandoning relationships that supported women and children. Dependent women and children have suffered greatly from these male desertions. Women's own autonomous living, by contrast, has, over time, brought women much more censure and hardship than praise.[40] Since women tend to be more financially dependent on men than men are on women even today, autonomophobia is understandably still more often a female than a male concern. Thus, men's autonomy has often done women little direct good and has instead imposed serious hardships on them.

On the other hand, many social relationships constrain and oppress women, indeed the very women who work to sustain them. Regardless of whether women want to devote their lives to maintaining close personal ties, gender norms have required this of them. Women have been expected to make the preservation of certain interpersonal relationships such as those of family their highest concern regardless of the costs to themselves. Women who have had important commitments other than that of taking care of family members were nevertheless supposed to subordinate such commitments to the task of caring for loved ones. Many men, by contrast, have been free to choose or affirm their highest commitments from among a panorama of alternatives. Indeed, men are sometimes lauded for just the sort of single-minded pursuit of an ideal that imposes sacrifices on all the people close to them.

Traditionally, the majority of women derived their primary adult identities from their marriages and families. For at least some groups of women, however, social and economic opportunities have broadened in the late twentieth century. Because of expanding financial opportunities in Western cultures at least, many women no longer need to accommodate themselves *uncritically* to traditional marriages or other relational ties in order to sustain themselves. As many feminists have well recognized, there is no reason to defend social relationships without qualification. There is nothing intrinsic to each and every social relationship that merits female or feminist allegiance.[41] The traditional relational work of women has included sublime joy and fulfillment but also abuse, exploitation, and subordination. There are some, perhaps many, relationships that women, too, should want to end.

Thus, the disruption of social relationships that can follow someone's growing autonomy is not itself inherently alien to women, nor is it a dimension of the ideal of autonomy that women today should automatically reject. What should matter to any particular woman in any given case is the worth of the relationship in question and how its disruption would bear on her and on innocent others. The old question, "Can this marriage be saved?" should be revised to "Can this marriage be saved from *oppressiveness*?" Some relationships should be preserved while others should be abolished. Even relationships that should be preserved can always be improved. Sometimes what disrupts social relationships is good for particular women. Since the socially disruptive potential of autonomy can at least sometimes be good for women, it does not constitute a reason on behalf of women for repudiating the ideal of autonomy.

Indeed, reflecting on her relationships or the norms or values that underlie them might be the *only* way a woman can determine for herself the moral quality of those relationships. A woman who does not reflect on her relationships, communities, norms, or values is incapable of recognizing for herself where they go wrong or of aiming on her own to improve them. Her well-being depends on those who control her life and on their wisdom and benevolence—regrettably, not the most reliable of human traits. Autonomy is thus crucial for women in patriarchal conditions in part *because* of its potential to disrupt social bonds. That autonomy is sometimes antithetical to social relationships is often a good for women. With all due respect to Audrey Lorde, as I noted earlier, the "master's tools" *can* "dismantle the master's house."[42]

Thus, although women still have occasion to fear *men's* autonomy, it seems that many women have good reason to welcome their *own* autonomy. When a woman is the one who is exercising autonomy, then even if its exercise disrupts relationships in her life, the value of her gain in autonomous living might well make the costs to her worth her while.

The value of autonomy, as I argued in chapter 3, is particularly apparent when one considers it from a first-person perspective. Although I might plausibly fear what increasingly autonomous *others* will do to the relationships between us, it would not make sense for me to reject autonomy for myself. I might choose not to exercise autonomy under certain conditions. I might, for example, devote myself loyally to an ideal that I can serve only by working with a group of persons who sometimes take specific actions I do not understand or endorse. I can hardly want to give up, however, the very option of so dedicating myself. To reflect on the standards or values according to which I will behave or live my life, as I do when resolving to dedicate myself to a particular ideal, is already to exercise a degree of autonomy. It would be self-defeating of me, at the same time, to reject autonomy altogether as a value for myself.

Once women admit that autonomy might be a value for us, it would be difficult to deny its value for persons in general. The capacity for autonomy seems instrumentally valuable as a means for resisting oppression and intrinsically valuable as part of the fullest humanly possible development of moral personality. In these respects it seems valuable for anyone. As well, there is a need for reciprocity. We cannot sensibly esteem autonomy in women while deprecating it in men. Yet this consistency does have its costs. Men's autonomy and the social disruption it can promote do sometimes threaten women's well-being. I have argued that when women have access to means for their own material support, this risk is lessened.[43] Women can then benefit from a generalized cultural idealization of autonomy and are not simply threatened by it.

There are, as well, certain mitigating possibilities that reduce, even though they do not eliminate, the likelihood that autonomy will cause social disruption. For one thing, autonomy does not necessarily lead someone to reject her prior commitments. Someone's increasing autonomy might instead enhance her appreciation of her close relationships, and, so, might lead her to reaffirm certain relationships on which others depend. As well, even if she comes to regard a relationship as seriously flawed, she might work to improve it rather than abandoning it.

These possibilities suggest that alongside of autonomy as a cultural ideal, we should also idealize the values and responsibilities that make relationships and communities worthwhile.[44] We should emphasize, for example, the ways in which close relationships are vital sources of care for the most vulnerable members of our society.[45] We should articulate these values in public dialogues in which all can participate, including those who might become autonomously skeptical about those social ties.

This balanced pursuit of the values of community *along with* the ideal of autonomy is a partial response to the contingent social disruptiveness of autonomy and the worry that such disruptiveness lessens the value of autonomy for women. There is no way, however, to alleviate this concern fully. Relationships one wants to preserve might nevertheless be disrupted by one's partner because of her—or one's own—increasing autonomy. This risk must be faced by persons and cultures who would idealize personal autonomy.[46] I have argued, however, that social disruptiveness is, at least, a mixed curse, one that harbors the potential for good as well as bad consequences.

As well, the mantra of "family values" that is invoked uncritically in so much public debate in the United States should remind us as feminists of the hazards of allowing any relationships, including those we most cherish, to be entirely insulated from the critical reflection of all their participants. Even care for the most vulnerable can usually be improved. It is a form of respect toward those with whom we most want affiliation to want *them* to find forms of commitment to us that reflect their most cherished values.[47]

In the next two chapters, I explore autonomy more specifically in the context of romantic and intimate domestic relationships.

III

INTIMATE RELATIONSHIPS

6

Romantic Love and Personal Autonomy

In the acknowledgment section of his book *Rediscovering Love*, psychiatrist Willard Gaylin writes: "It is impossible to acknowledge my wife's contribution to this book" because "in all things in my life, it is difficult to know where 'she' begins and 'I' leave off."[1] Why then didn't Gaylin list his wife as co-author and share the credit line with her? This sounds like a classic example of patriarchal relationships: a man takes all the public credit for what are actually the *joint* endeavors of him and his wife—and does it in the name of love.

Gaylin's omission might seem to be justified by the view of love presented in his book. In Gaylin's view, love involves the "merging of the self with another . . . creating a fused entity." Over time, on this view, the "barriers of the ego[s]" of two individuals in love break down, with the result that they lose their "separate senses of self" and forge a "common identity" characterized by "unsureness as to where I end and you, the person I love, begin."[2] If Gaylin and his wife are a merged entity in virtue of their love, then it might not seem necessary to name both of them as authors. Naming Gaylin alone would be sufficient, since Gaylin has become, through love, someone merged with "Mrs. Gaylin"—let us call her Mary Jones. To name Gaylin alone is now to name the both of them at once, an entity that comprises Willard and Mary.

This account of love, however, still does not justify omitting Mary Jones's name from the title page. An entity that comprises two individuals is wrongly named if known by the name of one of them alone. Rather than representing the merger of himself and Mary Jones, the name "Willard Gaylin" simply erases Mary's existence. Suppose, however, that "Willard Gaylin" were the correct name for their merger. This would mean that the reason Willard has trouble telling where he leaves off and Mary begins is that Mary no longer begins at all. She has lost her separate identity altogether in a merger that has produced merely one enlarged self, Willard Gaylin$_e$ ("e" for "enlarged"). Once again, we seem to be confronted with a classic variety of patriarchal relationships: the two shall become one, and that one is *him*.

In this chapter, I will focus on the ideal of a merger, fusion, or union of lovers in heterosexual romantic love. I do not doubt the existence of such mergers. I believe that they can and do occur, to varying degrees. My concern is to explore how these mergers occur and whether they are good things, particularly for women.

Philosophers are, perhaps, never quite so ridiculous as when we subject tenderly cherished human values and emotions to the microscope of analytic scrutiny. I now venture to do just that. Yet there are important philosophical points to make about the grounding of heterosexual romantic love in gender norms. The importance of this grounding for our investigation of autonomy may justify the trespass on delicate territory of the heart.

I remind you that this exploration, as with all philosophical works, issues from a particular personal standpoint. What I have to say is prompted and limited by who I am, what I have experienced, the particular others who have influenced my views, and the extent of my imagination. Any resemblance between actors conjured up in this chapter and persons I have known is probably not a coincidence.

Merger Mania

Love is "a strong, complex emotion or feeling causing one both to appreciate, delight in, and crave the presence or possession of another and to please or promote the welfare of the other."[3] Romantic love is love that is at least partly erotic or sexual in orientation.

The idea of a merger of identities between two romantic lovers is at least as old as the speech by Aristophanes in Plato's *Symposium*, which construes love as the quest for literal reunion with one's literal other half. Today's philosophers are more metaphoric about what merger means. Several contemporary philosophers regard the merger of two selves or identities into a "we" as an important feature or aim of romantic love, sometimes even the defining aim. Roger Scruton, for example, considers romantic love to be distinguished by a "community of interests" that erodes the boundaries between lovers. He thinks that the "course of love" involves an endeavor of cooperative, "mutual self-building."[4] For Robert Solomon, a merger of identities is the "dominant conceptual ingredient" in romantic love, and is a kind of "ontological dependency" that is the source of virtues made possible by romantic love.[5] Robert Nozick calls the merger of identities "intrinsic to the nature of romantic love."[6] In the view of Neil Delaney, it is one of three basic needs or interests that are involved in the pursuit of romantic love.[7]

For all these theorists, the ideal of a merger of two selves is a good, either intrinsically or instrumentally—and usually both. Now to some of us, this idea might seem crystal clear. It is not unfamiliar for lovers to murmur such sweet nothings to each other as, "you will always be a part of me," or "whenever you leave, I die a little," and similar sentiments conveying personal fusion. Others of us, however, might well find the idea baffling. Since two lovers do not literally merge bodily, the idea of merger might seem merely like a charming poetic metaphor but one lacking in serious ontological significance.

In the next section of this chapter, I raise and quickly dispose of a few quasi-ontological questions about the nature of romantically loving mergers. Then I suggest that romantically merged identity poses a problem for personal autonomy. I list some specific ways in which a romantic merger might diminish the autonomy of one or both of its partners. Then I connect the problem of autonomy in heterosexual romantic love to norms of femininity. I survey some changing cultural trends on these gender issues, and finally I consider some objections to my worries about women's loss of autonomy in heterosexual romantic love.

It is noteworthy that love is not the only means by which two separate selves can merge their identities. Romantic love might well involve unique sorts of mergers, especially in virtue of the special capacity of sexual intimacy to cross or blur the boundaries of embodied personhood and link selves profoundly. Also there may be forms of merger that are not based on romantic love. People who engage in joint undertakings, such as those involving dedication to shared ideals, may forge bonds of solidarity that merge identities without involving romantic love between the partners. My comments about romantic love may or may not transfer to these other domains of merged identity.

One, Two, or Three?

What might it mean for the identity of two separate individuals to merge in romantic love in such a way as to become a "we"? For the purposes of answering this question, I make certain assumptions. As noted in chapter 2, I assume, as for one thing, that there *are* individual selves, distinct persons with self-identities, who correspond more or less isomorphically with distinct human bodies. Human selves are embodied selves, and the distribution of them typically, although not necessarily, follows a democratic principle: one body, one self. I also assume that selves tend to cohere enough, most of the time, to make it sensible and plausible for us to talk of them as individual selves. In addition, as also mentioned in chapter 2, I assume that selves are at least sometimes capable of self-understanding without undue self-deception. In other words, I take a modified modernist, rather than a postmodernist, stance toward selves.

What might it mean for the identity of two separate individuals to merge in such a way as to become a "we"? Is the *we* of romantic love, in some sense, a new entity with an identity over and above those of the lovers? Or, rather, is it merely a metaphor that describes the mutual coordination of the lovers's still-separate identities and agencies? Nozick wavers between these two accounts. At one stage, he claims that a "new" identity is forged, one that is "additional" to those of the two lovers. Yet, at another stage, he claims that lovers orient themselves to each other in such a way that "each becomes psychologically part of the other's identity," and the identity that each partner had as an individual becomes altered in the process.[8] Solomon leans toward the latter view. He writes that romantic love expands the self, a development that, in his view, makes romantic love neither selfless nor selfish. Solomon emphasizes how the very contours of the self change and enlarge in romantic love.[9]

The old familiar dispute between individualists and holists thus reappears in the tenderly cherished realm of romantic love. One thing is clear: human lovers cannot merge so thoroughly as to obliterate their separate individual embodiments. Aspects of personal identity that were important to each before the romantic relationship brought them together as a couple still persist in their lives. As well, those romantic loves that end during the lifetimes of the lovers show that romantic mergers need not be permanent and may obviously be reversed or transcended.

A merger of identities is more than simply the sharing of activities or interests. Peripheral amusements and diversions, in particular, are irrelevant. What is shared must be important enough to a lover so as to pertain to her very identity. It must somehow constitute or define who she *is*. One sign that something pertains to identity might be that its sudden loss, say, through death or departure, would be experienced as a kind of bereavement, a deep wound in the lover's ongoing sense of stable personhood. Overcoming such a loss requires something experienced as a healing, one that may leave permanent emotional scars and may never be thorough.

Richard Schmitt finds some philosophers to be puzzled by the idea that two separate, and separately autonomous, individuals could constitute the sort of unity that romantic love is said to involve. Schmitt suggests that the puzzlement is eliminated by recognizing the obvious and mundane fact that lovers do many things together; they have many "joint projects." As such, they have many "feelings, desires, thoughts, choices, and actions in common." They are not, however, "self-identical; they are not numerically one person." Schmitt refers to their condition as one of "being-in-relation."[10]

It is important to recognize the degree of separateness that persists for beings in the relation of romantic love. Only very remarkable romantic love relationships contain no disagreements, disputes, or heated struggles, at some time or other. These disagreements seem more like antagonisms between whole persons than the internal struggles of a single self divided between conflicting loyalties. Lovers thus retain identities that remain at least partly individuated from each other, even if they experience themselves as merging to a substantial degree.

Neil Delaney suggests that what lovers really want when they seek to merge romantically is something analogous to a federation of states.[11] In a federation of states, two previously separate states retain some of their individual powers and capacities, but combine in joint ventures for the production of certain shared goals and purposes. A romantic merger of identities is somewhat like an interpersonal federation. On the federation model, a third unified entity emerges from the interaction of lovers, one that involves the lovers acting in concert across a range of conditions and for a range of purposes. This concerted action, however, does not erase the existence of the two lovers as separate agents with continuing possibilities of acting on their own, and for their own individual purposes. I take this to follow almost from the continuing fact of separately embodied agency alone.

Lovers may merge in part and by way of varied capacities. At least three sorts of such capacities can be distinguished. First, lovers may merge in *subjectivity*, that is, as the subject of experiences. They may share joys and sorrows, moments of ecstasy, insight, contentment, doubt, fear, anxiety, and even, in an odd way, loneliness. Second, lovers may merge in *agency*, that is, as persons exercising their capacities for action. They may engage in joint undertakings for various purposes and toward various ends. Third, lovers may merge in what I will call *objecthood*, that is, as the object of attention or concern, or the recipient of harms or benefits. Each lover may attend to and serve his or her needs as a couple. The attention may come from outsiders to the relationship or it could come from one of the lovers acting, to that extent, as a separate agent toward the couple of which she is a part.

A federation of states is, in some ways, importantly unlike a romantic merger. A federation of states is typically formalized in ways that are stable over time. How and when the states shall or may act in concert, and how and when they may not, is often clearly specified. In this respect, this metaphor is not helpful for our purposes. Romantic mergers can vary in degrees of stability and modes of action. They can be settled and stable or they can be highly dynamic, shifting, and unstable, needing constantly to be renegotiated and reaffirmed. At any one time, two lovers may merge in some respects but not others. Over time, the ways in which they merge may shift. In the respects in which they are not merged at any given time, they remain separate individuals, although, as individuals, they may still coordinate their activities and concerns.

Thus, two lovers may attend to their needs as a couple, for example by planning shared activities, but may do so individually, each acting alone to arrange time for them to be together. Or two lovers may act together as agents, focusing their attention and resources on meeting the needs that one of them has as an individual, health or career needs perhaps. Or two lovers may share sexual intimacies or other experiences as one and yet part the next morning to live their day separately and attend each to her own concerns. These stances or positions (of subjectivity, agency, and objecthood) can themselves become integrated. Out of our shared fear in the face of an unexpected emergency, my lover and I might act as one to fend off the impending danger.

When I speak of a merger of identities in this chapter, then, I will mean primarily a *flexible* interpersonal equivalent to a federation of states as understood above. It is crucial for my thesis that each lover remains, in some sense and for some purposes, a separate self with her own capacities for the exercise of agency. On this view, a romantic merger does not obliterate the separate existence of two lovers. Instead it produces a new entity out of them, but only to some extent, only at some times, and only for some purposes—while leaving them as two separate selves. Each lover remains, like each state in a federation, a separate self with capacities to make choices and to act on her own.

In romantic merger, then, there is not merely one self, nor are there merely the two original selves. There are three entities in a dynamic, shifting interplay of subjectivity, agency, and objectivity. There are the two individual lovers and there is the flexible romantic "federation," or merger, that they become. I am particularly interested in the impact of romantic mergers of identity on the on-going autonomy of the individuals who are parts of those mergers yet remain individual selves at the same time.

Problems with Romantic Mergers

Alan Soble scorns the ideal of romantic merger. In Soble's view, romantic merger has two costly consequences for love. First, it diminishes the auton-omy of lovers. Second, it makes impossible a type of loving concern that philosophers, theologians, and poets have all revered, and which Soble calls "robust concern." Robust concern is concern for another person for her own sake. Romantic merger diminishes autonomy and makes robust concern im-possible precisely because it obliterates the separate identities of two separate selves. In Soble's view, two lovers must have separate identities in order that each one may achieve personal autonomy or care about the other lover for her own sake.[12]

Soble's view that romantic merger undermines autonomy is particularly relevant in this context. Soble is right in principle to worry about this loss of autonomy. In practice, however, things are not so bleak. Soble's mistake is to focus only on the *ideal* of romantic merger as presented in romantic simplicity by writers who often do not admit that real love, even the best kind, is much more complicated than their idealizations suggest. The ideal of romantic merger is just that: an ideal. Two lovers merge; their hearts are one; they think as one, feel as one, act as one, react as one, and identify as one. "Make of our hands one hand, make of our hearts one heart," sing the ill-fated lovers in *West Side Story*.

Real human lovers, especially those whose love endures for some time, sel-dom if ever experience such pure and simple merger. Real romantic merger is complex. Human lovers, of course, remain physically separate selves. They also remain psychologically separate. Aspects of personal identity that were important to each before the romantic relationship brought them together as a "couple" still persist in their lives, often with a vengeance. The particular ex-periences, traits, views, and values that characterize one partner often do not characterize the other partner. They often have different occupations and re-sponsibilities. They may retain differing tastes and interests. They may not like the same friends. A separate biography could be written about each partner in a romantically loving couple. They can act in ways that have nothing to do with each other, no matter how deep and abiding is their romantic attachment.

Indeed, real lovers who spend too much time together and engage in too many joint projects may find their romantic love quickly evaporating. Only very remarkable romantic love relationships contain no disagreements, disputes, or heated struggles at some time or other. And since the vast majority of romantic loves do not last " 'til death do us part," the sort of merger that occurs in romantic love can end, permitting the lovers to recover clearly separate identities.

If I am right that actual romantic mergers are only partial, then Soble is wrong to think that romantic mergers simply abolish the separate identities and autonomies of two lovers. Merger is a matter of degree; lovers do not literally become one. If romantic mergers produce a new merged entity, a *couple,* this entity nevertheless makes up only a part of the lives of each lover. Each lover remains, to some extent and in some ways, a separate self.

Soble is right, however, to see a tension between romantic merger and separate identity. Insofar as, and to the extent that, one person is merged with another in romantic love, her separate selfhood is somehow blurred. Merged lovers are, on my view, partly separate selves and also partly merged beings. They constitute an "interpersonal federation." Thus we should ask what impact these romantic *partial* mergers of identity have on the personal autonomy of lovers.

Autonomy, to reiterate, involves reflecting on one's deeper values and concerns, reaffirming them, acting in accordance with and because of them, and persisting in doing so in the face of some minimum of opposition from others. To the extent that a lover is engaged in joint undertakings which are guided by the joint commitments and identity of the couple that she constitutes with her lover, she is *not* being guided by the commitments and identity that define her as an individual. The important point is that a romantic merger can unite two persons in different ways. One lover may shape the concerns and activities of the couple more intensely or more extensively than the other lover. And the commitments and values that define a couple's identity as a *couple* may be influenced more heavily by the values of one lover than they are by the other.

Scruton, Solomon, Nozick, Delaney, and others all portray the merger of identities in romantic love as a good thing. Although I will eventually agree that it *can* be good, I will first investigate the risks and dangers of such mergers. For it appears that romantically merged identity can *diminish* the autonomy of one lover even while enhancing the autonomy of her beloved. Gender identity being what it is socialized to be in our culture, the heterosexual romantic merger of identities compromises women's autonomy more than it does that of their male partners. But more on that later. First let us explore in some detail how autonomy can be diminished by romantic mergers.

How Romantic Mergers Can Diminish Personal Autonomy

Here are a variety of ways in which romantic merger might be manifested. Most are recognizable from the viewpoint of lovers themselves whereas some might be recognizable only to outsiders. Some of these items exemplify mergers in regard to subjectivity, some in regard to agency, some in regard to objecthood, and some a mixture of more than one dimension. The list contains much overlap and is not meant to be exhaustive. Also, these features may apply to nonromantic forms of love, and even to mergers of identity not based on love at all:

1. *Needs and interests:*   Romantic lovers come to care deeply about each other's needs and interests. For many philosophers, love involves coming to care about the good of the beloved at least in part for her own sake and in the same way that one cares about one's own good. This aspect of love is perhaps most fully a merger of identities when a lover's well-being and that of her romantic beloved become intertwined or pooled in such a way that each is or understands herself to be the subject of the good and bad things that happen to both of them.[13]

2. *Caring and protection:*   Lovers tend to contribute substantially to each other's well-being.[14] They are likely to bring each other pleasure and happiness through gifts, attentiveness, and the sharing of activities. They may go on to care for each other through difficult circumstances and to nurture each other's growth and development. In times of danger, they may protect each other. Sandra Bartky has suggested that caring for someone changes one's outlook. It creates a tendency to focus on and become absorbed by the perspective of the recipient of care.[15] In this respect, the caring that is part of love may carry its own distinctive dimension of merger.

3. *Deep mutual familiarity:*   Couples are often able to communicate with each other using seemingly insignificant bodily or verbal cues.[16] This suggests that lovers acquire such close knowledge of each other as to be able to recognize clear and unambiguous meanings in each other's small gestures or otherwise ambiguous signals. This sort of deep familiarity makes possible the communication that enables two persons to share perspectives and pursue common interests in the changing circumstances of everyday life.

4. *Attention:*   A merger of romantic love may involve changes in one's modes or objects of attention. One is normally alert and attentive to one's own circumstances, noticing, to a significant extent, those that are salient to one's needs and interests. One's attention might be drawn to dangerous conditions, for example, or to the sound of one's name amid background conversation. In romantic love, one's attention to circumstances can become guided by their salience for the needs and interests of one's beloved.[17] In addition, the focus of one's attention may follow one's lover's gaze or attentiveness when one is together with her.

5. *Decision making:*   Some of the decision making each would otherwise have made alone (or, at least, without the beloved) might be opened up to joint participation in which both lovers contribute to the final resolution. Nozick characteristically puts the point in terms of rights: each partner's *right* to make unilateral decisions on those joint matters is partly relinquished.[18]

6. *Division of labor:*   Lovers often undertake activities or joint projects requiring the coordination of different sorts of tasks. She steers while I navigate;

she prepares the appetizer and main course while I prepare the salad and dessert. After some practice, lovers may be able to coordinate their organized labor without much apparent monitoring.[19]

7. *Mutual awareness or consideration:*   Shared identity may involve a "sense of presence," a having of someone always "in mind" in a way that "defines one's sense of self to oneself."[20] One lover may always be thinking about her partner's needs or desires, or attending to and grasping the world as if from the perspective of her lover.

8. *Evaluative perspective:*   A merger of identities may have something to do with a merger of viewpoints. It may interrelate the perspectives of both lovers, their values or commitments, into a new and uniquely blended stance that differs from the perspective of each individual partner taken singly, a stance that each lover can take up when adopting the point of view of their *we.*[21]

Scruton emphasizes the ways in which one's ideals and values interweave with one's aim to merge with one's beloved. You desire your beloved's good and desire your beloved to *be* a good person. As well, you desire that your beloved similarly desire your good and regard *you* as a good person.[22] The desire to be regarded as worthy of love by one's beloved, in Scruton's view, delimits the project of love. New standards, possibly distinct from one's own, enter the scope of one's intentionality.

9. *Mirroring of self-concepts:*   Lovers tend to become concerned about how they appear to their lovers and what their lovers think about them. This is a specific and especially important version of the previous point. A lover may want her beloved to value her for things about her that she herself regards as both valuable and deeply defining of who she is.[23] Or she may simply come to understand herself as a mere reflection of how she thinks she appears in her lover's regard. Thus a person's self-understanding may become particularly infused with and refashioned by her understanding of how her lover regards her.

10. *Convergence of long-range plans:*   Lovers make joint plans for the future. They may plan projects that neither partner could or would consider undertaking alone, such as raising children. One lover may alter her own aspirations to accommodate her lover's ambitions. The more secure and abiding they understand their love to be, the more far-reaching may be their joint plans for future undertakings and the more their joint ventures may structure the major parameters of their lives: domestic and family relationships, places of residence, daily occupations and activities, development of talents, and life prospects.

This ends my rough list of ways in which the identities of romantic lovers may merge. It is important to note that there is a difference between a mere merger of identities and a *mutual* or *fair* merger. Romantic mergers that nurture and affirm us can promote our autonomy as individuals by promoting our self-understanding, self-esteem, and capacities to act effectively in concert with others. Romantic mergers that drain or erase us can reduce our autonomy as individuals by diminishing those same attributes.

Lovers may be very different from each other in the resources, capacities, and commitments they bring to their love. These differences can create imbalances of power, authority, and status within a romantic relationship. When two lovers become one, the one they become may very well be more one of them than the other. Or the merger may take place within one lover alone, so to speak. One lover alone may change in ways that incorporate aspects of the subjectivity, agency, or objecthood of her lover into her own self, thereby converting her into part of the enlarged self that now supports her lover's perspective and promotes her lover's well-being. At the same time, little or nothing of her lover may change to incorporate elements of her—or rather of what she once was, independently of her connection to her lover.

Each of the ways listed above in which identities can merge in romantic love can yield asymmetries that affect differently the identities and individual autonomies of two people who love each other. As with the list of merged identity features, this list is also not intended to be comprehensive, and the items overlap:

1. *Needs and interests:*   The needs or interests of one lover may come to take precedence over those of her partner as joint projects that both lovers work on together. Perhaps one lover's needs or interests simply are more urgent; for example, she suffers from a serious illness. Perhaps, however, one lover simply asserts her needs or interests more emphatically.

2. *Caring and protection:*   One lover may care better for the needs and interests of her partner than her partner does for her needs and interests. This would tend to make her partner's identity and concerns more definitive of their joint undertakings than would her own.

3. *Deep mutual familiarity:*   One lover may be better than her partner at reading the emotional and bodily cues conveyed by her beloved. The one who is better understood (by the other) is likelier to get a greater degree of recognition and understanding when reacting to situations or expressing her needs. Her reactions will thereby tend to become more definitive than her partner's of their joint concerns.

4. *Attention:*   One lover may be more alert and attentive to her surroundings or her circumstances than her partner. By noticing more quickly than her partner what they both need to take account of or react to, she sets a kind of agenda for their shared attention. The lover who is quicker to respond is more able to determine how they both grasp what is happening to them.

5. *Decision making:*   One lover may reach decisions more quickly, more surely or with more self-confidence than her partner. Or her decisions and choices may stand up better to subsequent scrutiny and evaluation, perhaps because she has a greater store of background knowledge about the conditions they deal with together. In such cases, she will probably emerge as the more decisive or more reliable partner in their joint undertakings.

6. *Division of labor:*   One lover may come to shoulder more of the workload of their joint projects or carry out what both view as the more important tasks between them. Actually, these are two different sorts of asymmetries regarding division of labor, and they are likely to have different effects. Handling the more important tasks may give one lover a higher status in their affairs; this often happens, for example, in a marriage in which only one partner earns income for the couple. By contrast, shouldering more of the burden of, say, domestic chores or emotional bonding in a relationship seems to reduce someone's status in the relationship and leave her less capable of setting the agenda for their shared future.

7. *Mutual awareness or consideration:*   Two lovers may differ in the degree to which they each have the other always "in mind" or incorporate the perspective of the other into their own. This point overlaps a great deal with the previous point about evaluative perspective. It seems likely that the lover who gets more consideration from her partner than she gives in return will have her identity and deep concerns come to preoccupy both of them and play a greater role in determining their joint tasks and undertakings.

8. *Evaluative perspective:*   A distinctly important form of asymmetric merger of identity occurs when one partner defers excessively and without corresponding reciprocity to the norms, values, or commitments of the other partner. This is always a risk in any relationship that intermixes an attentiveness to values with a loving attachment to a particular individual. One person's attachment to the particular person who is her lover may lead her to suspend wholehearted commitment to those of her values that conflict with her lover's values. For the sake of love, a person may abandon commitments that she should not abandon.

Bartky argues that emotional caring for someone creates both an "epistemic" and a "moral" lean in the direction of the one receiving care. One tends to become "engrossed" in the care recipient's perspective. Doubts about those views or values become difficult to voice since they would introduce a kind of distancing or disloyalty into the relationship. One risks accepting uncritically "the world according to him."[24]

Of course, a lover may have values or commitments she *should* revise. And the risk of inappropriate deference would not be particularly relevant to autonomy in case two lovers are roughly equal in their readiness to defer to each other over the course of time, to suspend conviction or cast shadows of doubt over their prior values and commitments. When they are not equal in the extent or intensity of their separate moral convictions, however, then the possibility looms large that the autonomy of the more deferential partner will be diminished by the relationship.

9. *Mirroring of self-concepts:*   One lover's own self-concept may play too little a role in her romantic relationship. Her partner's conception of her nature, her virtues and her shortcomings, may become the lens through which they together regard her. She may come to see herself more through her partner's eyes than through her own.

10. Long-range plans: Obviously, if the long-range plans of a couple are more a reflection of one partner's needs and interests than the other's, the identity of that favored one will have the greater determining influence on the projects that define and actualize the identity of the couple over the course of time.

There are other important sorts of asymmetries that may not fit neatly into any of the above categories:

11. Degree of adjustment required by the relationship: If someone has to give up many of her prior commitments in order to incorporate a romance into her life whereas her lover had to make only minor adjustments, then the relationship will make the former person a substantially different person from the one she was before, while leaving her lover substantially the same as before.

12. Voluntariness of the relationship: Intimate relationships can vary along a continuum between, on the one hand, joint undertakings sought with mutual voluntariness on the basis of affection and respect, and, on the other hand, hostile takeovers initiated by violation and maintained by domination. Perhaps the latter relationships are not really cases of "romantic love," but if the name fits at all (and Hollywood sometimes seems to think so), then clearly the personal autonomy of the less voluntary party would be diminished—indeed, *violated*—by the relationship.

13. Autonomy competencies: Two lovers enter their relationship with different autonomy competencies. One lover may be more discerning at self-reflection, say, while another may be more decisive in taking action. A lover, for example, who is more articulate in expressing her views and more adept at defending them may have greater say than her partner in determining what counts as a legitimate shared purpose or joint project. Linguistic competency is an important meta-attribute in autonomy; it is a particularly rich skill for self-representation, critical reflection, and imagining and evaluating alternatives. To the extent that lovers depend on dialogue to forge their plans and settle their disagreements, the lover who is less skilled than her partner at linguistic self-expression will often have a hard time communicating and defending her perspective to her lover.

14. Differential responses from others: Other persons give us feedback, both explicit and implicit, on how they perceive us. Most of us pay at least some attention to the ways in which others react to us, and for most of us, that information enters, to some degree, into our reflections on our character, commitments, and identity. If other people so closely identify a person with her lover that they ignore or disregard what distinguishes her from her lover, then the feedback they give her would promote in her a tendency to think of herself in terms that mirror her lover's separate identity rather than reflecting her own. She would thereby lose the sort of intersubjective feedback about her own self that helps each of us to explore and maintain our separate identities.

Asymmetric Mergers and Women

Love does not take place in a social vacuum. It is influenced by traditions, practices, and social and political institutions. It is guided by norms and stereotypes. Foremost among these are gender norms and ideals of romantic heterosexual love. The idea of a merger of identities is one of these norms—to women's frequent disadvantage.

Historically, women were usually *sub*merged by their mergers with men. In the common law tradition, marriage was covered by the doctrine of coverture, according to which a man and woman became one through matrimony and that one was *him*.[25] She became his "femme covert." Today's gender differences in romantic love, in the United States, are not primarily matters of formal law. They are more typically matters of cultural practice and gender socialization. Social institutions still tend to identify a marital unit in terms of the premarital identity of the husband. Women are, for example, still routinely expected to take their husbands' last names—never the reverse. This practice reflects the old marital traditions that erased a wife's separate public identity.

Marriage is the occasional outcome of romantic love, and women are still encouraged and expected to "marry up." A woman is encouraged to marry someone who is taller, stronger, older, richer, smarter, or higher on the social scale than she is. It she does so, this means that the personal resources, including status, that he brings to their love are greater than those that she brings to it. This imbalance in resources makes the romantic merger of identities riskier for her than for him. He is likelier to overrule or overpower her than she him in case they disagree or conflict. Her capacities for exercising autonomy could easily be stifled as a result.[26] (In lesbian or gay relationships, power imbalances may well occur, of course, but they would not arise in any simple way from the mere gender identities of the parties.)

Feminist philosophers have argued for quite some time now that romantic love harbors morally damaging asymmetries for women. In *The Second Sex*, first published in 1949, Simone de Beauvoir wrote that females and males are socialized to join asymmetrically in romantic love, the female to submerge herself in the identity, projects, and perspective of the free, active, self-determining male. Beauvoir's portrait of this female quest is grim: Denied the opportunity to be a transcendent subject herself, a woman seeks the absolute through association and identification with, and submission to, a man, someone who is permitted that free-standing subjectivity. According to Beauvoir, a woman in love longs for abolition of the "boundaries" that separate her from her male lover. She longs for her own "complete destruction," and for "ecstatic union" and "identification" with him. She submits to him "as if to a god" and seeks to be "another incarnation of her loved one, his reflection, his double." She seeks to *be* him, as epitomized by Catherine's declaration in *Wuthering Heights:* "I am Heathcliff." Aside from being doomed to failure, in Beauvoir's view, since "No man really is God," a woman thereby engages in profound bad faith: "She chooses to desire her enslavement so ardently that it will *seem* to her the expression of her liberty."[27]

Writing in 1970, the radical American feminist Shulamith Firestone also contended that women are exploited by men in the course of love. "(Male) culture," she claimed, "was built on the love of women, and at their expense. Women provided the substance of those male masterpieces; and for millennia they have done the work, and suffered the costs, of one-way emotional relationships the benefits of which went to men and to the work of men. . . . *(Male) culture was (and is) parasitical, feeding on the emotional strength of women without reciprocity.*[28]

More recently still, in 1988, psychoanalyst Jessica Benjamin argued that the historic asymmetries of heterosexual romantic love have not disappeared, "despite our society's formal commitment to equality." In her view, relationships between the sexes continue to be plagued by tendencies toward male domination of females. Masculinity is still culturally associated with autonomy and the position of subject, while femininity remains culturally associated with dependency and the position of object.[29]

Nonfeminist philosophers who write about love have not given the gender distinction much thought. Robert Nozick does suggest an important gender difference in the lived experience of romantically merged identity, but dismisses the topic without much commentary. What he suggests is that men typically feel that the *we* that they form with a beloved is part of them, contained within their own identities as a person, while women, by contrast, typically feel that the *we* that they form with a beloved contains them as a part of itself.[30]

Nozick's failure to comment on his own observation on this point is striking, since the difference he notes suggests that men feel as if they are somehow larger than, or more than, their romantic love relationships, while women, by contrast, feel wholly engulfed by them. As Alan Soble notices, the male model, on Nozick's account, does not even constitute a genuine merger of identities. A man who feels himself to be greater than the romantic love relationship in his life, by definition, would not feel his (whole) self to be merged in the relationship and would be less likely than his engulfed female partner to submerge his independent identity or interests to the collective decisions and projects that merger requires.[31]

Some thinkers would not regard this gender difference as a problem. They could invoke the old cliché that women, but not men, make love relationships into the overriding purpose of their lives. Lord Byron: "Man's love is of man's life a thing apart; 'Tis woman's whole existence." Balzac: "Among the first-rate, man's life is fame, woman's life is love." One might argue in response that women who obsess about love are merely making a virtue of necessity. Women have not been oblivious to the social obstacles that constrained their life choices and that made "marrying up" a rationally prudent life plan. As the mother of my high school friend Risa Dumbrosky used to advise us: "It's just as easy to fall in love with a rich man as it is to fall in love with a poor man!"

Women, in addition, are socialized to shoulder more of the burdens of sustaining close personal relationships than are men. Women usually bear a greater share of the emotional work needed for lovers to survive as a couple. This could happen because women are more dedicated to maintaining their love relationships than are their male partners. Or it could happen because their male partners pressure them into making greater contributions, for example, by threatening to leave the relationships for other women who are more "sympathetic" and "supportive." In addition, as Scruton admits, a lover might welcome his beloved's dependence on him and oppose those of her projects, such as a career, that could give her the chance to "live happily" without him.[32] Scruton does not appear to regard this attitude as a serious problem.

If two lovers approach their love equally committed to it and equally prepared to make personal sacrifices toward that end, then it does not matter for the sake of fairness or autonomy whether they are both deeply oriented toward the maintenance of relationships or neither is. If, however, one lover works much harder than the other to sustain their relationship, then the other partner is something of a freerider on her loving endeavors. Historically recent traditions of love and marriage place a heavier responsibility on women than on men for providing care and nurturance, and care and nurturance tend to be viewed even today as women's work.[33] Thus, women tend to give more care and nurturance to their male lovers than they receive in return (although norms and practices are changing). This sort of asymmetry tends to diminish women's autonomy more than that of their male lovers—and *that*, I maintain, is a moral problem.

Changing Trends

Few philosophers today would seriously disagree that the autonomy of each partner in a romantic love, and the equality and mutuality that this requires, are desirable values for relationships of romantic love.[34] They would assume that mutuality, equality, and personal autonomy can occur in romantic love relationships without threatening romantic love itself.[35] In addition, probably no philosopher would seriously claim that, whatever degree of autonomy was desirable in romantic heterosexual love, women should have less of it than do men.

This egalitarian attitude is common but by no means pervasive throughout American culture today. There is indeed a contemporary model of heterosexual love that places great value on the self-development and self-fulfillment of both partners. This model, however, has emerged only gradually and unsteadily over the course of the twentieth century. Marriage is not the same as romantic love, of course, but ideals of marriage tell us a great deal about how a culture views heterosexual romantic love. In 1909, an editorial in the magazine *Harper's Bazaar* asserted this ideal of marriage: "Marriage means self-discipline. Marriage is not for the individual, but for the race. . . . Marriage is the slow growth of two persons into one—one person with one pursuit, one mind, one heart, one interest . . . one ideal." Here we find the ideal of romantic merger full-blown with no emphasis on individual fulfillment.

The 1920s saw the development of the ideal of both marital partners fulfilling themselves in marital love. This idea subsequently declined for several decades, however, and did not pick up momentum again until the 1960s. Between the 1920s and the 1960s, more traditional ideals of love and marriage prevailed, ideals which deemphasized individual freedom and self-development.[36] Those traditions still persist today. Nevertheless, by the 1970s, the emphasis on self-fulfillment had again become quite prominent. A 1978 article in the *Ladies' Home Journal* warned against the ideal of marriage as "an all-encompassing blend of two personalities fused into one. A marriage like this leaves no breathing space for two individuals to retain their own personalities."[37]

According to the newest ideals of self-fulfillment in love and marriage, the personal development and fulfillment of both partners, female as well as male, is a primary value to be sought in heterosexual love. Predetermined sex roles and a sexual division of labor are less important than they used to be. Both the woman and the man in a loving couple are responsible for working to support the relationship. Such, at any rate, are the norms of love that many people now voice, even if their actual practices lag somewhat behind their expressed ideals.[38]

Part of this transformation included a shift from the nineteenth-century view that sex in marriage was mainly for procreation to the more recent view that sex is for enjoyment and communication between marital partners. According to a study by Michael Gordon of marriage manuals, it was approximately between 1920 and 1940 that sex was redefined as fun.[39] (Marriage manuals of later decades would go on to emphasize the complex skills needed to be a good lover. Thus, by the 1960s, according to another study of marriage manuals, sex had become redefined as *work*.[40] But I digress.)

Social researcher Francesca Cancian refers to the overall change in the ideals of love and marriage as a trend "from role to self." She finds ample evidence to suggest that the causes of the trend include "economic prosperity, increasing leisure and education, and the tendency of women as well as men to work for individual wages."[41] Cancian notes that the decades of strongest emphasis on personal freedom and self-fulfillment (that is, the 1920s and the decades since the 1960s) were either preceded or accompanied by a strong women's movement. This is not a coincidence.

Men's roles in heterosexual love and marriage have long afforded much wider latitude than women's roles for living according to their own distinctive identities and their deep self-defining commitments, whether at home, at work, or in public life. The crucial development of the past few decades has been the spread of the view that even in love and marriage, women's own selves are important. Women's identities, characters, and self-defining commitments have come to be viewed by many people as important, whether or not they are dedicating their lives to the care and nurturance of husband, children, or other loved ones. Women's own traditional commitments to love have even been enlisted to make this point. Thus, women's magazines in recent decades have advised women that they could not be genuinely loving people unless they each developed an independent self. This contrasts with advice to women from the 1950s, when they were routinely told simply to sacrifice themselves for their families, devote themselves to keeping family relationships intact and harmonious, and generally behave in ways that we would now group under the label of traditional female role.[42]

Traditional ideals present themselves as a set of moral duties: people should get heterosexually married and have children, and romantic love should be geared toward this end. Proponents of this traditional view believe that people should strive to fulfill those duties, regardless of what they happen to regard as their deepest identity, character, or concerns.[43] Persons who develop their lives around values and projects of their own that are not specifically geared toward family relationships are, on this view, selfishly individualistic. Merely living a life in accord with whatever happens to be someone's deepest sense of identity or character is not only *not* in itself valuable; on this traditional view, it is, in addition, often a threat to the stable marital love that *is* a matter of moral duty.[44] The only fulfillment of self through romantic love that counts as a moral value is the development of a self who makes a deep commitment to an enduring family life, thereby making concern for it a part of her identity. If aspects of someone's deep character are leading her away from the work of maintaining her marital love relationship, then, by these traditional standards, she should try to change those aspects of herself.

In our morally plural public culture, this traditional ideal of heterosexual love and marriage now competes with the newer ideal that emphasizes self-fulfillment in and through love. The debate is, in large part, a dispute over the location of the boundary between the moral duties that love requires and the moral discretion that it permits, between the realm of moral requirements and the realm in which personal autonomy may legitimately manifest itself with respect to love. Traditionalists regard marriage and romantic love as a realm of substantial moral requirements that often override the nonmoral preferences of individual lovers, even when these preferences stem from deep, self-defining commitments. Someone whose concerns lead her away from the work of maintaining her marital love relationship is failing to fulfill her moral responsibilities.

The newer self-fulfillment ideals, by contrast, are based on the premise that the deeply self-defining commitments of individuals should have substantial priority in governing how they interact with romantic partners. Assuming that someone's character is not generally immoral, a romantic relationship that she can preserve only by altering or giving up her self-defining commitments is probably not, on this view, worth preserving.[45]

According to Francesca Cancian, much social research suggests that, in the United States if not elsewhere, the ideal of self-fulfillment in romantic love becomes more prominent with the increasing affluence of a population. Economically poorer groups show a greater preference, on average, for traditional ideals of love and less interest than wealthier groups in ideals of self-fulfillment in love.[46] This may tell us something about one of the functions of romantic love relationships. When romantic loves endure over time, they allow individuals to pool their assets in order to cope with life's difficulties and to face risks and uncertainties in a world of scarce resources. The fewer an individual's own resources for coping with life's hazards, the more she needs an alliance with others for sheer survival. And the more she has to worry about sheer survival, the less important to her will be the living of a life that merely accords with her specific identity and self-defining character. Since women of all social strata earn lower incomes on average than similarly situated men, this effect will be stronger for women than for men.

Nevertheless, even if people who are materially disadvantaged take less interest in autonomy than those who are materially advantaged, this does not tell us that autonomy is of no value. It does suggest that the value of autonomy is secondary to other concerns, but this is hardly a surprising discovery. In any case, according to Cancian, research shows that the twentieth-century trend from role to self, to some degree or other, has occurred across all social strata in the United States.[47]

Romantic merger is a dimension of love that can threaten the personal autonomy of either partner in a heterosexual romance. We live, however, in a social context that still features lively traditional ideals pressuring women to a greater extent than men to sacrifice their own distinctive and separate interests for the sake of preserving love relationships. Traditions of love and gender still hold women more responsible than men for sacrificing their independent selves to sustain heterosexual love relationships. In such a context, romantic merger threatens women's personal autonomy more than that of men.

Of course, if a woman values her romantic love more than she does her other concerns, then it defines who she is and she does not (necessarily) lose autonomy by sacrificing her other concerns to preserve her love relationship. (I shall return to this idea shortly.) The point is that some of our existing ideals of love hold women more responsible than men for preserving love relationships *whether or not* these values deeply define the women themselves. This means that women experience more cultural pressure than men to *change* what is deeply defining of who they are, for the sake of heterosexual love, rather than simply being permitted to build their heterosexual relationships in accord with whatever happens already to define their identities. (It's the familiar story: he remains whoever he was before marriage, Mr. Whoever, while she becomes Mrs. Him.) It seems reasonable to expect that the lover whose pre-existing independent selfhood is more highly socially valued will be able to exercise greater control over whatever romantic merger she might forge with another. On my view, romantic heterosexual merger is dangerous for a woman not inherently but rather contingently, at this historical period, because of lingering norms of love and gender that undervalue both women's personal autonomy and those female aspirations that are not aimed at caring for others.

Possible Objections

I have suggested that because of traditional role pressures and expectations, women are more vulnerable than men to the loss of personal autonomy in heterosexual romantic love and that this difference is a moral problem. At least four objections can be raised to my view.

Objection #1: I seem to be construing autonomy in love as a zero-sum game, and this could be a mistake. One lover's gain in autonomy might have nothing to do with her partner's loss of autonomy. Women who are not very autonomous in love probably never were very autonomous outside of love, in the ordinary situations of their lives.

I agree that autonomy in love is not always or necessarily a zero-sum game overall. Often enough, however, it is.[48] Two lovers have only limited time and resources available for their joint projects and the life they build together. Time and resources that are devoted to the needs, interests, and life goals of one partner become unavailable for the needs, interests, and life goals of the other insofar as those concerns diverge. When the perspective of one lover prevails over that of the other in determining what they attend to and how they evaluate it, then the perspective of the other lover, in that regard, is thereby excluded. To the extent that the needs, concerns, and perspectives of two lovers harmonize, these conflicts will be avoided. If, however, harmony is achieved because one lover *gave up* more of her preromance commitments than did her partner, then once again autonomy within romantic love would exhibit a zero-sum dimension.

Objection #2: Over time, romantic love might enhance someone's capacity for individual autonomy, and this could offset whatever loss of autonomy she experiences in virtue of merging with the identity of her lover. Indeed, sometimes the loss of autonomy in the short run enables a gain in autonomy in the long run.

I agree with these claims. For one thing, romantic love can promote self-knowledge, a competency needed for autonomy. People often come to know themselves better through love. My lover, for instance, may discern features about me that I had never noticed, and communicate her insights to me—lovingly, I would hope! Or I may observe myself responding and behaving, in the course of love, in ways that teach me something about my deeper needs, capacities, or limitations.

As well, my sense of myself as a separate person may actually intensify in the course of love. As my lover and I focus loving attention on each other, we reinforce each other's self-esteem and sense of self-worth. Love that affirms me and conveys recognition of my virtues and talents inspires me to promote them and to try to diminish my shortcomings. An affirming love can thus increase the degree of my attentive focus on myself. In various ways, then, I may become more aware of who or what I am, and this sort of self-reflection contributes to personal autonomy apart from the effects of any merger of identity with my beloved.

Love can also promote the growth of competencies for autonomy. In this respect, even a merger of identity with someone who is more autonomous than oneself might become the very vehicle by which one learns through emulation and participation to become more autonomous. As I noted earlier, the competencies for autonomy include such skills as critical reflection, evaluation, and imagining alternatives. These skills are best learned from other persons who already know how to engage in them and can teach us by example or by instruction. Contexts of joint agency provide particularly intimate and intense opportunities for such learning. The shared activities and projects of love in particular engage us jointly with our lovers over the whole trajectory of agency: attending to situations, evaluating circumstances, making decisions, expressing our concerns in action, and living with the consequences of our choices. One's more autonomous lover may be able show how to maintain one's commitments in the face of opposition from others or how to imagine alternatives to them.

Thus, being for a while the less autonomous partner of a romantic merger of identities does not by itself preclude one from *ever* growing more autonomous. Indeed, the deference that is likely to arise in the less autonomous partner might well be the sort of attitude that permits one to learn from another. Whether or not love permits such growth in the less autonomous lover, however, depends on many factors, not the least of which is the support and encouragement of the more dominant or directive partner. My larger concern is with individual, and particularly women's, losses of autonomy over the whole course of a romantic love relationship, not merely with isolated occasions of it.

Objection #3: Autonomy may simply not be an important value for romantic love relationships. Thus, it might not be a moral problem when one lover's autonomy is diminished by the same romantic relationship that promotes her partner's autonomy. I acknowledged earlier that autonomy is not the only good. Perhaps in the context of romantic love, becoming more autonomous is beside the point. More important values may be at stake, values that could be jeopardized if both lovers try too hard to grow in autonomy competency. This objection questions whether autonomy is a value at all in romantic love, whether in the short run *or* the long run, and whether or not it involves a zero-sum game.

Martha Nussbaum suggests that temporary "phases" of loss of autonomy in intimate relationships can be all right, "even quite wonderful." The emotional and physical penetration of boundaries can, for example, be "a very valuable part of sexual life." Nussbaum, however, endorses the loss of autonomy only as an episode in the context of relationships otherwise featuring "mutual regard." She does not defend the persistent denial of one lover's autonomy by another.[49]

My account of autonomy, although socially grounded, is somewhat individualistic, as I discussed earlier. Too much individualism in relationships, however, may make relationships unworkable. Relationships define who we are. We do not have identities, characters, or self-defining commitments apart from relationships, although we might have mere desires and preferences. Relationships are thus necessary conditions for the very having of a stable self-identity. At the same time, in order to sustain these crucial, identity-conferring relationships, we may have to sacrifice or submerge some of our own desires and preferences, in particular those that would interfere with our efforts to preserve our relationships. As Objection #3 would have it, any desire or preference that interferes with our efforts to preserve our relationships should be abandoned because it undermines the very factors that are necessary conditions for our having, in the first place, stable identities worth acting on.

I grant, to this argument, that we do need social relationships in order to have the sorts of identities that become touchstones for personal autonomy. It does not follow, however, that we must derive these identities from any particular romantic love relationship. There are all sorts of relationships in our lives that can and do serve the purpose of socializing and building our characters and self-defining commitments. Whether or not one should make a particular romantic love relationship an enduring part of one's life and a deep self-defining commitment for oneself depends on whether the relationship nurtures or stifles the self that one already is. There is nothing inherently sacred about any one romantic love relationship, nothing that morally requires one to modify one's deeper self for the sake of entering it and merging (partly) with one's lover. The burden of proof is on those who insist otherwise, and especially on those who insist that women in particular are obligated to sacrifice themselves to promote heterosexual union.

Our culture, as I noted earlier, harbors a variety of ideals of marriage. Ideals of romantic love, especially of the traditional sort, have often seemed to take their bearings from ideals of marriage. It has seemed as if romantic love relationships have been viewed as testing grounds in which people's characters are trained up toward what is considered normative for them as marital partners. If marriage is viewed as a merger in which two identities become one and that one is primarily *his*, especially in the public world, then it might be reasonable for ideals of heterosexual romantic love to lead people toward developing the characters they will need for the marital state. Yet our culture no longer unanimously accepts the ideal of marriage as a union that preserves much of a man's identity while submerging the identity of the women. Once the male-dominant model of marriage is given up, there is no reason to derive ideals of romantic love from it.

Objection #4: Women themselves simply do not value personal autonomy as much as men do. What is more important for women, according to this view, are human relationships and their preservation. If women do indeed sacrifice more personal autonomy in romantic love than do men, perhaps this is no loss from their own subjective standpoints. Some women believe autonomy to be quite unimportant, perhaps a masculine preoccupation. There are feminists and nonfeminists who concur in claiming that women do not value individual autonomy as much as men do and instead place more value on human relationships and their preservation.[50] Women who lose more personal autonomy in romantic love than do men would not regard this loss as a real sacrifice.

This is a crucial objection to consider. The challenge is to be clear about the full nature of such an attitude. It seems to be a claim about women's deeper self-defining commitments and values. The claim is that women want to have and sustain love relationships regardless of whether or not they have to sacrifice other interests or concerns to do so. When we examine this attitude carefully, we shall see that, whether she knows it or not, a woman who holds this attitude would nevertheless be worse off if her romantic relationships diminished her autonomy than if they didn't.

There is, first of all, the empirical question of whether women in general really care more about relationships then they do about their autonomy. Empirical research does lend substantial support to this view. Much research shows that females at all ages have more close relationships than men and maintain them more closely that do men. Women are more likely that men at any age to have someone to whom they confide personal experiences and feelings. Women appear to be more competent than men at the emotional sensitivity and intimate self-disclosure that cement close personal bonds. Some social theorists have therefore argued that love and interpersonal relationships are defining aspects of women's, but not men's, identities and personalities.[51] If love relationships were really a paramount self-defining concern to women, then women would have little or no motivation to live a life built around any other projects.

Research data, however, do not show that *all* women make love relationships so central to their identities as to override all separate or conflicting concerns. The data give us only statistical correlations between gender and the degree of interest and personal investment in close relationships. Women who do have self-defining commitments that override romantic love relationships have no reason to sacrifice those commitments for the sake of love just because those commitments are unusual for their gender. In addition to leaving the normative issue unresolved, the data also do not show that women would unanimously reject personal autonomy as I have conceptualized it.

Even for women whose love relationships do define who they are—women who think they have no interest in personal autonomy—the data do not tell us that personal autonomy is unimportant. Let us then imagine a woman who does not value her own autonomy, or does not value it very much by comparison to other goods that she derives from personal relationships. In the course of a love relationship, she willingly sacrifices her own independent values and projects to sustain the relationship and to support her partner by investing her efforts in the realization of his values and projects.

The first thing to notice about such a woman is that she does not completely devalue autonomy. Rather, although she devalues her own autonomy, she actively promotes the autonomy of someone else, namely her lover. She helps to build a shared life with him that realizes his deepest commitments. Thus women in love who do not care about their own autonomy do not regard autonomy as completely valueless.

In addition, there is something puzzling about devaluing one's own autonomy but investing one's life in helping someone else to realize his autonomy. Perhaps such a woman finds herself to be personally fulfilled through successfully helping her lover to satisfy his needs and desires, attain his goals, and fulfill his commitments. If so, it seems that she lives vicariously through her lover's autonomous pursuits. The interest in *vicarious* autonomy, however, is not a complete disinterest in autonomy.

The vicarious pursuit of autonomy, however, raises its own problems. A woman who gives up her own separate identity for the sake of vicariously participating in the autonomy of some man exemplifies exactly Beauvoir's description of the (pathetic) woman in love. In Beauvoir's view, such a project is doomed to fail. No man is divine enough to deserve such a sacrifice. A woman will realize that fact soon enough, after which she will spend the rest of her life trying to hide, from others and herself, the sad pointlessness of her sacrifice.[52]

Our relationally oriented woman, however, may not really care about her lover's autonomy. Suppose that, more than anything, she simply wants her romantic relationship to last, and she will do whatever is needed to maintain its stability and harmony. One way to foster harmony in a love relationship is to bring one's needs, concerns, and values into concordance with those of one's beloved in order to minimize discord and conflict. She does this not to promote his autonomy but rather simply to preserve their relationship. She changes the less important aspects of herself in order to diminish threats to the relationship that might arise from value or viewpoint conflicts with her lover. Granted, the woman who does this is doing more sex/affective work than her partner (to borrow Ann Ferguson's phrase).[53] However, the relationship is supremely important to her. What she is sacrificing, perhaps her own former career goal, was never (in this example) so important for her as the love relationship has become.

Notice, however, that this example no longer clearly challenges my view that a woman's own autonomy is important within her love relationships. The relationship is now, by definition, the woman's overriding concern for which she will sacrifice other important values. The quest for close human relationships can certainly define a person's deep character, so that seeking to foster and sustain relationships could easily be the autonomous expression of such a person's deep sense of who she is and how she most wants to live her life. As such, it is a self-defining commitment for her. By acting in accord with that commitment, a woman does not actually give up autonomy; instead she shows a significant *degree* of it. Thus a woman who values her relationships more than she values autonomy, and who acts to maintain her romantic relationship, becomes autonomous after all.

It matters not that such a woman might have no self-conscious *commitment* to autonomy. On my view, someone can be autonomous without self-consciously seeking or even caring about autonomy itself as a value. Thus, the research data which show that women care less about personal autonomy and more about preserving close relationships than do men fail to show either that the personal autonomy of women in love is unimportant or that it is unrealized in their heterosexual relationships. Someone can achieve autonomy and maintain an intimate romantic relationship simultaneously so long as maintaining the relationship is something she really cares about and so long as her efforts to maintain it do not themselves involve sacrifices of her autonomy in other ways.Indeed, someone who really values close relationships may well be *unable* to preserve them if she lacks personal autonomy.

Thus, imagine again a woman who works to sustain a close, harmonious relationship by bringing her needs and concerns into concordance with those of her partner. Suppose now that her partner begins to neglect his relationship to the woman. He takes on projects and commitments that conflict with it: he stays late at the office every workday, he goes drinking with his buddies several nights a week, he takes up solitary hobbies, he schedules out-of-town business trips on her birthdays, he commits adultery. Our imaginary woman now faces a serious dilemma.

If she wants to preserve the relationship, she appears to have two basic choices. First, she could do what she usually does to maintain harmony in their relationship, namely, try to promote her lover's interests and to bring her own needs and concerns into concordance with his. Under the circumstances, that adaptation would necessitate *giving up* her deep concern to sustain their relationship for she would now be trying to promote the relationship-*threatening* concerns of her lover. In that case, however, the relationship would surely deteriorate. She would now be working for the very loss of that which we have defined her as wanting above all else—the maintenance of the relationship. It thus seems that her commitment to maintaining a love relationship could undermine itself if it involved deferring to her lover at all times, including supporting his tendencies to neglect or damage the relationship. This is surely an unwelcome outcome to those who celebrate women's supposedly greater concern for relationships than for autonomy.

The relationally oriented woman has another option, however. She could work to *modify* those of her lover's commitments that conflict with the maintenance of their relationship. Doing so, however, would amount to trying to direct the course of affairs for them as a couple in accordance with her *own* deepest self-defining values, and opposing his concerns in the process. This seems to be the only option available to her, given her aim of salvaging the relationship that we have defined her as caring about more than her own autonomy. A woman acting in this manner, however, would not exactly be forgoing her own direct personal autonomy. She would be promoting her commitment to relationships in the face of relationally threatening behavior by her lover. She would indeed be acting autonomously within their relationship.

A woman committed to maintaining relationships faces an additional difficulty, however—one that bolsters even further the argument that she needs to be significantly autonomous. Someone who has not acquired or practiced the *competencies* for autonomy will not be able to conjure up those skills simply for the occasion on which she might need them to preserve her relationships. In order to be ready to be autonomous when she needs to be (to protect the relationships that she values), a woman must have previously acquired the skills to do so. She could only have acquired those skills through sufficient practice. Like many other skills, she must occasionally exercise them in order to keep them from getting rusty.

Thus, in order to be truly capable of acting to sustain the relationships that matter most to her, a woman must be prepared to ward off threats to those relationships, including threats arising from the concerns and behaviors of her relational partners. She must have the ability to persist in the pursuit of what she cares about even in the face of some opposition by others, including her own partners. That is, in order to sustain the relationships she deeply cares about, she must possess some minimal level of autonomy competency that she is actively capable of deploying at least for its instrumental value, however much she might think that autonomy does not matter to her.

In this chapter, I explored some ways in which merged identity in romantic love can affect the personal autonomy of lovers. I surveyed a recent cultural ideal of love that places value on personal autonomy in romantic relationships, and I sketched out some persistent gender asymmetries that compromise those trends. Finally, I argued that even women who place overriding importance on romantic relationships need *some* degree of autonomy in love.

In the next chapter, I consider the breakdown of heterosexual intimacy in the form of woman battering, and I try to determine which cultural responses to these situations will preserve the personal autonomy of the affected women.

7

Domestic Violence against
Women and Autonomy

Women who are abused by their intimate partners have often sought help from the legal system and from professional caregiving services. In the past, the legal system virtually ignored the problem, leaving women to fend for themselves against violent partners. In recent years, partly as a result of feminist outcry and partly as a result of lawsuits against them, various legal jurisdictions have made efforts to respond more effectively to women's calls for help against abusive partners. While these efforts still need improvement, the legal response is generally better now than it was a few decades ago.

Certain types of cases, however, continue to pose legal challenges. These are cases in which the abused women[1] themselves act in ways that make it harder for the law to seek justice. Women may, for example, refuse to press charges against their abusers, making it difficult for prosecutors to gain convictions. Or women may return to live with their abusers, making it more difficult for police to protect them against future violence by those same abusers. Thus, *some* abused women act in ways that hinder even the still-inadequate efforts of the state to protect them or punish the offenders.

Suppose, fantastically, that the law had the resources, capacity, and will to provide full protection and justice to every abused woman who leaves her abuser or who cooperates in bringing him to justice. It would still not be clear how the law should respond to women who do not leave their abusers and who do not cooperate with the state in punishing them. Should the law continue to try to protect such women and to punish the offenders against the wishes of the women? Or should the law simply refrain from punishing offenders when that is what the victims want?

A related but different question is this: How should professional caregivers respond to women who seek help from them in coping with abusive relationships but who nevertheless choose to remain in those relationships? The aim of this chapter is to explore these two related issues. First, how should the *law* respond to women who are being abused by intimate partners but who do not

140

leave their abusers? Second, how should *professional caregivers* respond to women in those circumstances?

To anticipate, I shall argue that legal responses should lean toward penalizing abusers even when the abused women in question fail to cooperate with the law. Professional caregivers, however, should lean toward providing support for abused women who remain in abusive relationships, even if this hampers efforts by all concerned to control the abusers—with exceptions in case there is a risk of serious future abuse. That is, the law should tend to try to prevent domestic abuse with or without the cooperation of the victim while professional caregiving services should tend to support the victim even though this might hamper efforts by outsiders to help prevent her future abuse. Respect for the autonomy of abused women, and the different forms such respect can take, will constitute important considerations in exploring these issues.

The following discussion focuses only on women as abuse victims and only on those who are abused by intimate male partners. This is overwhelmingly the most reported sort of domestic violence, and there are good reasons to believe that it is the most commonly occurring sort. In 1994, according to statistics from the Department of Justice, as reported by social theorists Susan L. Miller and Charles F. Wellford, women experienced violence from an intimate partner at a rate almost ten times that experienced by men.[2]

Before answering my two main questions, we should first consider three other issues: How exactly does domestic violence diminish a woman's autonomy? Why do some women stay in abusive relationships they could safely leave? Is there anything *wrong with asking* why some women stay?

How Intimate Partner Abuse Diminishes Autonomy

Intimate relationships affect us in our very homes, our "havens in a heartless world" (to recycle a contemporary cliché),[3] the places where we are supposed to be safe, nurtured, and protected. In intimate relationships, we expose our bodies and bare our souls, making ourselves vulnerable at the very core of our beings. When one's haven *is* a heartless world, there is no further place of refuge, no sanctuary in which one can rest secure from the violence that threatens one's exposed and vulnerable core self.

Abuse by an intimate partner can include: (1) physical battering, ranging from shoving and hitting to attacks with lethal weapons; (2) emotional and psychological abuse, such as humiliation, isolation, threats to take the children away, or the killing of beloved pets; (3) financial control, such as withholding support money or stealing the abused person's own money; and (4) sexual abuse, such as rape or other forced sex acts.[4]

Autonomy, to reiterate, involves reflecting on one's deeper values and concerns and acting in accordance with them. It involves some capacity to persist in acting according to one's deeper concerns in the face of a minimum of opposition by others. One's reflections should, furthermore, have been made without undue manipulation or coercion.

Intimate partner abuse undermines autonomy in at least three related ways. First, intimate partner abuse is coercive; it threatens an abused woman's survival and safety. Intimate partner abuse denies to the abused person, in her very home life and her intimate bodily existence, the safety and security she needs to try to live her life as she thinks she ought to do. Instead of being able to live according to her values and commitments, an abused woman is reduced to seeking bare survival and security. Some philosophers have argued that a person cannot live an autonomous life unless she lives under circumstances that afford her a plurality of acceptable options and do not reduce her to the level of being governed by her basic needs, such as those of survival or security.[5] Basic survival and security are not commitments or self-conceptions that define us as particular persons; they are universal needs of all living beings. Merely to survive, even against great odds, is not (yet) to exemplify self-determination in any significant sense. I argued in chapter 1 that someone could still exemplify autonomy, when facing dangerous or tragic circumstances, by nevertheless acting, admittedly at great risk to herself, to preserve and protect what she cares about. Autonomy is thus not eliminated by dangers such as domestic abuse. It is certainly, however, much more difficult to achieve under those conditions and is, in that sense, undermined.

Intimate partner abuse undermines autonomy in a second way as a consequence of the threat it poses to an abused person's survival. This threat focuses an abused woman's attention constantly on the desires and demands of her abuser. An abused woman tends to develop a heightened awareness of what her partner wants and needs as she tries to accommodate his wishes and whims, all this as a way to minimize his violent reactions.[6] Such focused attention on what another person wants distracts someone from the task of understanding herself or being guided by her own self-defining concerns.[7] Her goals are survival and security, which are not, as such, autonomy-conferring goals. And her means of pursuing those goals involve mere deferential or heteronomous reactions to the abuser's actual or anticipated desires or moods.

Third, abusers are people who attempt in general to exercise inordinate control over their intimate partners. One significance of autonomy is that of not being consistently or deeply subjected to the will of other persons. Chronic abuse, however, is precisely a form of willful control by another person.[8] According to Angela Browne, the "early warning signs" of an abusive personality include possessiveness, excessive jealousy, quickness to anger, an insistence on knowing a woman's whereabouts and activities at all times, and a tendency to discourage the woman from maintaining relationships with others.[9] It is much harder for a woman to avoid subjection to the will of another if that other is an intimate partner with substantial access to her at private and vulnerable moments who tries continually to exert control over her.

Over the past several decades, professional caregivers and feminist activists have worked hard to reform the legal system and social support services so that these agencies will help abused women more effectively to avoid or end abuse.[10] Many counseling programs, for example, have emerged to rehabilitate batterers. Studies of the effectiveness of these programs suggest some degree of success, but the studies have been criticized for methodological weaknesses.[11] In the absence of programs with confirmably high or widespread success rates at rehabilitating abusers, much effort continues to be directed toward empowering abused women so that they can improve their own lives.[12] Some studies suggest that the only sure way for most women to stop being abused is to end their relationships with their abusers.[13] What professional caregivers and legal personnel often find, however, is that some women keep returning to their abusive relationships even after receiving the support of social services and finding out about opportunities to leave their relationships with relative safety. The question of how best to respond to abused women arises most acutely in such cases. To answer the question carefully, we need to know why some women stay in abusive relationships.

Why Ask, "Why Do Women Stay?"?

Some social theorists have argued that we should stop asking why women stay in abusive relationships. This question seems to blame the victim for the abuse she experiences and perhaps even to excuse the abuser. Instead of this question, it is argued, we should ask, "Why do men abuse women?"[14]

We should certainly ask why some men batter and abuse women, and we should continue to support the important research addressing this question. At the same time, there is value in asking the question why women stay—provided it is asked in the right way. The question is ambiguous in its presuppositions. It could be meant as a rhetorical question intended to *blame* an abused woman for the abuse she suffers. On this mistaken view, the abused woman's action of staying in the relationship is what enables the abuser to continue abusing her, and, for that reason, she is somehow morally responsible for the abuse.

The questions "Why do women stay?" or "Why does she stay?" could be meant, on the other hand, as sincere attempts to understand women's motivations. We assume, with good reason, that human beings tend to be self-protective. When someone defends herself against attack, this is understandable on the face of it. It requires no further explanation. Against this background expectation, it is reasonable to be perplexed when a competent adult seems to take no action to protect herself against attack and even knowingly remains in a situation that exposes herself to further danger. Such behavior does not make sense in those terms. Some further explanation is needed: more information, perhaps, about the behavior in question or the conditions under which it occurs.

It seems furthermore that there is indeed *something* wrong with the choice to stay in an abusive relationship. Exactly what kind of wrong is involved, however, must be specified precisely. Staying in an abusive relationship is not a moral wrong—unless it is morally wrong to endure mistreatment. This notion would require a self-regarding morality, a morality of duties to oneself. Even in the context of a self-regarding morality, it is not obvious that enduring mistreatment would be as wrong as inflicting mistreatment or that it would deserve the same degree of reproach. Without the backing of a self-regarding morality, we should say only that staying in an abusive relationship is at most a prudential mistake. It would be, furthermore, only a prima facie prudential mistake; the action in question could be justified if there were good enough reasons for it. The assumption to which we are entitled, then, in the absence of a self-regarding morality, is that a woman who stays in an abusive relationship that she could have safely left is *imprudent* if she thereby knowingly risks future abuse *for no good reason.*

To be sure, one should not belabor even this qualified point to a woman who has just entered the emergency ward with life-threatening wounds. In a more contemplative and detached context, however, we can certainly entertain the abstract, defeasible assumption that physically capable women should act to protect themselves (to the extent that they can do so) against foreseeable and unnecessary dangers. Many women stay in abusive relationships for understandable reasons, given the constraints under which they live (more on this below). The prima facie presumption that women do something prudentially wrong by remaining with their abusers can thus be rebutted by evidence in most cases. However, the possibility of rebuttal does not make the request for explanation wrongheaded.[15]

Taking responsibility for one's own well-being does not mean never being dependent on others. Indeed, in a world of scarce resources and human limitations, one's well-being requires depending on others for at least some things most of the time. Depending on others, however, should not lead someone who could defend herself to become utterly defenseless in her own right. There is something amiss about a person who could act to protect herself from a harm she is suffering but fails to do so. Such a failure calls for some explanation.

There might, furthermore, be value in a culturewide expectation that women *as women,* so far as they are able, should try to protect themselves against foreseeable and unnecessary dangers. According to traditional gender norms, women are relatively weak and defenseless and need men to protect them. Expecting or encouraging this dependence in women is part of the same gender role framework that celebrates dominant and controlling tendencies in men, the very tendencies that are at the root of most intimate partner abuse. When we assume that women should try to protect themselves to the best of their abilities, and when we go on to raise our daughters to do so, we are helping in part to reverse the very gender traditions that give rise in the first place to the problem of intimate partner abuse.[16]

So Why *Do* Women Stay?

Years ago, some psychoanalysts and psychological theorists argued that women stayed in abusive relationships because they were masochists. They enjoyed the abuse. This explanation has, thankfully, lost credibility in recent years due to mounting contradictory evidence.[17] Women rarely submit to abuse as something desired for its own sake. Nor are women typically mere passive victims of abuse. In general, they try to resist in some way. Even Lenore Walker's famous thesis of the early 1980s that abused women suffer from "learned helplessness"[18] has come under recent criticism. Edward W. Gondolf and Ellen R. Fisher, among others, argue that battered women are not passive or helpless and should not even be thought of as victims. Instead, they should be regarded as survivors, as people who try to resist abuse but encounter obstacles when doing so. Studies show, for example, that many abused women contact professional services for help in coping with their abuser but find these services to be either unresponsive or ineffective. Gondolf and Fisher suggest that professional caregivers may be the ones suffering from learned helplessness![19]

Empirical research in the past few decades has revealed that many women stay in abusive relationships because leaving the relationships would impose even greater hardships on them. Many abused women, for example, are financially dependent on their abusers; leaving the relationship would risk the loss of financial support.[20] Some women stay with their abusers in order to protect their children. A woman may feel that her children are simply better off for having a father in the home; perhaps the man is not abusive toward the children. Or an abuser may frighten a woman into staying with him by warning that he will get custody of the children in case she leaves.[21]

Finally, some abusers threaten to retaliate violently against their female partners for leaving. Sociologist Martha Mahoney calls this sort of abuse "separation assault." Separation assault consists of threats and violence that a batterer inflicts on his partner when she tries to leave, precisely in order to intimidate her into staying.[22]

Some women who leave violent men are pursued and harassed for months or even years afterward. Some abusive men murder their ex-partners. The first few months after leaving are especially dangerous. An abusive man may stalk his former partner, telephoning her family and friends repeatedly, showing up at her place of employment, hanging out at playgrounds and other places that she frequents. Some women who leave such vindictive men go into hiding, but the women's anxieties continue. They may worry constantly, afraid to enter their apartments, afraid to approach their own cars in parking lots, afraid of headlights that pull up behind them at night. These women sometimes report that living or hiding in fear of reprisal or death seems worse than remaining with the abuser.[23] Some women report that their abusers attempted to maintain a coercive tie for years after the actual relationship ended.[24]

Lack of financial means, worries about children's welfare, and fear of separation assault all provide indisputably legitimate, prima facie reasons for someone to stay in an abusive relationship. A woman who stays under such conditions has good reason to do so. She may have no better alternative. A professional caregiver trying to respect a woman's capacity for autonomy in such a case has a clear responsibility: support the woman's (rational) choice uncritically and, perhaps, try to help her to alter the circumstances that so constrict her life as to make staying in a dangerous relationship the optimal thing for her to do.

There are some other cases, however, that are less clear-cut, cases in which, to outsiders at any rate, the women seem somehow to be misguided. Abused women might, for example, misunderstand what is happening to them, a misunderstanding that can be perplexing to outsiders to whom the existence and nature of the abuse seems obvious. According to Kathleen Ferraro and John Johnson, many abused women deny that the abuse they suffered was really injurious. Or they deny that their partner was to blame for the abuse, perhaps by blaming alcohol or by blaming themselves for not being conciliatory enough. Abused women may also underestimate their abilities to survive on their own.[25]

Women may also be motivated to stay in abusive relationships by questionable normative commitments. Women may have what Ferraro and Johnson call "higher loyalties" to religious or moral norms that require, for instance, that a woman keep her marriage together despite high personal costs to herself. Or women may have what Ferraro and Johnson call a "salvation ethic," an outlook according to which a woman holds herself responsible for trying to "save" or "redeem" her abusive husband or partner from the "sickness" of abusiveness that "afflicts" him.[26]

Women who stay for these sorts of reasons are living their lives in accord with norms that are evidently very important to them. The women are, after all, risking their safety and security to adhere to those norms. On content-neutral accounts of autonomy, these women might well qualify as autonomous. Content-neutral accounts, as discussed in chapter 1, take no account of the substance of what someone chooses. On these accounts, someone is autonomous so long as her choice meets certain nonsubstantive criteria, such as being the result of reflection on her deeper values and commitments.[27] An abusive relationship is, of course, coercive. Someone's self-reflections and choices under those conditions are less likely than otherwise to be reliable reflections of what she really cares about. Yet it is not impossible to discern or act according to one's deeper concerns under coercive conditions. This possibility makes it imperative that a woman's "own" choices, even to continue enduring domestic abuse, should carry some weight in her interactions with the array of social agents who can become involved in domestic violence cases. The question is: What weight should her choices carry and which social agents in particular are best suited to take account of what the abused woman herself wants to do?

Earlier Feminist Legal Responses

In the 1970s and 1980s, feminists began arguing and litigating to make the criminal justice system abandon its previously shameful neglect of domestic violence against women. These efforts were successful, and, as a result, jurisdictions around the country began to improve their police and court practices to respond more effectively to domestic violence. The improved policies did not seem to help, however, in cases in which an abused woman asks police not to arrest her abuser or refuses to press charges against him once he has been arrested. When first reflecting on these sorts of cases, feminists assumed that these women really wanted to leave their abusers or press charges against them but refrained from doing so because the women lacked information about their legal rights or were pressured into backing down, perhaps by law enforcement personnel who discouraged them or by their own fears of retaliation from their abusers. Requiring law enforcement personnel to take the initiative in arresting and prosecuting batterers promised to solve these problems.

This view was supported by a landmark Minneapolis study, published in 1984, that suggested that arrest was more effective in deterring subsequent violence by domestic abusers than either of the two alternatives with which it was compared: mediation or removing the abuser from the premises for eight hours. Nationwide legal reform followed the publication of this study, and by 1996 all fifty states permitted a police officer to arrest someone without a warrant whenever the officer has probable cause to believe the person has committed a misdemeanor or violated a restraining order.[28]

In addition to police practices, legal reformers focused on the problem of inadequate prosecution efforts. Prosecutors had often been lax in pursuing criminal prosecution in domestic violence cases. Domestic violence advocacy groups argued that woman-battering was a crime and that it should be prosecuted like any other crime.[29] A crime is, in some sense, a harm to *society*, and "the state itself [is supposed to] bring . . . criminal proceedings" against those accused of crime.[30] Victims themselves do not have to press charges.[31] In recent years, in an effort to ensure that domestic violence is treated as a crime, "no-drop" prosecution policies have been implemented in many jurisdictions.[32] Essentially, these policies require prosecutors to make serious efforts to follow through with the prosecution of domestic violence cases that come to their offices.

The most stringent, and also the most controversial, sorts of no-drop policies call for prosecutors to go forward with a case "regardless of the victim's wishes," so long as there is enough evidence to do so. Stringent no-drop policies mandate some degree of participation by the victim, requiring, for example, that she be photographed to document injuries or provide the state with other evidence or information. Under these policies, a victim may also be forced to testify if the case proceeds to trial. Victims who fail to cooperate might be penalized. Cheryl Hanna notes that forced testimony is "unlikely given that 90% to 95% of all criminal cases end in plea bargains," but, in cases that do go to trial, this "extreme measure" may well be employed under a stringent no-drop policy.[33]

What are the success rates of no-drop prosecution policies? A stringent no-drop policy in San Diego is credited with lowering the annual number of homicides connected with domestic violence there from thirty to seven in the decade from 1985 to 1994. A stringent no-drop policy in Duluth, Minnesota, is credited with lowering the recidivism rate there. And programs in Seattle, Indianapolis, and Quincy, Massachusetts, have also been hailed as successes.[34]

For the rest of this discussion, I am going to assume that these findings are reliable and generalizable and that mandated legal procedures do tend to reduce the overall level of woman battering.[35] On that assumption, the original victims might benefit from less future violence from their abusers, and other women would benefit from a generalized deterrent effect. The primary argument for mandated procedures is thus that they tend overall to reduce the level of woman abuse. So what's the problem?

Reasons for and against Mandated Proceedings

One of the major arguments against mandatory arrest and no-drop prosecutions is that they may impose hardships and risks on an abused woman while at the same time undermining her autonomous capacity to choose or control the legal process that does so. The process proceeds without the woman's agency and possibly against her wishes. As an assistant prosecutor in Baltimore, Cheryl Hanna found that abused women want the abuse to stop but usually prefer the batterer to go into counseling than to be punished.[36] Punishment, if it occurs, would typically consist of jail time. Jailing the abuser would impose hardships on a financially dependent abused woman and her children. In addition, a trial itself can be a harrowing experience for a victim. Attorneys defending the accused batterer may cross-examine the woman about such embarrassing matters as her sexual preferences, in order to try to show that she "likes it rough."[37] And mandatory proceedings do not necessarily prevent abusers from retaliating against victims. The assumption that he won't retaliate against her for mandated legal proceedings against him may credit him with more rationality and integrity than he actually possesses.

A woman's loss of control over the legal process mimics in a way the disempowerment that the violence itself inflicted on her, so the loss of autonomy amounts to her "revictimization," this time by the law enforcement system. In addition, since the legal procedures are portrayed as being for her own good, imposing them on her amounts to paternalism. This interlocking set of hardships for the victim—disempowerment, revictimization, and paternalistic treatment—all stem from the way in which mandated procedures, by definition, largely ignore the victim's preferences and thereby seem to undermine her autonomy.[38] This is the major argument against mandated proceedings.

So on the face of it, we confront a dilemma: If the law *respects* the autonomy of abused women who don't want to cooperate and does not mandate their participation, it will be less effective in reducing woman abuse overall. On the other hand, if the law *mandates* the participation of reluctant abuse victims, it will fail to respect the autonomy of those particular women and may impose additional hardships on them. What should the law do?

The harms and risks that may befall an abused woman during criminal proceedings against her abuser are substantial and deserve serious consideration. I think, however, that they do not outweigh the major reason for mandated legal procedures, namely, a reduction in the level of woman abuse. Let us look more closely at the risks of financial hardship and retaliatory violence.

First, financial hardship. It is true that if an abusive man is put into prison, his family will suffer financially from the loss of any income that he contributed to the household. A family *always* suffers financially, however, when one of its adult, wage-earning members goes to prison for the commission of a crime. This problem is not unique to the families of domestic batterers, and it is not sufficient by itself to entail that no one ought ever to be imprisoned for harming others. We need some sort of policy to deter people from beating each other up. If imprisonment is successful as a deterrent (admittedly, a big "if"), then its value in deterring harmful acts may well outweigh the costs it imposes on the families of offenders. At any rate, there is no special argument based on family need for keeping woman batterers in particular out of prison—no more than there would be for any other offender whose family was financially dependent on him or her.

What about the problem of retaliatory violence? This problem is unique to domestic violence cases. The crime in this case is that of beating up an intimate partner, an action that is typically part of a pattern of behavior in which an abuser tends to blame his partner and "punish" her for things that go wrong in his life. It is certainly possible that the threat of being prosecuted might stimulate an abuser to be more abusive. Yet Cheryl Hanna argues plausibly that abusers might actually be more motivated to retaliate against their victims under a system in which the criminal law did *not* mandate victim cooperation. If an abuser knew that the victim's cooperation would not be mandated, then he would have a powerful incentive to try to scare her into dropping the charges against him, and this could increase the risk of retaliatory violence in nonmandated proceedings.[39]

Another argument against mandated legal proceedings is that they show disrespect, in the Kantian sense, to the abused women who are directly affected by those proceedings. An abused woman whose preference not to press charges was disregarded by the law would be used by the law as a mere means to gain criminal convictions for the sake of deterring future woman battering. We could try to argue that no individual woman should ever be used merely as a means to a social welfare end, even that of protecting other women.

It seems to me, however, that such "usage" cannot be avoided in these difficult cases. *Respecting* the preferences of current victims of domestic abuse and failing to prosecute their abusers would increase the risk of future abuse of both those current victims and other women. In that case, future potential victims would, in a sense, be "used" as a means to promoting respect for the preferences of current reluctant abuse victims. Whichever policy is adopted, *some* woman or women would be used as a means to the end of protecting or respecting some *other* woman or women. Trade-offs of this sort are unavoidable.

In any case, does the law even have a particular duty to respect the autonomy of those whom it affects? Even if it did, that requirement would not by itself tell us whether mandated legal proceedings are right or wrong, good or bad. The difference between autonomy in the short run and autonomy in the long run must be considered. Domestic violence, as I noted earlier, itself profoundly undermines a woman's autonomy. Anything that succeeds in deterring an abuser's future abusiveness promotes his victim's long-run autonomy. Thus, the short-run interference with an abused woman's autonomy that comes from a legal process over which she has no control may well be outweighed by her long-run gain in autonomy if the mandatory legal processes are successful in deterring her future abuse.

In addition, the law's treatment of each particular abused woman is a public matter with potential impact on many other women. The impact is at once both material and symbolic. Materially, the legal treatment of each individual domestic violence case has an impact on the level of domestic violence in the future. The best reason for mandated legal proceedings in domestic violence cases is their apparent effectiveness in reducing the level of domestic violence in a community.

Symbolically, the legal response to each case makes a public statement about how society regards the seriousness of domestic violence. Legal policies deal with whole populations. Feminists have long argued that woman abuse is the sort of harmful moral wrong that should be treated as a *crime* by society at large. Domestic violence is a public crime, not simply a private family matter, and this imposes a duty on the state to intervene with the full power of criminal law.[40] By "going public," we bring domestic life, where relevant, into the public sphere and make domestic violence an offense against the state, not simply against the abused woman. We thereby gain the right to legal protection against woman battering.

If feminists have been right that domestic violence is a public, political matter, then these acts should receive the same treatment under the criminal law as other crimes. The framework of the criminal law, however, changes the conception of a violent act. It is no longer merely an injury to a private woman. As legal theorists have argued, the overriding aims of the criminal justice system are to deter crime, to punish or rehabilitate criminals, and to seek justice. As Wayne LaFave and Austin Scott Jr. write in their textbook on criminal law, "The broad aim of the criminal law is . . . to prevent harm to society" and "to protect the public interest."[41] Respecting the autonomy of victims is not a particular aim of criminal law.

The status of citizen is the status of being a full member of the community. Citizenship transforms violence to oneself into an injury to the community of which one is a member. The community, organized as a state with a formal system of criminal law, may act to punish those who are found guilty of committing the violent acts. The advantage of the public criminalization of domestic woman battering is that the full power of the state may now be enlisted in protecting women against domestic tyranny. As Cheryl Hanna puts it, "One of the most important ways to curb domestic violence is to ensure that abusers understand that *society* will not tolerate their behavior."[42] In her view, it would be paternalistic and sexist to dismiss domestic violence cases based on victim reluctance while not doing so in other areas of criminal law.[43]

This incremental move toward full citizenship status for women, however, does carry a cost. One of the things we may have to give up is private control over the response to domestic violence done to us. Gaining respect for our autonomous—and our nonautonomous—preferences about how our abusers are to be treated ceases to be an overriding concern. It is important that in seeking to deter future crime, the criminal law does aim at promoting some of the conditions, such as personal safety and security, that happen to undergird the possibility of future autonomy for abuse victims. In any case, it was precisely because women alone *couldn't* control domestic violence that we needed legal protection in the first place.

To be sure, some feminists have recently argued in favor of retaining the public-private distinction on the grounds that it sometimes benefits women. In women's reproductive activities, for example, and in those consensual relationships in which consent and freedom are genuine, we should *want* the state to refrain from interfering in our lives.[44] As Laura Stein writes, there is more to the realm of privacy than simply individual men being "left alone to oppress women."[45] Surely, however, domestic violence is not an area in which women benefit from privacy. Left to our own devices, as we were for centuries, we were not able to stop woman battering. To combat it, women need supportive networks and institutions, including the criminal law. This protection, however, comes at a price. Part of the price is a loss of control over the legal consequences that follow domestic violence.

Granted, the criminal law may need to adjust its proceedings so as to respond more sensitively to the needs of crime victims in general. Women know this well from the area of rape law. A victims' rights movement in recent decades has called for such responsiveness across the board. This is not an issue that is peculiar to the crime of woman battering. If there were a good *general* argument against mandating the participation of crime victims, this would cover the case of domestic violence as well. I do not rule out that possibility. Cases of woman battering by themselves, however, do not seem to provide distinctive overriding reasons against mandated victim participation.

I therefore conclude that the deterrent and citizenship benefits to women in general of mandated criminal law proceedings in domestic violence cases outweigh the risks, hardships, and loss of autonomy experienced by those abused women who prefer not to cooperate with such proceedings. Criminal law procedures that genuinely reduced the level of woman abuse would incidentally also promote the (merely) content-neutral autonomy of women in the long run. The law should therefore do what it can to prevent men from abusing their intimate female partners, even if it must do so against the wishes of the victims and by mandating the victims' cooperation.

This does not mean that our society should disregard altogether the concerns of reluctant abuse victims. In the following sections of this chapter, I explore how professional caregivers (therapists, social workers, and so on) should respond to women who choose to remain in abusive relationships. We may find that the domain of caregiving, especially that of professional caregiving, is the appropriate institutional domain in which a society can respect the preferences of particular women without having to consider the impact of that respect on anonymous society at large.

Respecting the Autonomy of Women Who Stay

We now arrive at our second question: How should *professional caregivers* respond to a woman who chooses to remain in an abusive relationship that she may safely exit? I specifically focus on professional caregiving and not on nonprofessional caregiving such as that by friends and family members. How nonprofessionals should react to an abused woman who remains in an abusive relationship will be affected by many nongeneralizable factors, such as the caregiver's knowledge of the abusive situation, the nature of the caregiver's relationship to the abuse victim, and the caregiver's degree of readiness to support the abuse victim over the long haul.

Remaining in an abusive relationship is a self-endangering behavior. Professional caregivers can respond in a variety of ways to the self-endangering behavior of their clients. Broadly speaking, a caregiver can try to influence a client to avoid self-endangering behaviors or may refrain from trying to exert such influence. Influence can take the form of appeals to the reasoning and decision-making capacities of the client, or it can bypass those capacities and involve, for example, coercion or manipulation.

In the debate over how professional caregivers should respond to clients who endanger themselves, philosophers generally think that coercion and manipulation are inappropriate means for professional caregivers to use. Philosophers generally agree that caregivers may try reasoning with clients to persuade them to end their self-endangering behaviors. Indeed, some philosophers think that rational persuasion is the only morally permissible response by professional caregivers toward clients who act to endanger themselves. The typical objection to manipulation and coercion is that they fail to respect a competent adult's capacity for personal autonomy. The typical defense of rational appeals to the self-harming client is that such appeals do respect her capacity for personal autonomy.[46]

Some professional caregivers who work with female victims of domestic violence, however, have a different view of the matter. These caregivers do not try to influence, rationally or otherwise, the decisions of abused women who have chosen to remain in abusive relationships they could safely leave. Instead these caregivers support the women in whatever choices they make.[47] If this sort of intervention (which I shall call the "uncritical-support" approach) is at all sound, it suggests that the rational persuasion approach needs more defense. It must be defended not only against the usual alternatives of manipulative and coercive intervention, but also against the alternative of not trying to change the client's mind at all.

Earlier, when addressing the legal question, I sought a policy approach to these special abuse cases that does not undermine the general goal of providing the full protection of the law to women who do leave their abusers or who do cooperate with the legal system in seeking punishment for their abusers.[48] The legal response to particular abused women who remain in their abusive relationships must at the same time instantiate a general policy for all abuse victims, and this reduces the degree of flexibility and discretion that might be otherwise appropriate from those who implement the policy. Professional caregivers, by contrast, have more room for flexibility, since caregiving does not have to conform to consistent and uniform patterns. Professional caregivers have much more latitude and discretion to tailor their responses to specific needs of the client before them.

In general, there are good reasons both for supporting a woman who remains in an abusive relationship and for intervening in the relationship, against her wishes, to stop the abuse. I argued earlier that the law should be guided overall by responsibilities to reduce harms such as domestic abuse in a whole population. This consideration, along with certain empirical evidence, supported the conclusion that the law should mandate legal proceedings in domestic violence cases, even if this were to disregard, and thus fail to support, the preferences of particular abuse victims. Different social institutions, however, may have different roles to play in reacting to abused women and their situations. The role of the legal system need not be the same as that of professional caregivers.

So what should professional caregivers in general do? The choices before us are rational persuasion to try to change the woman's mind and uncritical support for whatever she decides to do about the relationship. The rational persuasion approach, first of all, has the advantage of aiming to respect someone's autonomy. It does so by appealing to her reasoning capacity and avoiding coercive and manipulative interventions into her perspective and her decision-making processes.

Second, rational persuasion can aim directly at trying to persuade an abused woman to leave her abusive relationship. Doing so would rest squarely on the assumption that there is something wrong with the content of her choice to remain in the relationship. The obvious wrongness of the choice consists in the facts that she thereby subjects herself to abuse and undermines her own autonomy. She is choosing to subordinate herself to the coercive and unjustified power of another party. When a woman's choice to remain in an abusive relationship is based on misguided norms that threaten to undermine the conditions for her (future) autonomy, then her choice appears to lack substantive autonomy. On a substantive conception of autonomy, substantive autonomy is the only sort of autonomy, so a choice to remain in an abusive relationship for no good reason would be a nonautonomous choice. Perhaps a professional caregiver should try to reason someone out of a nonautonomous choice.

On my view, as argued in chapter 1, however, both substantive and (merely) content-neutral autonomy are genuine forms of autonomy. A choice to remain in an abusive relationship, even if substantively nonautonomous, might manifest content-neutral autonomy. It might, that is, cohere with a woman's deeper values and commitments, such as her religious outlook, and, even under conditions of domestic abuse, it might be the product of a period of uncoerced and unmanipulated self-reflection. Such choices, even if content-neutrally autonomous, are, of course, not trouble free. Choices to live under autonomy-undermining conditions may habituate a person to a mode of living that diminishes her future content-neutral autonomy, for example, by promoting submissiveness to others.

The philosophical interest in autonomy is not merely about what makes particular choices autonomous in themselves but also about what makes for an autonomous life.[49] The substance of someone's choices affects her prospects for autonomy in the long run and is therefore important to autonomy somehow, whether as a constitutive part of someone's current autonomy or as a necessary condition for her future autonomy. So even if an abused woman's choice were content-neutrally autonomous, if it were not also substantively autonomous, then this would be a consideration in favor of giving her reasons to change her mind.

This tentative conclusion, however, depends on certain assumptions. It assumes certain things about the knowledge of the professional caregiver who is working with the abused woman, and it depends on certain assumptions about how reasoning actually operates in practice. These assumptions may be questioned in any given case. The problems with the reasoning strategy in practice may well outweigh its theoretical advantage. To grasp this point, let us explore the considerations that weigh against the strategy of rational persuasion and in favor of the more common professional caregiver strategy of uncritically supporting abused women who return to their abusive relationships.

First, professional caregivers in actual cases rarely have sufficient knowledge or understanding to be warranted in believing that they know better what an abused woman should do with her life than she does herself. A caregiver rarely knows for certain that the woman really misunderstands her situation or has dubious normative commitments.[50] If there is no strong contrary evidence (an important and defeasible assumption), an abused woman's own perspective on her life should be treated as the most credible of available alternative perspectives and should be respected as such.

Notice that this epistemic caution depends on the circumstances of the particular case. It does not show that there is anything wrong in principle with using rational persuasion to try to change an abused woman's mind. It also leaves open the empirical possibility that a very knowledgeable, very sensitive professional caregiver might, on occasion, indeed know better than a particular client what that client should do with her life. Some social theorists claim that abused women tend to minimize the extent of the abuse they suffer.[51] They might accordingly misunderstand the nature of their own relationships. A knowledgeable caregiver in a particular case might be better able than the abused woman herself to grasp the futility of the woman's relationship and to see that the woman's only hope for a decent life free of abuse is to leave it.[52]

This issue, however, does highlight the epistemic condition that must underlie any practical intervention—rationally persuasive, uncritically supportive, or otherwise—in the lives of abused women. No one in a professional caregiving capacity should try to change the mind of an abused woman unless the professional has good reason to believe that her understanding of the abused woman's situation is better than the woman's own view of it. Rational persuasion might be the right approach in those cases in which the epistemic requirement is met, but the number of such cases may well be small.

One reason to allow for the rare use of rational persuasion to convince a woman she should leave an abuser is that abusive men can become very violent. Abusive relationships can do much worse than undermine a woman's future autonomy; they can put a woman in mortal danger. Autonomy is not the only value that we should respect or promote in each other's lives. Helping to preserve someone's very life takes obvious precedence over respecting her autonomy. When the caregiver has good reason to believe the woman risks serious or fatal injury by staying with the abuser, even if in no other sorts of cases, then it seems appropriate for her to try rationally to motivate the woman to leave her abusive partner.

Professional caregivers agree that safety is a primary consideration, probably *the* primary consideration.[53] Yet those who favor the uncritical-support strategy tend to avoid rational persuasion even in pursuit of safety. Caregivers will, for example, help an abused woman to develop a "crisis plan" for dealing with future abusive incidents. The plan might well involve the woman's quitting the residence, but the departure is often conceptualized by the caregiver not as leaving the relationship but only as, say, leaving the premises during a dangerous incident.[54] This sort of proposal thus offers an abused woman a short-term plan for coping with immediate danger, not a long-term plan for changing the course of her life.

Why are some professional caregivers so reluctant to give women reasons to leave abusive relationships even when the caregivers have good reason to believe that great danger is imminent in the relationships? What exactly is the problem in such cases with trying to persuade someone rationally to change her mind? This brings us to a second consideration in favor of uncritical support: its alternative, rational persuasion, may well be an ineffective or counterproductive way to relate to victims of domestic violence. For someone to be capable of engaging with others in a rational debate over how to live her own life, she has to have supportive psychological conditions, for example, a minimal level of self-esteem and a relative absence of the stresses and anxieties that impair rational thought. How one's life should be lived is a profoundly sensitive topic for anyone to debate with professionals. For people in abusive relationships, the psychological wherewithal to engage in the debate may well be entirely absent.

Sociologist Mary P. Koss and her collaborators recommend viewing an abused woman as someone who is undergoing a severe, possibly life-threatening, crisis or trauma. On this view, she is psychologically healthy "at the core," but nevertheless, as a consequence of her traumatic abuse, may exhibit such ailments as depression.[55] On this view, women undergoing the trauma of abusive domestic relationships are in psychological distress and are not fully capable, at that time, of engaging in rational debates with professionals about such sensitive topics as their own future lives.[56]

Any suggestion to an abused woman, however tactfully formulated or cautiously articulated, that she has made the wrong choice about how to live her life might further diminish her self-esteem and undermine her confidence in her own agency. It might seem just like the criticism, scorn, ridicule, and contempt that her abuser already inflicts on her.[57] In *On Liberty,* Mill worries about the effects of censorship on those of "promising intellect" who happen to have "timid characters."[58] Mill does not seem to appreciate that even well-intended *rational argument,* in actual dialogue, can function to suppress the rational capacities of people of timid—or injured—characters.[59]

The strategy of uncritically supporting abused women is a reaction by many professional caregivers to years of victim blaming in family therapy and social services. Older approaches in family therapy frequently blame the victim for the abuse she suffers, for example, by focusing on the supposed personality traits of abuse victims that occasion or provoke the abuse.[60] Giving an abused woman reasons to leave the relationship can seem to her like another form of blaming; it can prompt her to have the thought that, because she remains in the relationship, she will be morally at fault for any future abuse she experiences.

To be sure, there is a difference, as I argued earlier, between being morally at fault for something and being merely one among many causal factors contributing to its occurrence. Domestic abuse cannot occur unless an abusive person has access to a domestic partner. By remaining in a relationship with her abuser, a woman makes herself accessible to her partner. This does not entail, however, that she is morally to blame for the abuse he inflicts on her. Yet this careful distinction might be one that an abused woman, in her traumatized condition, lacks the rational detachment to appreciate. She may be so overwhelmed by her trauma that she is incapable of grasping the subtleties of the reasons that a professional caregiver is using to persuade her to leave.

What I have been suggesting is that attempts at rational persuasion, however judiciously articulated or well-intentioned, may be experienced by someone who is damaged by domestic abuse as coercive or manipulative intrusions. Notice that this point about the coercive impact of rational persuasion is also an empirical consideration, like the previous point about the uncertainty of the caregiver's understanding. Whether or not rational persuasion seems manipulative or coercive to abused women surely depends on the circumstances of each case—and perhaps on the argumentative skill and subtlety of the particular caregiver.[61] Even if most traumatized persons have some difficulty in handling rational persuasion to get them to change their minds, so that rational persuasion under those conditions tends to be unduly intrusive, there is no reason to think that this is always the case or that trauma will always be extremely rationally disabling. Thus, considerations of psychological impact alone do not support the conclusion that it is wrong *in principle* to try rationally to persuade a woman to leave an abusive relationship. Again, however, the number of cases in practice in which attempts at rational persuasion are not intrusive may well be small.

A third reason in defense of the uncritical support strategy is that even if an abused woman's ability to handle rational persuasion is not seriously impaired, nevertheless, uncritical support may promote her capacity for autonomy in ways that rational persuasion fails to achieve. The ability of abused women to take control of their lives and cope successfully with abuse by an intimate partner depends, in large part, on having confidence in their own capacities for agency in the world. Whether abused women are able to view themselves in this way may well depend, in turn, on how others view them. If abused women are to cope effectively with abuse, they might first have to be regarded as effective agents by others. Professional caregivers can boost an abused woman's self-esteem by believing her account of her relationship or supporting her in choosing whatever is dictated even by her questionable normative commitments. Thus, uncritical support may be better than rational persuasion at promoting the psychological conditions that are necessary for someone's autonomy in the long run. In this vein, as I noted earlier, some caregivers insist that we should view abused women in general as active, not passive, survivors, not victims,[62] and capable of coping with and deciding how to live their lives.

The relationship between caregiver and abused woman is not merely an occasion for the abstract interplay of impersonal reason giving. Instead it is a social encounter between two persons, an encounter that may contribute to the ongoing development of the persons involved. The abused woman, as a traumatized person, is particularly vulnerable to the psychological impact of the caregiving encounter.[63] What uncritical support suggests to the abused woman is that she is a competent, active, and effective agent whose own understanding of her situation and whose choice about how to live her life are trustworthy.

To be sure, the aim of building the self-esteem of an abused woman is at odds with the rationale behind the second reason I gave on behalf of the uncritical support strategy. If abused women are so traumatized that they cannot handle rational persuasion, how then could they be competent and reliable agents? There is a tension between, on the one hand, arguing that abused women are so vulnerable that mere rational persuasion affects them coercively, and, on the other hand, insisting that abused women be viewed as active, competent agents.

Yet this tension may be resolvable in practice. There are many ordinary situations in which it is appropriate to show trust in someone's capacity for autonomy even while believing them to be incapable of it, for example, when giving young children some free rein to make decisions of their own. The opportunity to make their own decisions becomes, for children, a developmental stepping-stone toward the maturation of autonomy competency. In many cases, the trust given to the child's developmental capacity does no harm and even becomes a beneficial, self-fulfilling prophecy.

Suppose a caregiver avoids reasoning with an abused woman about the woman's choices, and does so based on the belief that the abused woman lacks the psychological wherewithal to engage in rational debate over how to live her life. If the abused woman were to discern the caregiver's underlying belief, this knowledge would surely undermine the woman's self-esteem rather than bolster it. A victim of abuse might well be attuned to the slightest verbal or nonverbal cues revealing someone's lack of confidence in her abilities. Caregivers who do not really believe that the abused women in their care are indeed capable of making reliable decisions thus might fail to inspire the woman's own self-confidence, even using the strategy of uncritical support.

Uncritical support that is carried off successfully and does not make an abused woman suspicious that the caregiver distrusts her abilities may still not promote the autonomy of an abused woman in all ways. As John Kultgen notes, an intervention into someone's life can promote some of the conditions or capacities necessary for autonomy while diminishing others.[64] The uncritical support strategy seems most respectful of a woman's content-neutral autonomy.[65] At best, it treats an abused woman's actual choices as respect-worthy in themselves and avoids anything that might feel like coercion to an abused woman at the time. Uncritical support, however, precisely disregards the substantive content of her choices. Yet the content of her choices might diminish her future autonomy.

The rationally persuasive strategy, which I tend to reject, does admittedly respect and aim at a woman's *substantive* autonomy. It aims to change a woman's mind so that she will choose substantively to live in a manner that will best promote her autonomy in the long run. Rational persuasion also respects someone's content-neutral autonomy by constituting an appeal to her reasoning power. It does this, however, only on the assumption that the woman at whom it is aimed has the psychological capacity to engage in debate about the sensitive matter of how to live her life. This assumption does not hold of all people under all conditions. Trauma victims, as I have been suggesting, may experience rational persuasion as further (psychological) abuse, and, thus, as the sort of manipulation or coercion that undermines content-neutral autonomy.

Furthermore, reasoning might be effective, if at all, on the basis of its psychological, rather than "logical" (in a broad sense) power. A caregiver's reasoning might prompt a woman to leave her abusive partner not because she grasps the rational force of the reasons for doing so but only because the caregiver's entreaties are psychologically manipulative. In that case, reasoning would have promoted the long-run substantive autonomy of the woman's choices at the expense of her current content-neutral autonomy. Thus, reasoning may fail to respect an abused woman's autonomy in the short run. Whether the trade-off is worthwhile no doubt depends on the circumstances of any given case. In addition, rational persuasion may prove counterproductive. Not only may it fail to motivate an abused woman to leave her abusive relationship; it may also prompt her to remain in the abusive relationship out of, say, resentment against the intrusiveness of the caregiver.[66] In that case, it will have failed to promote any form of the abused woman's autonomy.

Because it is hard to tell in any given case whether reasoning will be both noncoercive and effective, the wisest general policy is to avoid attempting to change abused women's minds through rational persuasion unless there is clear evidence in a given case that it would not adversely affect the woman's outlook. These occasions may well be rare. This is not to say that there is anything wrong *in principle* with the goal of trying to persuade an abused woman, using good reasons, to leave her abusive relationship—particularly in those unusual cases in which it can be done without seeming to her like undue pressure. The point is rather that reason-based appeals to change the minds of abused women can constitute undue pressure in most cases. Once again, uncritical support appears, on empirical grounds, to be preferable to rational persuasion in most cases of domestic abuse, but there is no reason to reject rational persuasion in principle.

My conclusion is thus that, mainly for practical reasons, professional caregivers should usually provide uncritical support for abused women who choose to remain in abusive relationships rather than trying rationally to persuade them to change their minds. The reasons are that: (1) professional caregivers seldom know best how abused women should live their lives; (2) rational persuasion can seem inappropriately coercive or blaming to trauma victims; and (3) uncritical support in the short run better tends to promote the psychological capacities needed for autonomy competency. Rational persuasion may, however, be a better strategy when the caregiver knows that the relationship threatens the woman with immediate and very serious danger. Also, we have found no principled reason to reject rational persuasion for those rare occasions on which a caregiver best understands an abused woman's life or the abused woman is strong enough to handle rational criticism of her own choices.

By contrast, legal policy must treat individual cases with consideration for the material and symbolic impact of that treatment on a whole population. I have argued that legal policy should aim at reducing the harm of domestic violence in a population even when this requires mandating the reluctant legal cooperation of abuse victims. Legal policy does not have as much flexibility as professional caregiving does to respond to each case based only on what is good for the victim at hand. Fortunately, the law and professional caregiving may take different approaches to the problems of domestic violence. Somewhere among the combined interventions of these two social practices, both the capacity of abused women for autonomy and the actual choices they make can gain respect.

IV

THE LARGER POLITICAL SYSTEM

8

John Rawls and the Political Coercion of

Unreasonable People

Political power "is always coercive power," writes John Rawls.[1] *Political Liberalism* is a study of how to justify the state's use of that coercive power against its citizens. Coercive state power is legitimate, for Rawls, so long as reasonable and rational persons reasoning under certain constraints would agree to its exercise.

More specifically, political coercion is justified so long as it accords with a political conception of justice that free and equal citizens would endorse in their capacity as reasonable and rational persons, in an overlapping consensus that spans their diverse moral, religious, and philosophical commitments, their "comprehensive doctrines."[2] Reasonable and rational persons constitute, for Rawls, what I will call the "legitimation pool," the pool of persons whose endorsement would confirm the legitimacy of Rawls's political liberalism—or whose rejection would confirm its illegitimacy. In considering whether or not to endorse a system of political power, citizens exercise their personal autonomy with respect to political life.

Suppose that someone contends that she cannot accept Rawls's conception of political liberalism from the standpoint of her comprehensive doctrine. Rawls's response to this contention would differ substantially depending on whether or not that person was reasonable. If the person was reasonable, then her rejection of Rawls's political liberalism would count for him as a serious reason to consider revising it. If, however, the person was unreasonable, the result would be quite different. Rawls's description of his method of legitimation takes no account of the possible rejection of his political conception by unreasonable people. Their rejection appears to carry no theoretical weight.

If a state's legitimacy depends only on the endorsement of reasonable and rational persons, that means that a state that is endorsed only by its reasonable citizens is thereby entitled to exercise its coercive power over *un*reasonable citizens *without* their consent. In that case, how do those citizens remain free and equal? And in what sense are they politically autonomous?

The mere fact of someone's unreasonableness does not by itself create this tension for political liberalism since an unreasonable person might nevertheless endorse the system. Granted, her actual endorsement, on Rawlsian grounds, would be irrelevant to the legitimacy of the liberal state. Nevertheless her political autonomy is, in some liberal sense, not violated by liberalism's exercise of its political power over her since she consents to it. My focus of concern is directed to those unreasonable persons who *withhold* consent from political liberalism. It is their political autonomy that seems to be violated by Rawls's legitimation methods.

Rawls, of course, is not the only philosopher who seeks political legitimacy in the consent of reasonable persons only. Thomas Scanlon and Thomas Nagel, for example, also frame the problem in these terms.[3] Rawls, however, gives the concept of reasonableness a very elaborate explication. Thus his exclusion of the unreasonable merits special attention.

It is crucial to be clear about what Rawls means by "reasonableness" since he uses this word as a term of art. A fuller discussion follows shortly, but briefly, for now: Reasonable persons are those who seek fair terms of social cooperation with others and who think that reasonable people living under free institutions will disagree about fundamental matters of religion, morality, or philosophy. *Un*reasonable persons are those who lack one or both of these attitudes. Not only are we not required by Rawls to take seriously the political views of unreasonable persons. As well, he would have us impose on those persons the coercive power of a state which they reject, provided only that that state has been ratified in the right way by reasonable persons. Indeed, as I shall point out below, the legitimate state may even infringe on some of the basic rights and liberties of unreasonable persons. Such persons thus appear to lose political autonomy in several ways. This is a foundational concern for any theory that calls itself "liberal."

To be sure, given the enormous diversity among human viewpoints, the exclusion of unreasonable people from the legitimation pool makes the search for legitimacy more manageable than it otherwise would be. This consideration, however, is a practical one only. It is not a principled reason for excluding anyone. Rawls, by contrast, elevates the exclusion of the unreasonable into a matter of principle in his quest for political legitimacy. The question is whether Rawls's principled exclusion of the unreasonable is inconsistent with any of the aims or values of the system he seeks thereby to defend. Since Rawls views a social contract as "a hypothetical agreement . . . between all rather than some members of society," the prospects for internal consistency here are not promising.[4] This problem will form my primary concern in this chapter.

Rawls on Reasonableness and Rationality

First, let us recall more fully what Rawls means by reasonableness and rationality. In Rawls's ideal society, citizens are both reasonable and rational. Rational persons adapt means to their given ends and adjust their ends in light of their overall life plans. Rationality alone is not sufficient to make citizens just since rational agents do not necessarily seek fair cooperation "as such" nor "on terms that others as equals might reasonably be expected to endorse."[5] Those concerns are subsumed instead under the virtue of reasonableness.

Reasonable persons are willing to "propose and honor fair terms of cooperation," and "to recognize the burdens of judgment and to accept their consequences."[6] The "burdens of judgment" are the sources of possible limitation and error involved in the exercise of human reason. These sources include the variability and finitude of human experience, the ways in which those experiences underdetermine our judgments about them and permit differing interpretations, and the chance influence of divergent norms.[7]

Reasonableness is public in a way that rationality is not. Our reasonableness is our readiness to participate in the public world and therein negotiate, and abide by, the fair terms of social cooperation with others that will ground our social relationships with them.[8] The distinctive moral power of reasonableness is a sense of justice, and the distinctive moral power of rationality is a conception of the good.[9] "Someone who has not developed and cannot exercise [those] moral powers to the minimum requisite degree," writes Rawls, "cannot be a normal and fully cooperating member of society over a complete life."[10]

Rawls's method of political legitimation is developed with regard to his idealized account of liberal society. Does it tell us anything about actual, imperfectly liberal societies? There may well be reasonable and rational people in actual societies who reject their own would-be liberal systems because these systems are unacceptable from the standpoints of their comprehensive doctrines. In an imperfectly liberal society, we might learn something about the imperfections of the system from reasonable and rational persons who reject it. Rawls apparently thinks, however, that the opinions of *un*reasonable persons do *not* tell us anything informative about whether a system is legitimate or not. It seems that regardless of whether an actual society is ideally liberal, imperfectly liberal, or illiberal, the political opinions of unreasonable people simply do not count.

In the real world, of course, people might be unreasonable because they have grown up under unjust institutions rather than under the free institutions postulated in Rawls's ideal society. Real-world unreasonableness has a different sociohistorical context than does the ideal-world variety. This surely *diminishes* the justification for excluding unreasonable persons from the legitimation pool. People who become unreasonable as a result of growing up under unfair institutions certainly constitute good evidence of the unfairness of those institutions. This would still not entail, of course, that the content of their opinions as such revealed anything reliable about what was wrong with their imperfect institutions. If bad institutions made people fascists, this might be good evidence that something was wrong with the institutions under which they were raised but it would not confirm the truth of their fascism.

In this discussion, I will focus mainly on unreasonableness and only occasionally on irrationality. I will also interpret Rawls's view of reasonableness as requiring both of the attitudes that Rawls sets out, the quest for fair terms of social cooperation and the belief that reasonable persons may disagree about fundamental comprehensive matters. Someone is unreasonable if she rejects either (or both) of these two attitudes.

The twofold nature of the notion of reasonableness does raise a curious question of detail however. What if the two attitudes that make up reasonableness part company? What about those who are reasonable in one way but not in the other? Could someone who seeks fair terms of social cooperation nevertheless reject the idea that reasonable people can disagree about fundamental comprehensive matters? Alternatively, could someone who believes that reasonable people can disagree about fundamental matters nevertheless not seek fair terms of social cooperation? If these two variations are possible, then we may need a ranking of these attitudes to determine which is more central to the liberal concern for political legitimacy. Reasonableness is, in any case, surely a matter of degree, and we should want to delineate the minimal threshold level of reasonableness that entitles someone to be free of any state coercion except that to which they would consent. I leave these questions about degrees of reasonableness for another occasion.

Liberalism, Consent, and Political Autonomy

Our focus is on Rawls's method of excluding unreasonable people from the legitimation pool, that group of persons whose support, or its lack, tests Rawls's conception of political liberalism. It is useful to recall why anyone's consent matters to political legitimacy. In the liberal tradition, the legitimacy of state power is linked to the value of the political autonomy of citizens. Liberalism, in theory at any rate, considers its citizens to be free and equal. Free and equal citizens have political autonomy, among other things, when they themselves specify the fair terms of their own social cooperation.[11]

In real life, citizens rarely congregate to formulate from the ground up the terms of their social cooperation. Mindful of this reality, liberalism settles for the mere *consent* of the governed to arrangements that have been worked out by a very few among them. In principle, these arrangements must still be justifiable from the standpoint of each citizen. In the words of Jeremy Waldron, liberalism requires "that all aspects of the social world should either be made acceptable or be capable of being made acceptable to *every last individual*" (emphasis mine).[12] Waldron continues: "If there is some individual to whom a justification cannot be given, then so far as *he* is concerned the social order had better be replaced by other arrangements, for the status quo has made out no claim to *his* allegiance."[13]

In Thomas Nagel's view, the quest for universal citizen consent to a political system is definitive not simply of *liberal* political philosophy but of political theory in general. The "ultimate aim of political theory," writes Nagel, is to find a way "to justify a political system to everyone who is required to live under it."[14] Thus liberalism in particular, and perhaps political theory in general, seeks to make us an offer that no one can refuse.

Liberalism, however, aims not merely to win allegiance. The mere allegiance of citizens can be the product of compulsion or indoctrination. From a liberal perspective, such consent does not by itself demonstrate or constitute the legitimacy of a political order. The requisite allegiance must be warranted. That warrant must furthermore be recognizable from the standpoint of the consenting citizen. Each citizen must be able to consent to the social order in virtue of her *recognition* of its justification. Thereby a citizen exercises genuine political autonomy.[15] Thus Nagel writes:

> The pure ideal of political legitimacy is that the use of state power should be capable of being *authorized* by each citizen—not in direct detail but through acceptance of the principles, institutions, and procedures which determine how that power will be used. This requires the possibility of unanimous agreement at some sufficiently high level, for if there are citizens who can legitimately object to the way state power is used against them or in their name, the state is not legitimate.[16]

The idea that all citizens of a large-scale political system would ever consent to their system, however, is a hopeless nonstarter. Few people in the real world have consented in any significant sense to the societies in which they live. Even with the exponential growth of cybersociety and current technologies of communication, it would be a daunting prospect to get every adult citizen in a large modern society to consider political liberalism (or any other political philosophy) and express an opinion on it. (Let us not forget how many people still lack computer literacy, not to mention old-fashioned reading and writing literacy.) In practice, only the consent of *some* persons is a realistic possibility.

As is well known, liberal theorists have devised various notions to cope with this practical problem. The recent favorite is the notion of hypothetical consent, its current popularity owing much to Rawls's first book, *A Theory of Justice*.[17] Hypothetical consent is the consent someone *would* give to a political order under appropriate, and specified, conditions. For Waldron, hypothetical consent can decrease the wrongness of illegitimate state intervention in someone's life.[18] Waldron argues that if someone, who happens not to have consented to being treated in a certain manner, *would* have consented had she been in a position to do so, then treating her in that manner is "less wrong" than it would be if she would not, even hypothetically, have consented to it.[19]

For most modern liberals, hypothetical consent is construed in terms of the *reasons* for accepting one political arrangement rather than another. As Waldron notes, "Liberalism is also bound up in large part with respect for rationality."[20] The idea of rationally reconstructed, hypothetical consent solves the problem created by the practical impossibility of sampling the political opinion of every adult citizen. The rational reconstruction need only be devised and endorsed by a few intellectuals who take the liberty of determining on their own what an entire citizenry *would* endorse whose members, implausi-bly, were all reasonable, rational, and had the leisure to enter the dialogue.

That last sentence is, of course, ironic. The strategy of imagining rationally reconstructed hypothetical consent faces well-known difficulties. "Real peo-ple," suggests Waldron, "do not always act on the reasons we think they might have for acting: the reasonableness of the actors in our hypothesis may not match the reality of men and women in actual life."[21] That to which people ac-tually consent may well not match that to which a handful of intellectuals *think* it would be rational for them to consent. Waldron suggests, nevertheless, that the liberal probably has to assume some minimum of "reasonableness" on the parts of people "if the project of social justification is to get off the ground at all."[22] This modified approach, we should note, is not a matter of liberal principle but rather a pragmatic concession to the practical limitations of our ability to test political conceptions.

Rawls's conception of reasonableness, in particular, does not apply to every-one. Some people, for example, do not accept the burdens of judgment and be-lieve instead that "reasonable" people will *not* disagree on conceptions of the good or other comprehensive moral, religious, or philosophical matters.[23] Per-haps concomitant with this view, some people believe that the one true faith should be forcibly imposed on all persons as part of the political system itself, even on those persons who do not accept its tenets. Rush Limbaugh, for exam-ple, urges the political enforcement of specifically Judeo-Christian values.[24]

Attitudes such as these pose a problem for liberals. Modern liberal democ-racies are pluralistic. They contain persons with various political values. Some citizens of liberal democracies believe that the system ought to be "acceptable to every last individual" (to reiterate Waldron's words). Others, by contrast, believe that the system ought to impose certain values on all citizens, regard-less of whether or not those values are acceptable to every last individual. One and the same political doctrine is not likely to satisfy both of these groups simultaneously.

Waldron recommends that liberals acknowledge that their "conception of political judgment will be appealing only to those who hold their commit-ments in a certain 'liberal' spirit."[25] Those who lack the liberal spirit are not likely to find such a system acceptable. Such persons would consistently con-sent to political liberalism only if they were to abandon what Rawls would call their illiberal comprehensive doctrines. This creates a problem for liberal theories that rely on a notion of hypothetical consent, *even if* rationally recon-structed. It seems viciously circular to try to justify a liberal doctrine in terms of the hypothetical consent of a citizenry, if the condition grounding that hy-pothesis is that citizens do not hold the illiberal commitments they do in fact hold. Such illiberal commitments can be deeply important to people, enough so to shape their very identities. Disregarding those commitments in the ra-tional reconstruction would be like saying that all citizens *would* consent to political liberalism if only they were not the illiberals they actually are.

The quest for liberal legitimacy thus raises a problem analogous to other liberal paradoxes. If one values liberal tolerance, for example, one must nevertheless not tolerate those expressions and modes of living that would undermine toleration itself as a social practice. If one values liberal free expression, one must nevertheless withhold it from those whose expressions would undermine the very practice of free expression. It appears, similarly, that if one is seeking fair terms of social cooperation among persons who are free and equal and who are assumed to disagree reasonably on fundamental comprehensive matters, then one must not allow persons who *reject* this goal or these assumptions to hijack the legitimation process. In each case, a liberal principle comes up against its limiting case: the freedom given readily to those who do not threaten the system must be withheld from those who would use it to destroy the system.

Yet this very necessity nevertheless seems inconsistent with the liberal goal of resting on the consent of *all* the governed. In Rawls's view, the legitimacy of a political system is sufficiently established even if it is endorsed by only the reasonable and rational among its citizens. Reasonableness, however, is defined in terms of the very values and assumptions from which Rawls derives his political liberalism. Yet, how satisfactory or meaningful is the consent of a citizenry if the process of representing or obtaining consent excludes the opinions of those persons who, because they start with nonliberal attitudes, are the very ones who might vote "no"? By excluding from the legitimation pool exactly those persons who do not accept the political values and basic tenets on which Rawls grounds political liberalism, Rawls rigs the election in advance.

The exclusion of unreasonable persons from the legitimation pool thus seems to beg important questions in the defense of liberalism. And the liberal commitment to political autonomy appears to be undermined by withholding political autonomy precisely from those persons who reject the system that advocates it.

The Fate of Unreasonable People

Let us now clarify the fate that awaits those who are unreasonable in Rawls's political liberalism. There is more at stake than simply being excluded from the legitimation pool.

Rawls distinguishes between "the fact of pluralism as such and the fact of reasonable pluralism."[26] His emphasis is on the latter. Reasonable pluralism is the diversity of *reasonable* views about fundamental matters of religion, morality, and philosophy. Rawls is particularly concerned to exclude from the legitimation pool those who hold *un*reasonable views. Under this heading, Rawls includes "doctrines that reject one or more democratic freedoms." In a footnote that is crucial for our purposes, he suggests that the way to treat unreasonable doctrines is to *contain* them "like war and disease—so that they do not overturn political justice."[27]

How does one "contain" a doctrine? This requires regulating and controlling the media in which it is expressed and promulgated—books, magazines, cyberspace, and so on. More significant, it requires suppressing those who hold the doctrine, in particular, suppressing their expression and/or enactment of it. At the same time, however, Rawls contends that "it is unreasonable for us to use political power . . . to repress comprehensive views that are *not* unreasonable" (emphasis mine).[28] Rawls's recommendation to "contain" the unreasonable doctrines that reject democratic freedoms thus contrasts markedly with the basic rights and liberties that his system accords to doctrines that are "*not un*reasonable."

Thus, while supporters of reasonable doctrines will enjoy basic rights and liberties, supporters of certain unreasonable doctrines, in particular those that reject democratic freedoms, will be treated like the bearers of a pestilence. Their political autonomy will be denied in two ways. First, they will be excluded from the legitimation pool, that collection of citizens whose consent to the political system confirms its legitimacy. Second, in daily life, they will be · denied the full protection of its basic rights and liberties, particularly freedom of expression.

Who Are the Unreasonable?

Mindful of what lies in store for unreasonable people, we may now attempt to evaluate the full theoretical and practical significance of Rawls's view. One useful initial strategy is to try to determine *who* the unreasonable persons are. There are at least two relevant possibilities here, and they foreshadow contradictory intuitions.

First, we should worry about a liberalism that ignores, from the outset, the political views of certain groups among a citizenry. Despite some manner of commitment to the notion of free and equal persons, liberal democracies have historically found specious grounds, such as race and sex, for excluding various groups of adults from political participation and full civil rights. This practical inconsistency in the history of the tradition should make us wary of any seemingly principled reason for yet again excluding certain groups of persons from something so important as the legitimation pool.

Second, however, we should also worry about those persons among a citizenry who seek on their own, independently of the formal political process, to dominate others or to impose a social order that degrades, marginalizes, or oppresses others. There is no reason to suppose that all oppressive tendencies in human relationships originate with bad government. We must also beware of individuals who, as such, harbor their own oppressive tendencies or convictions and for whom political freedom would provide an opportunity to act oppressively. Indeed, part of the valuable potential of a formal political process is its capacity both to curb any possible human proclivities toward dominating or oppressing other persons and to deny political influence to those who manifest such tendencies.[29] And one important form of political influence is to count publicly as someone whose opinion helps to decide the legitimacy of a political system: in other words, to be a publicly recognized member of a legitimation pool.

To summarize these two initial concerns: it appears at the outset that there are both bad and good reasons for excluding particular persons from the legitimation pool. Race and sex are bad reasons, and we want to make sure that no one is excluded, either intentionally or inadvertently, on grounds such as these. We must make sure that our legitimation strategy invokes only good reasons, if any, for excluding people. On the other hand, being someone who wants to dominate others looks like a good reason for being excluded from the legitimation pool. We must also ensure that the application of those good reasons is not overinclusive—that is, that it does not exclude by mistake any persons who do belong in the legitimation pool.

How do Rawls's legitimation methods apply to those groups that have historically been excluded unjustly from real-world liberal political processes? The category of "reasonableness" should alert us to possible dangers in such application. Some of the groups historically denied the rights and privileges of liberal citizenship were disenfranchised at least partly because they were regarded as irrational, as poor reasoners, and as people who could not achieve the detached impartiality needed to reflect on the common good. Women, for example, fell into this camp.

Does Rawls's exclusion of unreasonable persons mean that women's voices once again count for little or nothing in the search for liberal legitimacy? Part of the answer depends on the extent to which the stereotypes of women as poor reasoners persist today. Even if they do persist, the beginning of the twenty-first century in the United States shows a marked improvement in the public regard for women's reasoning capacities. Compared to former decades, the public now widely acknowledges a substantial level of female achievement in many fields that are regarded as involving reason, for example, the professions.

Recall that by "reasonableness" Rawls means two things: first, the willingness to seek fair terms of social cooperation, and second, the acknowledgment that reasonable people can disagree on fundamental matters of religion, morality, and philosophy. Our question must be: Do these particular sorts of attitudes have anything to do with the various public images and conceptions of women?

The gender stereotypes studied by psychologists are rarely as specific as the traits that constitute Rawls's conception of reasonableness. As is well known, men have been stereotyped in terms of agency and instrumentality; desirable adjectives for men include independent, forceful, ambitious, aggressive, competitive, dominant. Women have been stereotyped, by contrast, in terms of emotionality and social relationships; desirable adjectives for women include affectionate, compassionate, warm, gentle, understanding, and tender.[30] These common feminine stereotypes do not obviously support the view that women are unreasonable in either of Rawls's senses.[31]

Indeed, rather than supporting the idea that women are unreasonable in Rawls's sense, conventional gender stereotypes seem instead to support the idea that they are quite reasonable. Consider, for example, the stereotype of women as sociable. This idea seems to suggest that women would cooperate with those to whom they relate socially and would want the forms of cooper-ation to be acceptable to all concerned. In more specialized contexts such as psychoanalysis and political theory, women have sometimes been stereotyped as less conscience driven than men, as having a weaker sense of justice.[32] This suggests that they might be more capable of tolerating, and regarding as rea-sonable, others who hold religious, moral, or philosophical doctrines differ-ent from their own. This idea is reinforced by the stereotype of women as com-passionate and understanding.

My suggestions about how women would fare under Rawls's approach to unreasonable people are based on mere associations of ideas. They are by no means logically entailed by the stereotypes in question—not that stereotypes are ever very logical in their operations. However, even if the common stereo-types of women suggested that women were quite reasonable, this would not directly tell us anything about real women. Stereotypes are hardly the best guide to empirical truth.

Do real women deny the burdens of judgment any more than men? Do real women, any more than men, think that reasonable people will *not* disagree about fundamental matters of religion, morality, or philosophy? Do real women reject fair terms of social cooperation any more than men? Doubtless, there are individual women who avoid fair terms of social cooperation. It does not seem, however, that women outnumber men in the ranks of savings and loan swindlers, junk bond peddlers, fraudulent accountants, and so on. If any gender group shows widespread tendencies to eschew fair terms of social co-operation, it is not women.

There is still another way, however, in which women might be unreason-able in Rawlsian terms. "Womankind," according to one old school of philo-sophical thought, is "the everlasting irony in the life of the community [who] changes by intrigue the universal purpose of government into a private end . . . and perverts the universal property of the state into a possession and orna-ment for the family."[33] On this Hegelian view, women are incapable of impar-tial political participation because they cannot rise above loyalty to their own family members. Women simply favor "their own" and do not treat all citi-zens as abstract equals. If women really are, to a great degree, guided politi-cally by such partial loyalties, then they would scarcely seek fair terms of so-cial cooperation with other citizens. They would try instead to promote the welfare of their own loved ones through the political process. If women really favored their "own" substantially more in the political process than men, while men much more readily attained an impartial civic attitude, then women might indeed be more unreasonable than men and might merit exclu-sion from the legitimation pool.

What can be said about this possibility? Lacking empirical evidence on the question, I will offer an unsystematic, uncontrolled personal observation. As women now participate in the public political cultures of many nations, they do not appear to do so with any more partiality then men. Though some women have been involved in self-serving political scandals, anyone familiar with such politicians as Chicago's legendary *first* Mayor Richard Daley knows that many men have attained levels of nepotism and cronyism in public life that are unrivaled by any woman.[34] When it comes to self-serving partiality and taking care of one's own, the myth of men's public *im*partiality should be consigned to the ranks of the Tooth Fairy.

The overall relevance of gender to Rawls's conception of reasonableness thus seems to me to be as follows. There is no overt or covert gender bias built into his conception. Nothing about the ways in which Rawls defines reasonableness excludes real women as a group from the legitimation pool—any more or any less than it excludes men as a group. Granted, some persons might misapply Rawls's views because they mistakenly stereotype women as unreasonable. The philosophical tradition, as Genevieve Lloyd has argued, traditionally defined reason by excluding whatever were, or were considered to be, feminine traits.[35] Someone could, for example, interpret Rawls's requirement of cooperative fairness so as to exclude whatever it is that women do when relating socially with others. Anyone who is predisposed to think that all the interesting forms of fair social cooperation are the products of male collaboration will simply find a way to interpret the interest in fair terms of social cooperation in such a way that women's cooperative endeavors have nothing to do with it.[36] In such cases, however, the fault would lie with the mistaken gender stereotyper and not with Rawls's method for confirming the legitimacy of political liberalism.

Thus, the case of women does not give good reason to worry about Rawls's exclusion of unreasonable persons from the legitimation pool. Other examples are not so sanguine, however. According to a common attitude in traditional political theory, economically poorer classes are so absorbed with their own plights that they cannot be trusted to consider the wider public good when participating in the political process. The assumption has often been made that wealthier classes are able to surmount self-interest and base their political decisions on the common good. Although this line of reasoning could easily support welfare rights and greater efforts to better the lot of the poor, it has also been used as an excuse for excluding the poor from the political process by establishing property qualifications as a requirement for participation. This latter strand of thought in the liberal tradition simply dismisses the poorer classes as incapable of the attitudes required by liberal citizenship.[37] On this view, the poor seek only self-serving and unfair terms of social cooperation and are, therefore, by Rawls's criteria, unreasonable.

Thus, Rawls's conception of unreasonableness has, at best, mixed results when applied to real groups of people. Women should not be excluded from the legitimation pool under any sensible interpretation even of female stereotypes. Yet at least one of the groups historically disenfranchised by liberal democracies, namely, the poorest classes in a society, might qualify as unreasonable in Rawls's sense. Accordingly, they could be excluded from Rawls's legitimation pool. This is a disturbing outcome of his theory.

Let us turn to the other point I wish to raise about the sorts of real people who might be excluded from Rawls's legitimation pool. Suppose that Rawls's criteria of reasonableness excluded persons who want, as individuals, to dominate or oppress others. By contrast with the previous result, this would be an intuitively welcome outcome of his exclusion of unreasonable people. Let us see if Rawls's views do have this implication.

Rawls's criteria of reasonableness would exclude those persons in a liberal democracy, for example, who (1) insist as part of the public culture that their comprehensive beliefs are true; (2) want to impose their comprehensive doctrines on others; (3) reject the basic, liberal democratic political values, such as the liberal ideal of persons as free and equal; and (4) do not believe that the fundamentals of the political system need to be justified to all. In more Rawlsian terms, these latter persons in particular would lack a full sense of justice; they would lack the willingness "to act in relation to others on terms that [those others] can endorse." Such persons would lack a sense of justice sufficient to make them "fully cooperating members of society."[38]

What about people with comprehensive doctrines that devalue women and subordinate them to men? Such doctrines do not construe all persons as free and equal. Some of those doctrines, as interpreted by some of their supporters, would deny to women the same measure of political freedom and equality that is granted to men. According to Rawls's criteria, the adherents of such doctrines appear to be unreasonable and should accordingly be excluded from the legitimation pool. Rawls himself, however, does not spell out these implications of his views and he does not apply them consistently. Susan Moller Okin argues that Rawls actually vacillates in his reaction to such groups in those cases in which the doctrine in question is a familiar religion.[39] Thus, despite his strong statement about the containment of doctrines that themselves would deny basic freedoms, he appears willing to include the real-world adherents of some of those doctrines in his legitimation pool.

Despite Rawls's vacillation on this issue, his principles, in the context of his ideal theory at least, do appear to call for excluding the believers, for example, of male-dominant religions from the legitimation pool. Such doctrines conflict with the idea of persons—*all* persons, women as well as men—as free and equal. The same would apply to those who hold comprehensive doctrines that privilege some racial, ethnic, or religious group above others. Rawls does note that comprehensive doctrines that require the "repression or degradation of certain persons on . . . racial or ethnic" grounds conflict directly with the principles of justice and are apparently unreasonable.[40] If it is unreasonable, on Rawlsian grounds, to believe in racial inequality, then it is surely also unreasonable to believe in gender inequality. By holding Rawls to his own principles, we would be able to exclude sexists (along with racists) from the legitimation pool.

These various thoughts about who the unreasonable persons are thus yield mixed results. On the one hand, we face the happy prospect that persons committed to certain systems of social domination will be excluded from the legitimation pool. On the other hand, we also face the worrisome risk that Rawls's principles in combination with long-standing stereotypes about groups such as the poor would lead to the exclusion of some of the very sorts of persons who have historically been unjustifiably disenfranchised by liberalism. Intuitively, it is therefore not clear whether the impact of Rawls's exclusion of un-reasonable people would be benign or malign overall.

In addition, these thoughts about application do not settle fully the question of whether or not any unreasonable persons *should* be excluded from the legitimation pool. Even if the rubric of "unreasonable people" did turn out to fit the right-wing religious fundamentalists who worry many philosophers,[41] this by itself does not show that denying political autonomy to the unreasonable ones is internally consistent with politically liberal principles. It is to that problem that I now turn.

The Main Problem

In a nutshell, the problem is this. The unreasonable persons who are excluded from Rawls's legitimation pool are defined as such by their rejection of certain ideas and attitudes. These ideas are themselves basic conceptions and values that define a liberal democratic tradition. They include, to reiterate, first, the view that reasonable persons are affected by the burdens of judgment and will therefore disagree over fundamental comprehensive matters, and, second, the concern to seek fair terms of social cooperation. The problem is that anyone lacking these ideas or political values is not merely unreasonable; more specifically, they are also *illiberal*.

Thus Rawls's legitimation pool for political liberalism is defined precisely in such a way as to exclude those whose prior (illiberal) commitments would lead them to reject political liberalism. As Samuel Scheffler has noted, this attempt to justify liberal principles "appears to presuppose a society in which liberal values are already well entrenched. It is not clear that political liberalism provides any reason for establishing liberal institutions in societies that do not already have liberal traditions."[42]

If Rawls is not to engage in serious question-begging, he needs a conception of reasonableness that is politically neutral, one that is not defined in terms of the politically liberal values he seeks to defend. The challenge for Rawls is to find good but politically *independent* reasons for eliminating so-called unreasonable people from the legitimation pool. Can this be done?

Let us consider more closely one of the defining attitudes of a reasonable person, the quest for fair terms of social cooperation. What exactly does this rule out? Rather obviously, it rules out seeking unfair terms of social cooperation. More specifically, it rules out seeking terms of cooperation that give some persons undeserved advantages while others are made to bear undeserved burdens.

The problem is that matters of fairness and deservedness are themselves political notions. Few people would admit that they wanted social systems that gave them unfair or undeserved advantages. Most people would characterize the terms of social cooperation they seek as fair. Most of the people who believe that women should be subordinated to men either believe that men are smarter and stronger than women and therefore deserve to rule, or they believe that the traditional female social roles that many of us regard as socially subordinated to men's traditional social roles are equally valued within these traditions and not subordinated at all.[43] When I describe these views as aiming at women's (undeserved) subordination, I am using *my* terms, not those of their exponents. Thus, the terms of social cooperation that I regard as inegalitarian or hierarchical might well seem, to some other persons, as quite fair indeed.

These differences of opinion precisely exemplify the sorts of diversity out of which *Political Liberalism* seeks the emergence of an overlapping political consensus. Persons raised under the so-called free institutions of actual liberal democracies find themselves manifesting not only moral or religious diversity but political diversity as well. Many religious, moral, and philosophical doctrines themselves harbor political content. (Political philosophy is, after all, a type of philosophy.) Indeed, most of the important and intractable cultural battles of recent years have emerged from the clash of incommensurable political views entailed by diverse moral, religious, and philosophical doctrines.

Rawls recognizes that comprehensive doctrines often have political implications. Indeed, he discusses the comprehensive doctrines that would be discouraged or excluded altogether within his ideal society.[44] It seems, however, that he does not recognize how this insight undermines the very legitimacy of his legitimation method. It does so, to repeat, in two ways: first, it reveals that Rawls's conception of unreasonableness, which is used to exclude certain persons from the legitimation pool, is question-begging because it is already biased in favor of persons with basic liberal values; and, second, it reveals that one of the very features making a doctrine "unreasonable" in Rawls's conception of it, namely, that it is coercively imposed on persons who reject it, turns out to be a feature of the very political liberalism that is supposedly legitimized using Rawls's methods.

To be sure, for those of us steeped in the political culture of liberalism, the people who reject some of its basic political values are an unsavory lot indeed. I myself distrust people who insist dogmatically that their religious "truths" apply to my life contrary to my own convictions. I fear people who seek terms of social cooperation that simply enhance their prospects at my expense. I, frankly, would be overjoyed to find good reasons for keeping these sorts of people out of *my* legitimation pool. Unfortunately, I cannot find principled but politically neutral reasons for doing so.

In Rawls's view, the public culture of a liberal democratic society lacks any "public and shared basis of justification" that could establish for all citizens the truth of any particular comprehensive doctrine. Accordingly, in liberal public culture, no one can make good the claim that her comprehensive beliefs are true. Thus when someone attempts to impose her beliefs on others in the public sphere of a liberal pluralist society, she is thereby attempting to impose them on at least some persons for whom those beliefs are not publicly justifiable. Those who are reasonable, according to Rawls, must count anyone who would attempt to do this as *un*reasonable.[45] Thus, another trait that indicates unreasonableness is the readiness to impose one's comprehensive beliefs on others to whom those beliefs are unjustified and unjustifiable, given the available, publicly shared resources for justifying doctrines.

It is ironic, however, that if we substituted the word "political" for that of "comprehensive" in the description of the trait that I have just given, we would have a description of what Rawls himself is trying to do on behalf of political liberalism. That is, Rawls's ideal society would impose its coercive power consensually only on reasonable persons at best, while for unreasonable people, including all those with illiberal prior commitments, political liberalism would be an unjustifiable and nonconsensual imposition. Unreasonable persons are to feel the coercive power of the liberal state despite their possible lack of consent, since its legitimacy is for Rawls established without their consent or even their participation in the legitimation dialogue.

Rawls's approach is therefore similar in one respect to the very viewpoints that he regards as unreasonable, namely, in that he seeks to justify the use of coercive (liberal) power over some of the individuals who reject its tenets. From their points of view, it is *Rawls* who appears, by analogy with his own characterization of it, to be *unreasonable*.

Rawls imagines an ideal society with genuinely free institutions, such that persons growing up under them would come to endorse the political values and principles that underlie those institutions. Rawls's ideal society aims for political stability and the stable perpetuation of its distinctive sorts of institutions. The dream of political stability has long attracted political philosophers who long for a better social world. In most cases, however, political philosophers have recognized that no society could achieve stability without noble lies and not-so-noble forms of censorship or coercion that would impede the destabilizing influence of dissident ideas and social movements.

Liberalism promised to surmount those restrictive tendencies by grounding itself on a political philosophy that no one could refuse—not because they were coerced into endorsing it but rather because they were convinced of its justification. Unfortunately, most of the methods for showing that liberal principles are indeed convincing seem hedged with provisos that precisely exclude from the outset exactly those persons whose prior convictions *would* lead them to refuse.

Let us be thoroughly clear about the nature of this outcome. On my interpretation of it, one appealing implication of Rawls's conception of unreasonableness is the exclusion from the legitimation pool of some of the very sorts of people whose comprehensive doctrines should trouble those of us committed to equalities of gender, race, and so on. This heartening outcome, however, rests precisely on starting points that contradict the political conception that the method is supposed to justify. The political autonomy that liberalism promises to all persons, and the social contract that Rawls wants, namely a "hypothetical agreement . . . between all rather than some members of society,"[46] are both restricted in the end to those who begin with liberal political values.

There is no Archimedean point, as we all know, from which to begin the search for political legitimacy. We begin this endeavor as persons defined by commitments that are often religious, moral, or philosophical *and* political. Political liberalism wins consent only by excluding from the outset those very persons whose illiberal convictions would lead them to reject the system. Political liberalism, furthermore, would impose its coercive power on the non-liberal persons who reject its legitimacy—just as those persons, if they had the chance, might seek to impose their own political conceptions on their own dissenters, including liberals.

Nor can political liberalism claim that one of its distinctive values is a respect for the political autonomy of *all* its citizens. Each political doctrine, including political liberalism, would suppress the political autonomy of some of the citizens who lived under it, in particular, all those whose opposition threatened to destabilize the system. Political liberalism would do so in part by excluding those dissidents from the legitimation pool and in part by suppressing their free expression in daily life. In Rawls's political liberalism, the suppressed persons are the "unreasonable" ones who seem to deserve their fate. Yet this dishonorific term masks the fundamentally political and contested nature of this very notion.

It is hard to avoid the conclusion that political liberalism is simply one more political doctrine among many, with no greater politically independent claim to anyone's allegiance than its political rivals. If I myself continue to defend liberalism, it is because I reason in the manner acknowledged by Rawls, that is, from the standpoint of my own historic tradition and also because I have not abandoned hope of a wider *moral* liberalism as a final court of appeal.

9

Cultural Minorities and Women's Rights

What should a liberal democratic government do when the traditions and practices of a cultural minority within the society violate the rights of female members of that minority, in particular, such rights as would warrant protection by the government of the larger liberal society?

In recent decades, many voices have called for liberal governments to stay out of the internal lives of their cultural minorities. Even many liberals themselves lend support to this view by arguing that the supposedly individualistic liberal tradition actually tolerates to a certain degree group rights and special protections for cultural minorities within liberal societies.[1] On this view, a cultural minority is sometimes entitled to practice its cultural traditions without interference from the overarching liberal government even when those traditions violate rights that are recognized and protected in the larger society. The difficulty, of course, is to determine how far this doctrine may be carried and where to draw the line that separates what liberals should tolerate from what they should not or need not tolerate.

The situations of women and girls are important areas of concern for all cultures, so it is no surprise that they are especially affected by cultural minority practices. Cultural minorities that reside within liberal democratic states featuring powerful capitalist economies may find that the only areas of life in which they can hope to exercise some communal control over their lives and practice their cultural traditions unimpeded are areas commonly treated as matters of "privacy" by the surrounding liberal society. Thus, as Susan Moller Okin notes, the practices of many cultural minorities tend to focus on marriage, sexuality, family, and reproduction—aspects of life that affect women extensively.[2] Minority cultural traditions, however, do more than simply have a strong affect on women and girls. Okin writes that *"[M]ost cultures have as one of their principal aims the control of women by men"* and that "many . . . of the cultural minorities that claim group rights [in liberal societies] are more patriarchal than the surrounding [liberal] cultures."[3]

Ayelet Shachar observes that women's reproductive role is crucial to the survival of cultural communities because most cultural groups "acquire members first and foremost by birth" rather than by voluntary participation.[4] Cultural groups, accordingly, have a variety of practices by which they control women's "personal status" and reproductive activity. Shachar suggests that the central aim of these practices is to determine "how, when, and with whom women can give birth to children who will become full and legitimate members of the community."[5] While this particular function may well be what best explains the existence of cultural traditions concerning personal status, marriage, sexuality, and reproduction, the actual scope of those traditions often exceeds the precise aim of simply determining new members to the community. Minority cultural traditions often seem to impose a wide-ranging set of constraints on women's lives.

In the United States, for example, many men from cultural minorities have been prosecuted for crimes against women or girls from their own communities, and have benefited by using what Okin calls "cultural defenses." That is, they have defended their behavior on the grounds that it was the accepted practice of their respective cultural communities. Thus, Hmong men, when tried for kidnap and rape, claimed that their actions exemplified their tradition of "marriage by capture." And some Asian and Middle Eastern men, when charged with murdering their own wives, used a cultural defense that justified those actions on the grounds that their wives had either committed adultery or treated the husbands badly. Cultural defenses have also been used successfully in cases in which mothers of Japanese or Chinese background murdered their own children and subsequently claimed to have been attempting to carry out the practice of mother-child suicide as a culturally condoned response to their shame at the marital infidelities of their husbands. In Okin's view, these cases all reveal minority cultural practices that embody the attitude that women's worth lies in their sexual and domestic service to men. In all the cases that Okin cites, the defense used expert testimony about the defendant's cultural background, as a result of which the charges were either dropped or reduced, or the sentences were reduced.[6]

In such cases, writes Okin, the women and girls in question "*might* be much better off if the culture into which they were born were either to become extinct (so that its members would become integrated into the less sexist surrounding culture) or, preferably, to be encouraged to alter itself so as to reinforce the equality of women—at least to the degree to which this is upheld in the majority culture."[7]

Okin does not think that women are treated splendidly in Western culture either. Far from it. As Okin points out in response to critics, she has spent much of her academic career "critiquing Western political thought and practice, including much of liberalism."[8] She does believe, however, that Western liberal cultures protect the rights of women and girls better than do many of the cultural minorities living in their midst. And she rejects the idea that women from cultural minorities should be less well protected than women from the cultural majority against such problems as male violence.[9]

Katha Pollitt agrees with Okin. Pollitt is disturbed by the way in which the cultural rights movement in liberal societies often centers on preserving practices that subordinate women and girls; it is often these sorts of practices that liberals are asked to tolerate for the sake of sustaining cultural minorities. Pollitt wonders: "How far would an Algerian immigrant get if he refused to pay the interest on his Visa bill on the grounds that Islam forbids interest on borrowed money?" No one in mainstream U.S. society would allow money or profit to be sacrificed to the interests of cultural minorities. It appears, however, that the women and children of those minority groups "are another story."[10]

The principal aim of this chapter is to identify a common ground between liberals and defenders of cultural minorities that can serve as the basis for a mutually acceptable, yet still liberal, policy toward the treatment of women and girls by the cultural minority groups to which they belong. A secondary aim is to defend the very project of a liberal policy by responding to some of the criticisms that Okin and others have received for defending women's rights in apparent opposition to some minority cultural traditions.

Why Expect Common Ground?

To some people, a search for common ground between liberalism and cultural minorities may seem hopeless, given that multiculturalists often vehemently reject liberalism and liberal values. Not everyone, however, will be pessimistic about this strategy. Jeffrey Reiman, for one, has argued that multiculturalist critics of Western liberalism do in fact rely, in their criticisms, on central values of the very same liberal tradition they criticize.[11] One of those values is what Reiman calls "individual sovereignty." This is the capacity to live one's life free of the domination of others. Reiman's "individual sovereignty" is akin to autonomy, the key value of my later argument.

In an analogous vein, Uma Narayan has observed that critics of Western liberalism appeal in their arguments to the ideals of equality and rights, just as do Western liberals. Yet these are ideals which both liberals and multiculturalists concur in regarding as quintessentially Western liberal values. Narayan and Reiman construe this concurrence of values differently, however. Whereas Reiman might agree that such values are both distinctively Western and distinctively liberal, Narayan regards them as having a more cross-cultural pedigree.[12] Western societies, as we all know, historically denied the liberal values of equality, rights, and autonomy to various groups, most notably white women, all blacks, poor people, and colonized peoples. These disenfranchised peoples had to struggle *against* liberal governments in order to win in practice the equality, rights, and autonomy to which those systems were committed in principle. The length of historic time these struggles took and the degree of resistance put up by supposedly liberal governments to granting those rights suggests that equality and human rights might not be inherent or essential features of the historic tradition of Western liberalism *in practice*.

It is also useful to remind ourselves that liberals disagree profoundly over the question of how to elaborate and defend the values that liberals typically champion. There is not merely one liberalism; rather there are many liberalisms. Equality, rights, autonomy, justice, and liberty are all variously interpreted by liberals themselves. Liberalism is no more monolithic or homogeneous than are the minority cultures that sometimes challenge the authority of liberal governments. What are called "liberal values and principles," then, are simply values and principles that happen to figure prominently in many versions of liberal ideology today, but that could be defended from any number of philosophical points of view. This even includes the liberal legitimacy principle that I emphasized in chapter 3, the principle that a system of political power is legitimate only if those who live under it consent to it. What counts as consent, among other things, is subject to numerous conflicting interpretations.

Rights constitute another liberal value that is widely debated among liberals themselves. Rights in general are entitlements to specified forms of treatment by others. What rights there are, what grounds justify attributing them and to whom, and what value they afford those who bear them are among the many questions about rights that rights-based political and moral philosophies seek to answer. Liberalism, however, offers no univocal set of answers to questions about rights. There are, however, common tendencies that differentiate liberal approaches to rights from others that might be taken up. Rights may be borne by individuals or by groups. Liberalism, however, has historically tended to attribute rights to human individuals. Thus, individual rights predominate in and epitomize the liberal tradition. One profoundly important sort of right borne by human individuals consists of human rights. Human rights are entitlements to specified forms of treatment by others that the rights bearers each have simply by virtue of being a human person. In principle, one does not have to earn human rights; one merely has to be a human person. Among those individual rights are rights against unwarranted bodily harm and abuse.[13]

Thus, quintessential "liberal" norms and values such as rights, equality, and the idea that legitimacy is grounded in popular consent are subject to debate and varying interpretation among liberals themselves. In addition, versions of these concepts may be found in other cultural traditions not specifically known as liberal.[14] Thus, there are some values and principles that liberals tend to share with some multiculturalists, values and principles that provide common ground on the basis of which we can try to resolve dilemmas about how liberal societies should treat cultural minorities in their midst that violate women's rights.

One such shared value is revealed by a line of argument, primarily multicultural in inspiration, that is used against liberals by defenders of those cultural minority practices that seem to violate women's human rights. To anticipate, the cultural minority defense is this: *Cultural practices that violate women's rights are nevertheless justified when the women in question want to live under those practices and choose to do so voluntarily.* I shall explore this argument in detail below. At present, a word on the liberal significance of the argument is in order.

The above argument evokes clearly liberal ideas. For one thing, it evokes the liberal principle of political legitimacy. In chapter 3, I recommended that we deconstruct that principle into a list of statements about all the significant groups living under any particular political system. On this approach, a political regime is legitimate only if all significant groups that live under it consent to it.

John Stuart Mill's famous liberal principle of legitimate state authority allows it to reach as far as, and no further than, human behavior that causes or threatens harm to others, with harm understood as the violation of rights.[15] Although the realm of liberal privacy, in historical practice, has been associated with certain social domains such as that of the family, there is no principled liberal reason why this should be so. In terms of Mill's principle, the legitimate sphere of governmental activity is any human behavior that causes or threatens harm to others by violating their rights. Such behavior can certainly occur in the context of family life, as well as in the related contexts of marriage, sexuality, and reproduction, and can pertain to all matters of personal status associated with these forms of human activity. Thus, it makes sense, from a liberal point of view, to extend the liberal conception of legitimacy to all these social institutions, as well as any others in which human beings can violate each other's rights.

Combining that extended understanding of the liberal legitimacy principle with my earlier suggestion to consider the perspectives of each significant group living under a political regime, we get the following result: No social institution or practice in which people can violate each other's rights is legitimate unless all significant groups that have to live under it consent to it. The opinions of the women who must live with each cultural minority practice that has to do with personal status, marriage, sexuality, and reproduction thus become crucial to determining the legitimacy of those practices.

To be sure, a number of issues of detail would have to be specified before this guideline could be applied in practice. For one thing, we would need a clear idea of what constitutes acceptance as legitimate by a group. Is it enough that a simple majority of the group's members regard the practice as legitimate? Or should the number be larger than a simple majority? Should only actual consent count? Or is rationally reconstructed hypothetical consent adequate? In other words, the usual problems with consent arise as questions about our proposal for determining the legitimacy of social practices. The general standard I have articulated is thus far an abstract ideal that could ground an ethical stance that, in turn, could become the basis of liberal political policy toward cultural minority practices. The challenge is to make this standard acceptable to non-liberal cultural minorities.

Clarifying the Question

Before I elaborate on the shared value that seems to provide common ground between liberal and nonliberal cultures on the question of violating women's rights, it will be useful to consider a different line of argument that, if successful, could obviate the need for finding any common ground for deciding the issue.

Will Kymlicka argues that cultural minorities which are voluntary immigrant groups are obligated to comply with the liberal principles of a host liberal state so long as they understood before immigrating that this compliance would be expected and they nevertheless voluntarily chose to immigrate.[16] There is a great deal to be said for this argument. It illuminates the background framework of the question about what a liberal democratic government should do regarding the illiberal practices of cultural minorities in its midst. At first glance, it might seem that this question arrogantly presumes that the liberalism of the larger culture needs no defense. The question, however, does not inherently presuppose such an assumption. In the overall and ongoing human project of comparing and evaluating political ideologies and systems, liberalism needs as much defense as any other approach. What is presupposed instead is the liberal democratic background framework; it is simply taken as a given. The point is that the scope of general laws in an established and stable political system extends to everyone residing in the system in question. In the context of a liberal democratic political system, the practices of cultural minorities that become controversial are precisely those that, in some respect or other, violate general laws applicable, in principle, to everyone in the society. Exemptions from general laws must be justified, and the presumptive terms of justification are those that define the established and stable political culture of the larger society.

The reasons for granting exemptions from general laws have to be intelligible and reasonable from the standpoint of the system that makes and enforces the law, or else it will not be rational for that system to grant exemptions to its general laws. Of course, the laws themselves must also be intelligible and justifiable in the very same system or they should not have been enacted in the first place. Should liberal societies enact general laws that prohibit capture and rape, behaviors that lead to Hmong marriages? Should liberal societies enact general laws that prohibit girls under, say, sixteen years of age from being married off by their parents? Should liberal societies enact general laws that prohibit parents from arranging for the mutilation of their children's bodies? While the relevant concepts need specification (What counts as mutilation? Does male circumcision count?) and proposed specifications will be debated, the questions nevertheless have to be answered somehow. Without legal restrictions of these sorts, there will be no limits to what cultural groups may do to their female members (nor to their male members, for that matter). However fuzzy the borders between what is permitted and what is prohibited, it does not seem unreasonable to have general laws against rape, capture (kidnapping), forced childhood marriage, or the mutilation of children.

At any rate, it is also possible to separate the question of whether a particular, general law is justifiable in a liberal system from the question of whether, assuming its justifiability, there should be exemptions made for any population groups. The latter question need not be confined to liberal political systems. It may be asked of any political system that contains minority groups whose cultures differ in important ways from that of the majority. Thus, for any society, one may ask: "What should an X government do (where "X" is some nonliberal political ideology) regarding the non-X practices of cultural minorities in its midst that violate an X law that is otherwise generally applicable?" In the case of a nonliberal host society, this question would be answered in accord with the nonliberal traditions and legitimate reasoning based upon it that were part of the political culture of that host society.

The question with which I began this chapter is thus an internal question; it presupposes an existing political framework that is not being challenged at the time of the question. This omission may, although it need not, represent a background presumption that the political culture of the host society is ultimately defensible. Even such a presumption would not mean that the host society's political system is *never* to be put into question. When it comes to something as important as political ideologies and systems, every contender merits strict scrutiny, and the more powerful the contender, the more extensively it should be scrutinized. If the answer as to how to treat a cultural minority depends in any way on the taken-for-granted ideology of the host society, then the answer is a contingent one; it's ultimate defensibility depends on whether or not that host ideology can ultimately be justified. This is true whether the host society is Islamic, Hindu, Marxist, socialist, or of any other ideological persuasion—including liberal.

In the world today, liberal societies attract large numbers of voluntary immigrants. It is therefore commonplace worldwide for the problem of justifying cultural minority practices as exemptions from general laws to arise in cases in which the background political culture is liberal. Actual cases calling for the limited internal justification of exemptions to general laws will therefore often take liberal political frameworks for granted. However, this is not always the case.[17]

When a cultural minority remains voluntarily in a host society with a political culture different from its own, this fact may lend support to the idea that the host political culture is ultimately defensible. After all, if the members of a cultural minority who disagree on some matters of social life with a particular host society nevertheless choose voluntarily to remain in that society despite significant options to live elsewhere, the minority group seems to saying by its behavior that it continues to regard the host political culture as legitimate. In such a case, voluntary (past) immigration combined with voluntary continued residence would stand as a kind of minority endorsement of the host political culture. Thus, it is not unreasonable for Kymlicka to argue that voluntary immigrant minorities should not be exempted from having to obey general liberal laws that enforce liberal rights.

Unfortunately, the argument based on voluntary immigration has its limits. Kymlicka recognizes that there are several types of minority groups to which it does not apply without qualification. Prominent among these are national minorities, that is, indigenous peoples and other institutionally complete communities that have been overtaken by conquest, colonization, or federation. The argument also does not apply without qualification to nonvoluntary immigrant groups such as slaves and their descendants, nor does it apply readily to political refugees. In Kymlicka's view, it also does not apply to immigrant groups that have had long-standing legal permission to maintain nonliberal practices within liberal societies.[18]

Kymlicka's voluntary immigrant argument has other difficulties. For one thing, it may be difficult to apply in practice because voluntariness can be a matter of degree. Immigrant groups may have fled economic hardship or political suppression, or both. They also may not have been able to find other nations willing to admit them in sufficient numbers for them to reconstitute a viable community. Since immigration may be only partly voluntary, it is reasonable to ask what degree of voluntariness is enough to make one obligated to obey the laws of a host society? As well, immigrants often migrate together in families, whose decision to migrate may have been made by some but not all family members, and perhaps by only a single adult family member. The other family members, children most obviously and often wives as well, may have had no other choice but to stay with their family units. Thus, involuntariness of immigration may be real and substantial yet be unrecognizable to outsiders who would therefore misapply Kymlicka's guideline in those cases.

More important for my purposes, if voluntary immigrant groups were to be covered by general liberal laws governing the treatment of women and girls while certain other cultural minorities were exempted from compliance with those laws, the result would be a two-tiered system of protection for women and girls in the liberal society as a whole. Women and girls who were fortunate enough to be members of voluntary immigrant groups in a liberal society would be eligible for protection of their liberal rights under the host state, while women and girls who were members of national minorities or other exceptional groups would lose this protection. Why should the degree of protection received by particular women and girls depend on the random outcomes of the ethnocultural lottery?

Moreover, the voluntary immigrant argument rests not on values of the cultural minority itself, but on something more like a presumption of state sovereignty. Because a liberal state forms the larger host culture (in the cases we are considering), its laws are the ones with which voluntary immigrant minorities should comply. The burden of proof lies on those who would justify an exemption from general laws, and they must make their case in terms acceptable to the sovereign host political culture. This is not the only way in which the justification of minority cultural practices can proceed. It is also possible, and perhaps politically more respectful, to see whether the case for exemption—or for minority compliance—can be made in terms acceptable to the cultural minority as well as to the cultural majority. Plumbing the depths of thought between both cultures may reveal, as I observed earlier, value convergences at a deeper level, convergences that can be the basis for some sort of compromise.

Common Ground: Women's Choices

My proposal, then, is that both nonliberal and liberal cultures defend social practices with arguments based on the consent of those who have to live under and with the practices in question. In the context of a liberal society, it is particularly the consent of those women and girls whose legal rights are violated by some cultural practice that I urge as the paramount standard for determining the legitimacy, and legal permissibility, of that practice. The reason for thinking that this clearly liberal standard expresses common ground between liberalism and cultural minorities within liberal societies is that defenders of cultural minority practices frequently already treat the favorable choices of women and girls in the community in question as a justification for minority cultural practices.

This argument has been used to defend minority cultural practices as they occur within liberal societies and it has been used to defend those same practices in their indigenous homelands, especially in the face of postcolonial and globalizing threats. Leila Ahmed and Anouar Majid, for example, each illustrate this line of argument by emphasizing that many younger Islamic women choose to wear the veil voluntarily. They do so, according to Ahmed and Majid, to symbolize their repudiation of both colonialism and secular nationalist postcolonial elites. This voluntary wearing of the veil is, in Majid's words, a "recuperation and affirmation" of a "heretofore marginalized identity."[19] Ahmed and Majid both thus give normative significance to Islamic women's own choices to wear the veil. Ahmed and Majid discuss veiling as it occurs within Islamic societies and their argument displays the emphasis given to women's choices by defenders of Islamic, and not liberal, traditions.

Bhikhu Parekh offers another example of the argument. He agrees that clitoridectomy should not be practiced on children, who are "helpless victims," but argues that it is quite acceptable when chosen by "adult, sane, and educated women" who might opt for the surgery because of commitments to their religion or their mothering roles. Parekh also refers to "well-educated white liberal women" in Britain who converted to Islam or returned to traditional Judaism as well as examples of Muslim girls in France and the Netherlands who "freely" chose to wear head scarves for various reasons, all as a way of defending the respective practices in question. Finally, he suggests that polygamy does not violate "any central liberal values" to the extent that it is based on "uncoerced choice" by both the women and men involved.[20]

Western anthropologists Sandra Lane and Robert Rubinstein offer another example of the argument. Although Lane and Rubinstein are Westerners themselves, they urge Westerners to adopt a more tolerant attitude toward "traditional female genital surgeries," such as clitoridectomy, to which they refer in controversial fashion as "female circumcision." One of their contentions is that many, if not most, of the women in the communities that practice this surgery do voluntarily and often wholeheartedly embrace the practice. Lane and Rubinstein interviewed many Egyptian women who expressed no anger whatsoever over having had genital surgery performed on them. These women planned to have it performed on their daughters. They thought that natural adult female genitalia were disgusting and could not imagine that a man would want to marry a woman who had not undergone the surgery.[21] Lane and Rubinstein also claim that even *feminist* groups in Egypt are generally not particularly concerned about female genital surgery as an issue and tend to focus on other issues instead. Accordingly, Lane and Rubinstein chastise "Western feminists [who] make female circumcision a preeminent concern, with little or no regard for the priorities of Arab and African feminists."[22]

Apart from the question of feminist priorities around the world, a crucial source of common ground between liberals and defenders of nonliberal cultural practices is thus revealed by the argument that cultural practices that violate women's rights are nevertheless permissible if the women in question accept them. The common ground in question involves an important sort of respect for women, in particular, respect for women's choices and perspectives. From a liberal standpoint, respect for people's actual choices is relevant to the principle of respect for their personal autonomy. While many liberals base the respect for people's choices on the rationality that is presumed to lie behind those choices, this is not true of all liberals. Martha Nussbaum, for example, finds importance in the mere fact that people are "active and striving beings" whose strivings have "some importance, some dignity," and thus deserve respect as such.[23] Thus, many liberals and at least some defenders of what could be minority cultural practices within liberal societies concur in thinking that the attitudes of female participants, whether rational or not, toward those cultural practices are important touchstones for evaluating the practices.

What are the presuppositions and implications of this common ground of respecting women's actual choices and perspectives? One possibility is that it presupposes a minimal level of confidence that women's decision-making capacities will lead them to live decent lives. If someone's underlying capacities for making choices were not minimally capable of guiding her to live a decent life, then, in the view of many, there would be no good reason for others to consider her choices or preferences when designing the legal or policy arrangements under which she is to live.

However—and this is the point at which my argument becomes more controversial—women would have the capacities for making choices that were, in general, reliable, only if at least two conditions were met. First, women's choices would have to be made under conditions that promoted the general reliability of their choices. This would require that women be able to choose among a significant and morally acceptable array of alternatives and that they be able to make their choices relatively free of coercion, manipulation, and deception. Second, women must have been able to develop, earlier in life, the capacities needed to reflect on their situations and make decisions about them. The right sorts of opportunities and guidance must have occurred in order for women to have developed these general skills of practical reflection.

In liberal philosophy, respect for people's actual choices serves a crucial value, the value of personal autonomy. Personal autonomy, to reiterate yet again, is the capacity to reflect on one's deeper values and commitments and to act and live one's life accordingly. The reflection must be relatively free of coercion and manipulation, and the agent must have a capacity to persist in acting according to her deeper concerns even in the face of some minimum of opposition by others. The ideal of autonomy thus requires both certain personal competencies and certain "external" conditions among which those competencies can develop and manifest themselves.

The ideal of autonomy is a debatable requirement for a good human life. As I noted earlier, many of the world's peoples do not explicitly subscribe to this conception of the good, and some explicitly reject it. Some multiculturalists would resist my claim that their arguments invoke the value of personal autonomy. In some multicultural quarters, autonomy has been stigmatized as a distinctive vice of liberal individualism. How can the ideal of autonomy function as a common ground between liberals and cultural minorities if those minorities reject the value of autonomy?

Yet why *else* base the legitimacy of cultural practices on the choices of those who must live with and under them? If those choices are important as such, it must be because there is something important about how people choose to order their own lives. This something is what gives value to people's own perspectives as a basis for shaping their own social arrangements. As Nussbaum puts it, a respect for people's choices credits their own strivings for themselves with importance and dignity, and accords respect to the persons in question. Without defending autonomy by name, the multicultural insistence that women's own choices to live by their cultural traditions counts toward justifying those traditions implicitly relies on a commitment to autonomy nonetheless. It thus appears that, disclaimers aside, not all defenders of cultural minorities really reject autonomy in all possible ways.

This finding gains support from the observations of Sawitri Saharso regarding South Asian cultures. Saharso notes that South Asian cultures do not particularly esteem individual autonomy and do not socialize females for autonomous behavior within social relationships. Nevertheless, according to Saharso, the child-rearing practices of these cultures do in fact promote what Saharso, borrowing from Katherine Ewing, calls "intrapsychic autonomy."[24] This encompasses the mental capacities for autonomy and, in particular, for an awareness of one's own feelings and thoughts, one's "inner world of self," especially when these thoughts have a socially unacceptable character and are difficult to act on.[25] Reflecting on and understanding one's values and commitments is a necessary condition for autonomy on my account. If Saharso is right, South Asian cultures are indeed socializing females for some of the requirements of autonomy competency despite lacking the public acknowledgment of this cultural practice.

The defense of cultural practices in terms of women's choices to live under them seems to rest on a content-neutral conception of autonomy in particular. Content-neutral conceptions of autonomy, to reiterate, are those that define autonomy in terms of either the manner by which a person makes choices or the internal integration or structure of her choosing self. She must reflect on her choices and commitments in light of her deeper values and concerns, and she must be relatively free of coercion, manipulation, and deception when making her choices. On a content-neutral conception of autonomy, if a person's choices manifest her deeper cares and concerns under these appropriate conditions, then the person's choices are autonomous.

A substantive conception of autonomy adds to this content-neutral conception a requirement pertaining to the contents of what a person chooses. According to the substantive conception, someone realizes autonomy only if she makes choices which, in their *substance* or *contents*, are consistent with the value of autonomy itself. A choice, for example, to live in a thoroughly subordinated, servile, or slavish manner is, on this approach, a choice that fails substantively to accord with the value of autonomy and is, therefore, not genuinely autonomous even if it meets all content-neutral criteria. So-called content-neutral autonomy is, on the substantive view, not genuine autonomy after all.

Both content-neutral and substantive ideals of autonomy may be used to support the idea that people's actual choices deserve respect. In the absence of further information, people's actual choices may, for all we know, exemplify autonomy, either in a merely content-neutral sense or also in a substantive sense, and therefore merit the respect due to autonomous choice. However, the content-neutral view supports this conclusion more easily, since, on the content-neutral view of autonomy, fewer conditions have to be met for someone to be autonomous. If the default position is to assume that someone's choices are autonomous until proven otherwise, it will be easier to prove otherwise on a substantive view of autonomy since there are more ways in which choices may fail to be substantively autonomous than they may fail to be content-neutrally autonomous. This point is of special relevance in regard to minority cultural traditions that seem to harm women.

When a woman voluntarily accepts, say, the practice of female genital surgery because she thinks it makes females more attractive to men, as did the Egyptian women interviewed by Lane and Rubenstein, the content of her choice seems on its face to lack substantive autonomy. Her choice defers to what pleases men and is a choice that would permanently eliminate from a woman's life the option of certain sorts of pleasurable and satisfying experiences. Whether such choices do lack substantive autonomy is debatable. My point, however, is that even if a woman lacks substantive autonomy, it does not follow that she lacks content-neutral autonomy. She may wholeheartedly prefer the practice of female genital surgery to the alternative of not having the surgery, in accord with her own deepest values and concerns, and may have reached that conclusion through careful reflection devoid of undue coercion or manipulation by others.

In chapter 1, I argue that content-neutral autonomy is sufficient to deserve the name of genuine autonomy; it crosses the threshold marking the minimal conditions for autonomy. One does not have to endorse the content of some-

one's choice in any way, let alone think it consistent with the value of autonomy itself, to regard it as deserving the default respect due to any choice not
yet known to be nonautonomous. The consent of women in a minority culture
to their own cultural practices that seem to violate their rights provides, on the
face of it, a significant degree of justification for the cultural practices in question, so long as that consent is content-neutrally autonomous. If women in a
cultural minority consent to practices that violate their liberal rights, and do
so under conditions promoting content-neutral autonomy, then the liberal society at large has at least one good reason to permit the practices to continue,
namely, respect for the content-neutral autonomy of the women in question.
And this line of thought is harmonious with a liberal perspective whether or
not it is uniquely distinctive to liberalism.

There is, of course, the usual limit to liberal respect for consent, even consent that has occurred under conditions promoting content-neutral autonomy. Liberalism, at least in principle today, does not recognize literal slavery
and would not uphold a contract or other formal decision by anyone to enter
a condition of servitude. This liberal restriction leaves ample room for the argument that the oppressive conditions under which some must now live make
those persons de facto slaves to particular others who are able to dominate
them. Liberal political systems in practice do not weed out all oppressive social arrangements. However, if anyone "chooses" de facto slavery under oppressive conditions, then she has not made her choice under conditions promoting content-neutral autonomy. Her choice would therefore not command
respect for its own sake under liberal conceptions of what is required by respect for autonomy. Would anyone think it ought to command such respect? It
seems safe ground to assert that, from both liberal and nonliberal perspectives, the choices of women that deserve default respect are those made under
conditions promoting the women's content-neutral autonomy.

Recall that, within liberalism, personal autonomy contributes to justifying
political authority. Jeremy Waldron expresses this view when he claims that
liberalism is "fundamentally" a theory that views consent by "all those who
have to live under" a "social and political order" as a necessary condition for
its moral legitimacy.[26] Liberalism, in principle even if not always in practice, is
committed to the idea that major social institutions and practices should be
acceptable to those who are its sustaining participants. Any institutions and
practices that are legitimately regulated by law and public policy come under
the scope of this ideal of political legitimacy. Thus, the ideal of political legitimacy, now linked to women's consent in particular, emerges as another aspect
of what is at stake in the common ground that, I argue, obtains between certain defenders of cultural minorities and liberals over the question of women's
rights within cultural minority traditions.

The next important question is: Where does this common ground lead us?
It allows us, for one thing, to pursue the following line of thought: If we find
ourselves valuing and respecting women's capacities for making choices, then
it seems reasonable to care whether the conditions under which women are
developing their capacities and making their choices are the right sorts of

conditions. In accordance with the ideal of autonomy, choices deserve the respect due to autonomy only if they are genuinely autonomous. More modestly for practical purposes, we should say that people's choices deserve respect and consideration if there is no positive reason to think those choices are *not* content-neutrally autonomous. The default position is to presume autonomy unless there is good reason to think otherwise. (There might be some reason for respecting nonautonomous choices but it would not be that they deserved the respect due to autonomy. Such respect would have to be defended on some other basis.)

If a group of women consistently choose to live in ways that violate their own rights, we should first try to assess the conditions under which the women are making their choices. As noted in the first chapter, there are at least two sorts of conditions required for autonomy: those that promote autonomous choices by persons already possessing autonomy competencies, and those that foster autonomy competencies in the first place. When seeking to determine whether the women of a community live under those two sorts of conditions, we should ask questions such as these: Do the women have genuine alternatives among which to make important choices? Are their choices subject to coercion, manipulation, or deception? Were the women culturally enabled to develop the capacities that the exercise of autonomy competency requires? Extreme poverty, malnutrition, violence and abuse, lack of educational opportunities, and forced childhood marriages to adult men are conditions that tend to undermine or destroy the women's capacities and opportunities for the exercise of autonomy.

What should a liberal society do when such autonomy-disabling conditions affect the women of cultural minorities? Kymlicka suggests that liberal societies may impose certain limitations on the protections they grant to cultural minorities.[27] One requirement is that minority groups not restrict the "basic civil or political liberties" of their own members—in particular for this discussion, the rights of women and girls in the minority groups. Kymlicka's guideline has the effect, therefore, of allowing the liberal state to suppress any minority cultural practices that violate women's rights.

To this guideline delineating the limits of liberal toleration, I add the amendment mentioned earlier, which was designed to accommodate the viewpoints of women in cultural minorities. Cultural minorities should not be allowed to engage in practices that violate women's rights or general laws *unless the women themselves consent to those violations*. This amendment may now be specified still further. The consent of the women in minority cultures within liberal societies must occur under conditions of *genuine content-neutral autonomy*. If positive evidence reveals cultural conditions that impede the development of autonomy competencies in women or that prevent its exercise, then the consent of women living under those conditions does not justify the rights-violating practices. Whether particular conditions count as autonomy-impeding is, of course, open to debate. The possibility of such debate over what promotes or impedes autonomy in practice, however, does not undermine the abstract point.

Possible Objections

I have argued that one common ground between liberals and defenders of cultural minorities within liberal societies is revealed by the argument that women's consent helps to justify practices in which the women are involved, even practices that appear to violate the women's own rights. Although I have drawn attention to examples of this argument in the writings of those who defend cultural practices that are not specifically liberal in origin, it may still seem that my presentation has been constructed from a liberal perspective and is biased against non-Western views that might diverge from or compete with liberalism. Many Third World, or Southern, and postcolonial writers frequently charge that Western liberals arrogantly presume the value and universal appropriateness of liberalism. Parekh, for example, criticizes Okin for displaying this sort of attitude in her discussion of the dangers of multiculturalism for women; he calls for Okin to show that liberal values are worth accepting. Parekh argues that Okin misses the deeper importance of multiculturalism by focusing only on the relatively minor issue of minority group rights within liberal societies. Multiculturalism, claims Parekh, is "a revolt against liberal hegemony and self-righteousness" and a challenge to the universal rationality and validity claimed by the liberal tradition.[28]

Azizah Y. al-Hibri accuses Okin of writing "from the perspective of the dominant cultural 'I'" which presumes the universality of its principles, reduces the "*inessential other*" to an Orientalist stereotype, and struggles with the "burden" of "immigrant problems."[29] Bonnie Honig suggests that Okin views the issues through a "liberal feminist lens" which equates feminism with "liberal brands of equality and individualism," thereby occluding other forms of feminism. As well, writes Honig, Okin displays a "faith" that Western liberal regimes are more "progressive" than other regimes in their treatment of women, a faith that prevents Okin from understanding other cultures at the level of detail that might reveal the limits of "liberal ways of life."[30] Abdullahi An-Na'im hears the "sense" of an "ultimatum" in Okin's suggestion that women might be better off if cultures which cannot change so as to promote the equality of women were to "become extinct" (Okin's terms).[31] Complaining in general about liberals who "have a way of occupying the high moral ground," Homi K. Bhabha criticizes Okin for emphasizing selective data that yield "patronizing and stereotyping" portraits of minority cultures. Okin, he writes, gazes down on non-Western cultures "from above and elsewhere" and portrays them as existing "in a time warp," ignoring the complexities of their own indigenous traditions of feminism and protest as well as the hardships they suffer from their legacies of postcolonialism and the forces of globalism.[32]

Western feminists in general, many of whom are not liberals, are sometimes accused of exhibiting stereotypical liberal vices such as those attributed to Okin. Ofelia Schutte suggests that Western feminists, though more sensitive than they were some years ago to cultural differences, nevertheless still speak about women's emancipation with universalist aspirations.[33] And liberals in

general, many of whom are not feminists, are frequently charged with inordinate hubris. Bhabha refers to the "way in which the norms of Western liberalism become at once the measure and mentor of minority cultures—Western
liberalism, warts and all, as a salvage operation, if not salvation itself. With a
zealousness not unlike the colonial civilizing mission, the "liberal" agenda is
articulated without a shadow of self-doubt."[34] It is also articulated, Bhabha
continues, without any acknowledgment of either the feminist and reformist
strands that exist within nonliberal cultures or the internal debates going on
within those cultures over how to "translate" "gender and sexual politics in
the world of migration and resettlement."[35]

What is the significance of these charges for the debate about minority cultures within liberal societies? Most superficially, there is an issue of political
effectiveness. Okin might be right that some minority cultural traditions in
liberal societies egregiously violate the rights of female members of their own
communities. Yet even accurate messages can lose political struggles by failing
to win the support of those they aim to benefit. Okin's message could fail to
win the support of cultural minority women and girls if it exudes a colonial arrogance that offends those women and girls. An-Na'im captures this point
well when he suggests that Okin's proposal might be "resented as hegemonic
imposition, whether among minorities in the West or in non-Western societies, thereby becoming counterproductive for gender equality in practice."[36]

Beyond the question of political effectiveness, Okin's critics raise a variety
of issues distinct from her original question regarding cultural minority practices within liberal political systems. Some of these issues pertain to the general moral evaluation of cultural practices while others pertain to the sorts of
attitudes that Western liberals show in dialogue with those who are either not
Western, not liberal, or neither. We can differentiate at least three distinct
questions: *First*, there is the specific question which Okin focuses on and with
which I began this chapter, namely, what should a liberal society (or any other
sort of society, for that matter) do, in law and public policy, when a cultural
minority within it seeks exemption from compliance with general laws or constitutional principles, particularly those that protect women's rights? *Second*,
how can liberal (or any other) laws, policies, practices, or systems be evaluated or justified either politically or morally? *Third*, what attitudes should
people from one culture show to those in another culture when discussing the
evaluation of cultural practices (or any topic), given the international histories
of colonization, political and economic domination, and severe global economic inequality?

Okin begins her discussion with the first question, asking what the law or
public policy of a liberal society should be when a cultural minority seeks exemption from general laws for practices that violate the rights of its female
members. As asked by Okin (and myself), this question presupposes a liberal
framework. As I suggested earlier, however, the question could be asked in regard to any political system. Someone might, for example, wonder what an Islamic state should do when a cultural minority within it seeks exemption from
compliance with general laws in order to engage in practices that violate such

women's rights as are generally protected in the Islamic society at large. One legitimate way to answer this question is to presuppose an Islamic political framework and to derive an answer from the legal, political, and other normative resources available in the society's Islamic traditions. There is nothing wrong in principle with asking, about *any* political system, the limited question of how to deal with subcommunities that seek exemptions from its general requirements. Those communities which seek exemptions for themselves are not, as such, challenging the ideology of the larger political system. They are simply seeking to make exceptions of themselves. Construed in that way, the question takes for granted that the political system in question is sovereign and legitimate in the territory in question and merely seeks a policy for potential exceptional cases.

Because the first question does not force debate over whether a host political system is legitimate, it could seem that asking this question from the standpoint of a liberal system expresses an arrogant presumption that liberalism is the best political system for everyone and is beyond reproach. The first question, however, to repeat, does not carry these presumptions. This is not to say that people who in fact ask that question are not assuming the value of liberalism. The point is that the question itself does not presuppose it. It may be asked of any political system how that system should treat internal cultural minorities who want exemptions from general laws in order to practice their minority cultural traditions.

I suggested earlier that a more culturally respectful way to answer the question is to seek common ground with cultural minorities and find a normative basis that all parties could accept from which an answer could be generated. I argued that cultural practices that violated the rights of women and girls should be tolerated by a liberal political system in case the women and girls who have to live with the practices in question choose to do so under conditions that promote female autonomy. I thus urge that the answer be based, as far as possible, on values that are acceptable to cultural minorities. This strategy is meant to embody and express respect by a liberal system for nonliberal cultures in its midst.

At the same time, the answer must also be based on liberal values. My aim is to find a principle for dealing with minority cultural traditions violating women's rights that is acceptable both to liberals *and* to members of cultural minorities. Why should the answer be acceptable to liberals? Because the question I am raising pertains particularly to cultural minorities living in liberal political systems. If the system of general law in question is a liberal system, then so long as that system remains sovereign and is treated as legitimate by most of those who have to live under it—including the cultural minority in question—then the choice of what to do about illegal minority traditions must be acceptable in terms of the values of the larger liberal system in which the law and any exceptions to it take place. To say this is not to presume arrogantly that liberal values and rights are universally applicable and need no defense.

It is possible to opt for a different strategy in responding to the first question. It is possible to challenge either the law or liberal right that the minority cultural tradition violates, or the liberal political system as a whole that underlies the law or right. Nothing bars this response. It may be that *no one* should comply with the law in question. It may be that the political system as a whole is fundamentally unjust. This line of thought needs, however, to be developed. It requires either a critique of the particular law in question or a wholesale critique of liberalism, or both. Without that additional argument, the challenge is incomplete. The burden of proof does not lie only with those who would defend liberal rights and laws. In the context of a sovereign liberal state, any minority group that seeks exemption from general laws on nonliberal grounds must also make its own case.

Notice that the claim that a particular liberal law, or that liberalism itself, needs defense in its own right does not actually answer the first question. The first question narrowly asks how a political system with a liberal character should respond to a cultural minority practice that violates the liberally recognized rights of female members of the minority group. To challenge either the rights in question, the general law that is being violated, or the liberal character of the whole system is to change the subject. It shifts debate from the first to the second question listed above, the question of how to justify liberal laws and principles. These alternative issues are critically important ones. They are different issues, however, from the question of what a *liberal* system should do when cultural minority practices violate the rights of females in the minority. In the same way, one would also change the subject if one were to claim that an Islamic law, or Islam itself, needs defense when the question is, narrowly, what an Islamic society should do regarding minority traditions that are illegal in that society.

Thus, the first question (what should a liberal society do regarding illegal or rights-violating minority cultural traditions?) does not, in itself, force debate about whether the larger liberal framework is legitimate. On the other hand, it also does not call for an overall moral evaluation of cultural minorities. The first question pertains only to those cultural minority practices that violate general laws or constitutional principles. In the United States, to take a counterexample, public school children are seldom required to wear uniforms, and when they are not, no legal or constitutional issue is raised by the head scarves that Muslim girls might wear to public school. No U.S. law bars women or girls—or men or boys!—from wearing either the Muslim head scarf or the full veil.[37] The question of how a liberal society should treat cultural minorities that violate female rights is simply not raised by cultural traditions such as full or partial personal veiling when they involve no legal violations. In these cases, cultural minorities are legally free to do as they wish.

The second question, asking how cultural practices should be evaluated or justified, differs from the first question in various ways. For one thing, it does not presuppose any particular sort of political system as the sovereign context of the practices being evaluated. The second question is open to cross-cultural evaluation and there are no types of political terms that have any claim to priority in the cross-cultural, moral evaluation of cultural practices. Moreover, any cultural practices may be held up for this sort of evaluation.

Whereas the first question is limited to cultural practices that violate general laws or rights upheld by a larger society, the second question is of potentially unlimited scope. The Islamic practice of veiling, for example, is of no legal or policy concern to a liberal society that lacks dress codes for public schools or other public places; however it is a legitimate subject of cross-cultural *moral* analysis.

In the cross-cultural moral evaluation of cultural practices, liberal principles should not be presupposed. They have no necessary cross-cultural authority. They require as much defense as any other moral, religious, or ideological terms that might be invoked in such discussions. And liberal cultural practices may, and should, be morally evaluated no less than any other cultural practices. When assessing the views of someone such as Okin on cultural practices, it is necessary to know what sort of question she is trying to answer. If her focus of attention is on how a particular political system should deal with minority cultural practices that violate general laws, then she is answering the first question and is not arguing unreasonably by limiting her arguments to the terms and principles of the system involved in the case at hand. By contrast, if her focus of attention is on a moral assessment of cultural minority practices, then she is answering the second question and arguing unreasonably by limiting her arguments to liberal terms.

The third question shifts attention from the assessment of practices or laws to the attitudes people from one culture show to people from another culture when they engage together in the evaluation of cultural practices. Some of Okin's critics are objecting more to what they regard as Okin's attitude in cross-cultural dialogue than they are to the content of her views. Liberal arrogance, as well as arrogance on behalf of anything Western, capitalist, and European-derived, is of special concern because it has historically played a role in rationalizing the one-way history of global colonization and economic domination by certain Western liberal democracies.

Cross-cultural discussions about cultural practices are complex and multifaceted. They are not simply intellectual engagements in which scholars forge third-person-observer, theoretical accounts of cultures from which they are all equally detached. Such discussions are also, at the same time, cross-cultural encounters among individuals with cultural identities, encounters that are themselves parts of the cross-cultural relations that are in process in the world today. Someone's attitude in dialogue is an important facet of her overall engagement with people of other cultures when discussing cultural practices. To promote thoughtful understanding of the issues, however, it is crucial to keep the issue of cross-cultural attitudes distinct from those of the political or moral evaluation of cultural practices. For someone to argue that the principles of political system X require that system to prohibit minority cultural practice Y is not, in itself, to show arrogance toward the minority culture in question. As well, the argument for prohibition is not undermined even if the arguer fails to defend political system X and shows arrogance in presenting her argument. The defense of the larger political system, in this case, liberalism, and the attitude of a discussant who is a member of that system are crucially important issues, but they are different issues from the question of whether the larger political system should permit minority cultural practice Y.

Of course, the question of liberalism's legitimacy may itself be posed as the primary issue, as it is in the second question. It goes without saying that liberal laws and liberal cultural practices should be subjected to critical scrutiny, both on political grounds and on general moral grounds. Indeed such scrutiny already occurs. One particular focus of concern, in scrutinizing liberal laws and practices, should be the quality of life of women and girls who live with those practices. As I suggested earlier and numerous others have suggested before me, there is no reason to presume that the actual practices of a liberal society necessarily provide for all its members the values to which liberalism is committed in principle. Thus, Bhabha points to the high rate of domestic violence in Britain to show that Western liberal culture is not as superior as he thinks Okin suggests.[38] And An-Na'im reminds us that the fullest dialogue about human rights will address issues of equality regarding race, religion, language, and national origin as well as that of gender. Majority liberal cultures are hardly exemplary in the areas of race and class relations.[39]

Widening the discussion to include the topic of the legitimacy of liberalism provides us with a context for appreciating al-Hibri's question to Okin, "Why is it oppressive to wear a head-scarf but liberating to wear a miniskirt?"[40] Superficially the question is irrelevant to Okin's discussion of how a liberal society should deal with minority cultural traditions that violate women's rights. Furthermore, no one in the dialogue over cultural traditions, least of all Okin, has ever seriously said that miniskirts are liberating. Al-Hibri's question is relevant, however, to the wider dialogue we should all be having about the treatment of women and girls in *all* cultural traditions. It is a form of respect by Western liberals toward non-Westerners or nonliberals to make sure we engage in that wider dialogue.

The wider dialogue is particularly a response to the second question: How should we evaluate political systems and cultural traditions? That dialogue should not presume liberal principles; all principles must be defended. To ensure that this dialogue about cultural practices is a genuine and mutual dialogue, liberals must acknowledge their willingness to entertain criticisms about their own social and political institutions.

Even in the context of a liberal society, if government regulation of minority cultural practices is legitimate from a liberal point of view, then there is no reason to limit this regulation to the practices of cultural minorities. All cultural practices, both minority and majority, should be vulnerable to regulation if they violate the rights of those who are affected by them. In addition, all members of a society, both majority and minority, must somehow consent to such regulation. Otherwise, on core liberal grounds, it is not acceptable. There is no reason why cultural minorities should accept government regulation of their cultural practices if majority cultural practices are not being equally monitored for rights violations. Concern for the well-being of women and girls living in a liberal society should apply to women from all cultures: Third World, postcolonial, Southern hemisphere, Eastern tradition, First World, post*colonist*, Northern hemisphere, Western tradition, and so on. Indeed, no cultural tradition anywhere is, or should be, exempt from attempts by insiders or outsiders to understand or assess the place of women and girls within it—or that of men and boys, for that matter.

I have argued that liberalism shares with certain defenders of cultural minorities a key value: respect for women's perspectives and thereby for women's autonomy. I have also argued that this common ground opens up fruitful lines of further thought. But what about those defenders of cultural minorities who fail to give any normative weight to women's choices or perspectives and who defend cultural minority practices on entirely different grounds? Is there no possibility of dialogue there?

There is, I believe, the possibility of dialogue, but it occurs at a more basic or foundational level. This is the level at which one asks the question: *Why* should women's perspectives *not matter* in the defense of cultural practices? Remember that we are talking about the women who have to live under those practices. Why should it not matter what those women think or feel about the practices that determine the course of their lives? Why should any group of women have to live under social conditions they have no opportunity to revise or reject?

A complete disregard for women's perspectives is demeaning and deeply disrespectful to women. On this view, either the women would be regarded as somehow *incapable* of making generally worthwhile choices or the women would be regarded as *irrelevant* to moral community, as beings whose perspectives made no normative difference. Neither of these attitudes should escape the demand for justification. There is no reason for liberals to be embarrassed in calling for justification of such attitudes across what seem to be cultural barriers. If my earlier arguments are correct, there are many defenders of nonliberal practices who agree that women's perspectives are critical when justifying cultural practices.

As I noted earlier, Jerome Schneewind's historical account of the development of the ideal of autonomy[41] shows that it emerged in the West as an antiauthoritarian notion. A conception of morality as autonomy, or self-governance, came increasingly over the seventeenth and eighteenth centuries to replace the previous conception of morality as obedience. According to the view of morality as obedience, human persons are not equally capable of grasping what morality requires or moving themselves to act accordingly and, indeed, most are not capable of this at all. On this view, to be assured of acting morally, most people need to submit to the authority of certain others, such as kings, priests, husbands, or fathers, who are the privileged interpreters of morality for those beneath them on the moral hierarchy. By the end of the eighteenth century, however, the idea had taken hold among some Western thinkers (although it was still a very long way from full implementation) that all normal individuals are equally capable of grasping what morality calls for and of moving themselves to act accordingly.

Moral knowledge and motivational capacities of individuals are at stake in this debate. The conception of morality as autonomy, or self-governance, enlarges the social space within which each person is thought capable of adequately directing her own moral behavior without having to be dominated by others. The idea that people are capable of doing so supports the idea that it is desirable to allow them to do so, and perhaps, more strongly, that they are *entitled* to do so.

It seems plausible to consider the ideal of personal autonomy in the same light as that of moral autonomy in this respect. According to the ideal of personal autonomy, typical or average adults are entitled to act and live their own lives without being dominated by others in major areas of their lives. Major areas of life include and are not limited to matters of sexuality, marriage, and reproduction. Thus, to say that autonomy is not ideal for a cultural group, or a cultural subgroup, such as the women in the group, seems to presuppose either that the members of that group are not capable of discerning how best to live their lives or they are not capable of motivating themselves accordingly.

The conversation between liberals and those who defend cultural minority practices must start at the foundational level of identifying the members of the moral community whose perspectives are to count in legitimating whatever practices a culture would sustain. All (or nearly all) cultures of any substantial size or complexity have social hierarchies that organize various important aspects of social life. These hierarchies are the social means by which conflicts between persons are resolved and people are moved toward socially productive activity that preserves the communal life. All hierarchies involve elites, that is, persons who have positions of privilege in the possession of knowledge (or the assumption of it) and power. Elites within any social hierarchy are those with the power to shape, in accord with their own beliefs and values, the lives of whole communities of people affected by the hierarchy in question.

Members of elites are those with de facto access to the benefits and privileges that rights tend to confer. They have great leeway to shape and implement normative values and requirements in their communities. Their choices and commitments, made for the whole community, determine key aspects of the normative lives of their groups. Social, political, and economic elites include spokespersons for the group whose articulations on behalf of the group are accepted as authoritative expressions of what the group as a whole believes or values. Thus, elites get to exercise substantial autonomy in practice, even if this trait is not idealized for the culture as a whole. That is, even where autonomy is not recognized as a culturewide value, the elite, decision-making members of the community still enjoy the practical equivalent of autonomy, and the cultural protection of its embodiment in them. At the same time, these same protections are denied or unavailable to other members of the community. The practical significance of the autonomy enjoyed by elites is that they get to control important dimensions of the lives of other members of the group. The status of elites in a community manifests the community's reliance on the moral competence of those elites, on their capacity to discern what morality requires and to act accordingly. Subordinated members of the community, by contrast, lack communal recognition of their moral competence.

Okin worries, for example, about all cultural groups that accord less concern, respect, and freedom to their women and girls than to their men and boys.[42]

A cultural group that subordinates some of its members is treating those subordinates as prima facie incapable of grasping how to live their lives (including their moral lives) and of motivating themselves accordingly. To the extent that women are subordinated to men in the traditions and practices of a community, a community expresses its collective view that women are incapable of this achievement—or less capable, at any rate, than men. Around the world, women are generally subordinated to men, not only in the political and economic spheres in which women's lesser participation alone might render them less capable on average of directing their own lives, but also in the spheres of sexuality, marriage, reproduction, and family—spheres of life in which women *specialize*. This subordination, we should note emphatically, is hardly absent from U.S. culture, as witness the recent convention of Southern Baptist messengers who made it an explicit point of their doctrine that wives should "submit graciously" to their husbands.[43]

Of course there might be other issues on which liberals could find common ground with multiculturalists who disregard women's perspectives. Liberals might, for example, share with multiculturalists a belief that, as a matter of justice, some cultural minorities deserve protection from the larger society as compensation for a past history of unjust treatment by the larger society. Liberals might also share the common multiculturalist worry that small, fragile cultural minorities will disappear if their ways of life are not shielded from regulation by a vastly more powerful surrounding liberal state. To a liberal, these concerns need not be morally irrelevant.

At the same time, however, liberals should not forget to consider the perspectives of minority *women*. Why should a culture's survival or its compensation by the larger society come at the price of the rights and autonomy of its female members? For a liberal, to ignore the perspectives of minority women would be to fall far short of liberalism's own philosophical commitments to respect the perspectives of all persons. It would be to regress back to the shameful period of liberalism's own illiberal past practices.

Thus, a liberal culture should respect and tolerate the practices of cultural minorities in its midst even when those practices violate the rights of females in those minority groups, but only so long as the females themselves choose to participate in those practices and do so under conditions that facilitate autonomy. Those conditions must include the presence of genuine alternatives for the women's choosing, the absence of coercive and manipulative interferences with the women's reflections on their cultural practices, and socialization that is capable of developing in the women real autonomy competency. Without these background conditions to enable the women's choices to be autonomous, liberals are not required to respect those choices on grounds of the autonomous nature of the choices (although they might be required to respect them for other reasons).

Two final issues must be addressed. First, my recommendation does not consider the complexities involved when cultural practices violate the rights of its girl children, its female members below the age of majority. Many cultural practices are imposed on females well before they are adults. Female genital surgery and very early forced marriage are two such examples. There is good reason to doubt that females (or males, for that matter) at these preteen ages could make genuinely autonomous choices. They would not have sufficiently developed their capacities for self-reflection, for understanding their alternative options, or for being able to make choices on the basis of their own values and concerns. They might not be free of manipulation or coercion, and they would hardly be able to persist in pursuing what they care about in the face of a minimum of opposition from others. How should liberalism deal with minority cultural practices that violate the human rights of female (or male) minority children?[44]

One possibility is that the attitudes of adult women in a cultural minority could function to represent the attitudes of the girl children regarding the cultural practices that violate the human rights of those children. On my individualistic account of personal autonomy, however, this view is precluded. Someone's autonomous choice could be represented by another party only if that other party had been "authorized" by the original person to represent the original person's position. If children are incapable of autonomy, they certainly are also incapable of authorizing anyone to represent their autonomous choices. There are reasons to entrust the care and social representation of children's interests to certain adults, usually their parents, but these reasons are not based on the presumed autonomy of, or authorization by, the children. There seems to be no way around the conclusion that in the case of cultural minority practices that seem to violate the human rights of girls in the minority group, the surrounding liberal society must decide whether to tolerate those practices based on considerations other than the (present) autonomy of the girls or the autonomy of the women in the culture who may endorse the practices. The case of children is a continual challenge to liberal notions of political legitimacy, rights, and autonomy; it is an issue that will have to be addressed elsewhere.

The second final point to consider is a seeming inconsistency between my recommendation in this chapter that liberal systems tolerate some cultural minority practices that violate women's rights and my defense, in chapter 7, of the use of mandatory domestic violence legal procedures even in the face of rejection of those procedures by abused women. Why should it be all right for a liberal political system to be swayed by the choices of women in cultural minorities to live with rights-violating practices but not be swayed in the culture at large (as I argued in chapter 7) by the choices of women who choose to continue living with their abusers and to shield them from legal sanctions?

My answer is twofold. First, while woman abuse may indeed be a widespread practice in a particular culture, it is not the sort of practice that constitutes a tradition in the honorific sense of the term. By "tradition in the honorific sense of the term," I mean practices that are ritualized or ceremonial in nature, that involve people engaging together in shared and repeated patterns of complementary activity, or that partly define a culture or gives it its distinctive identity. Woman abuse, to be sure, is a tolerated *practice* in many, if not most, cultures. This is not, however, sufficient to warrant protection from a larger liberal system as a cultural *tradition* in the honorific sense. Thus, my recommendations regarding the legal treatment of woman abusers are meant to apply to liberal societies at large across all their internal cultural barriers and are not affected by the arguments in this chapter, which pertain to cultural traditions in the honorific sense.

Second, I assume that woman abuse is not a practice that the women of any culture would choose to uphold. At most, I expect, many individual women are resigned in the face of it and feel that they must endure it, that there are no alternatives. As I suggested in chapter 7, individual women may have prudent reasons, under constrained circumstances, for acquiescing in domestic abuse from their male partners, for example, financial dependence, worries about children, and fears of retaliatory violence should they leave their abusers. None of these attitudes suggest that women, under conditions that promoted their autonomy competency and provided genuine alternative options they could actually choose, would choose to be treated abusively. Thus, the requirement I defend in this chapter as a justification for tolerating cultural minority practices by a liberal society, namely, that the women of the minority group choose under autonomy-promoting conditions to live with those practices, would hardly be met by the practices of woman abuse, whether these practices took place in cultural minorities or in the larger liberal society.

In this book, I have presented a conception of autonomy based on a core idea of self-reflection. I defended that conception against a variety of objections that could be raised against it and explored its significance in a number of contexts ranging from romantic love and intimacy to large-scale political practice. I paid particular attention to the significance of autonomy for women and I aimed especially to show how a socially embedded yet individualized ideal of autonomy could be of great value to women struggling finally to end gender domination.

Notes

Chapter 1

1. For stylistic reasons, I shall not always use both terms, "choice" and "action," and I shall interchange the terms "actions" and "behavior" as if they were equivalent. Choices may be autonomous, even if someone is blocked by circumstances from carrying out her choice effectively in action. As I use the term "behavior," it may pick out actions collectively or choices and actions collectively. What makes any of these autonomous are, I maintain, the same sorts of features. The distinctions between these notions are, therefore, not significant to my account of what autonomy is.

2. See, for example, Harry Frankfurt, "Freedom of the Will and the Concept of a Person," *Journal of Philosophy* 68 (1971): 5–20; Harry Frankfurt, *The Importance of What We Care About: Philosophical Essays* (Cambridge: Cambridge University Press, 1988); Gerald Dworkin, *The Theory and Practice of Autonomy* (Cambridge: Cambridge University Press, 1988); various of the essays in John Christman, ed., *The Inner Citadel: Essays on Individual Autonomy* (New York: Oxford University Press, 1989); and John Christman, "Autonomy and Personal History," *Canadian Journal of Philosophy* 21 (1991): 1–24.

3. Charles Taylor has attempted to articulate the sort of autonomy that is possible when we choose how to cope with momentous life choices for which our prior articulated commitments give us inadequate guidance. See, for example, Charles Taylor, "What Is Human Agency?" in Human Agency and Language, Vol. 1 of Charles Taylor, *Philosophical Papers* (New York: Cambridge University Press, 1985), pp. 15–44. The novelty in such choices is different from choices in which our prior commitments, concerns, or sense of self give us adequate but routine guidance.

4. John Christman, "Autonomy and Personal History."

5. I myself once asked this same question of similar accounts by Frankfurt and Dworkin; Marilyn Friedman, "Autonomy and the Split-Level Self," *Southern Journal of Philosophy* 24, 1 (1986): 19–35.

6. Joseph Raz, *Engaging Reason: On the Theory of Value and Action* (Oxford: Oxford University Press, 1999), pp. 22–23.

7. Harry Frankfurt, by contrast, construes the requisite reflection as a matter of volition. See Harry Frankfurt, *Necessity, Volition, and Love* (Cambridge: Cambridge University Press, 1998).

8. Richard Rorty expresses and addresses these concerns in *Contingency, Irony, and Solidarity* (Cambridge: Cambridge University Press, 1989).

9. Rosalind Hursthouse, "Arational Action," *Journal of Philosophy* 88, 2 (February 1991): 57–68.

10. Bennett W. Helm, "Integration and Fragmentation of the Self," *Southern Journal of Philosophy* 34 (1996): 43–63; and Bennett W. Helm, "Freedom of the Heart," *Pacific Philosophical Quarterly* 77 (1996): 71–87.

11. See, for example, Catriona Mackenzie, "Imagining Oneself Otherwise," *Relational Autonomy: Feminist Perspectives on Autonomy, Agency, and the Social Self* (Oxford: Oxford University Press, 2000), pp. 124–50.

12. The classic sources on this subject are Alasdair MacIntyre, *After Virtue*, 2nd ed. (South Bend, Ind.: University of Notre Dame Press, 1987); and Michael Sandel, *Liberalism and the Limits of Justice* (Cambridge: Cambridge University Press, 1982).

13. MacIntyre, *After Virtue*, pp. 220–21.

14. Michael Sandel, *Liberalism and the Limits of Justice*, p. 179.

15. I borrow the term "autonomy competency" from Diana Meyers, *Self, Society, and Personal Choice* (New York: Columbia University Press, 1989). My account differs somewhat from hers, however.

16. See chapter 4 for a fuller discussion of the social reconceptualization of autonomy and for references to relevant literature.

17. My account of autonomy does not construe autonomy competency in terms of the ability to give an account of oneself to others. For an excellent example of this last view, however, see Joel Anderson, "A Social Conception of Personal Autonomy: Volitional Identities, Strong Evaluation, and Intersubjective Accountability" (Ph.D. diss., Northwestern University, 1996). For an analysis of theories of autonomy that require accountability to others, see Margaret Walker, *Moral Understandings: A Feminist Study in Ethics* (New York: Routledge, 1998), pp. 150–52.

18. See Steven Lukes, "The Meanings of Individualism," in *Figures on the Horizon*, ed. Jerrold Siegal (Rochester, N.Y.: University of Rochester Press, 1993), pp. 1–22.

19. See chapter 3 for the argument that nonselfish individualistic dimensions of autonomy are part of what makes autonomy advantageous as an ideal for members of subordinated and oppressed social groups.

20. Joseph Raz construes autonomous persons as "part creators of their own moral world"; Joseph Raz, *The Morality of Freedom* (Oxford: Clarendon Press, 1986), p. 154.

21. Marina Oshana's discussion of this issue is very helpful; see Marina Oshana, "Personal Autonomy and Society," *Journal of Social Philosophy* 29 (spring 1998): 94–95.

22. See Jon Elster, "Sour Grapes—Utilitarianism and the Genesis of Wants," in *The Inner Citadel: Essays on Individual Autonomy*, ed. John Christman (New York: Oxford University Press, 1989), pp. 170–88.

23. For defenses of substantive conceptions of autonomy, see Paul Benson, "Feminist Second Thoughts about Free Agency," *Hypatia* 3 (1990): 47–64; Paul

Benson, "Autonomy and Oppressive Socialization," *Social Theory and Practice* 17 (1991): 385–408; Sarah Buss, "Autonomy Reconsidered," *Midwest Studies in Philosophy* 19 (1994): 95–121; and Sigurdur Kristinsson, "The Limits of Neutrality: Toward a Weekly Substantive Account of Autonomy," *Canadian Journal of Philosophy* 30, 2 (June 2000): 257–86.

24. John Kultgen, *Autonomy and Intervention: Parentalism in the Caring Life* (New York: Oxford University Press, 1995).

25. This caution is presumptive but not necessarily decisive. Whether it is the last word on how to treat someone under specific conditions depends on the nature of the conditions and on the full meaning and consequences of the treatment. In chapter 7, I will argue for an important exception to this presumption for contexts of domestic violence.

26. Perhaps no form of respect should require manifest autonomy. I postpone this issue for another time.

27. Natalie Stoljar, "Autonomy and the Feminist Intuition," in *Relational Autonomy: Feminist Perspectives on Autonomy, Agency, and the Social Self*, ed. Catriona Mackenzie and Natalie Stoljar (New York: Oxford, 2000), p. 95.

28. Raz, *The Morality of Freedom*, pp. 373–74.

29. Hannah Arendt, *Eichmann in Jerusalem: A Report on the Banality of Evil* (New York: Viking Press, 1964), p. 233.

30. Charles Taylor, "Responsibility for Self," in *The Identities of Persons*, ed. Amelie Oksenberg Rorty (Berkeley: University of California Press, 1976), pp. 281–99.

31. These thoughts are indebted to Claudia Card's work on evil; see Claudia Card, "Complicity and Gray Zones" (unpublished ms., 1999).

Chapter 2

1. Daniel C. Dennett, *Consciousness Explained* (Boston: Little, Brown, 1991), esp. chap. 13, "The Reality of Selves."

2. Judith Butler, *Gender Trouble: Feminism and the Subversion of Identity* (New York: Routledge, 1990).

3. Obviously this consideration is not sufficient to warrant the assumption that there are selves.

4. Of course, they need not be attributable to her alone. They should, however, be attributable to her separately from their attribution to other persons.

5. Dennett, *Consciousness*, p. 418. Italics mine.

6. Ibid., pp. 428–29. Italics mine except for "*representation*."

7. Ibid., p. 418.

8. Ibid., p. 413.

9. Ibid., p. 76.

10. Butler, *Gender Trouble*, p. 144.

11. Ibid., p. 145.

12. Ibid.

13. Dennett, *Consciousness*, p. 418.

14. Ibid., p. 241.

15. The degree of emphasis on selves can, of course, vary and individual human identity can incorporate some degree of emphasis on interrelationships with other human beings.

16. There is no problem in my continuing to use "we" language to describe how selves are constructed, since I do not advocate or rely on the assumption that selves are *merely* discursive or narrative constructs.

17. The other version of this argument is that selves in themselves lack capacities for doing what autonomy requires, in particular for accurately understanding themselves. I take up this objection next.

18. I discuss the social reconceptualization of autonomy in chapters 4 and 5. I argue, for one thing, that the required social context or antecedents of autonomy do not preclude the role of individuation in autonomy.

19. See John Christman, "Autonomy and Personal History," *Canadian Journal of Philosophy* 21 (March 1991): 1–24.

20. Jean Grimshaw, "Autonomy and Identity in Feminist Thinking," in *Feminist Perspectives in Philosophy,* ed. Morwenna Griffiths and Margaret Whitford (Bloomington: Indiana University Press, 1988), pp. 90–108. See also Axel Honneth, "Decentered Autonomy: The Subject after the Fall," trans. John Farrell, in Axel Honneth, *The Fragmented World of the Social,* ed. Charles W. Wright (Albany: SUNY Press, 1995), pp. 261–71.

21. Lee Ross and Richard E. Nisbett, *The Person and the Situation: Perspectives of Social Psychology* (Philadelphia: Temple University Press, 1991), pp. 139, 8–9, and 4. I am grateful to Eddy Nahmias for bringing this literature to my attention.

22. Ibid., pp. 79–81.

23. Ibid., pp. 138–39, 150.

24. Ibid., pp. 79–81.

25. Ibid., pp. 11–13, 163–67, 19.

26. It is not clear why Ross and Nisbett think that attributing goals and preferences does not commit the fundamental attribution error while attributing (other) personality traits does do so; this may be an inconsistency in their account.

27. Lorraine Code, "The Perversion of Autonomy and the Subjection of Women: Discourses of Social Advocacy at Century's End," in *Relational Autonomy: Feminist Perspectives on Autonomy, Agency, and the Social Self,* ed. Catriona Mackenzie and Natalie Stoljar (Oxford: Oxford University Press, 2000), pp. 181–209.

28. In chapter 4, I contest this interpretation of mainstream autonomy theory. Citations to the critical literature and to mainstream literature are given there.

29. Code, "Perversion of Autonomy," p. 200.

30. The philosophers that Walker mentions are Charles Taylor, Bernard Williams, and John Rawls; *Moral Understandings,* p. 132.

31. For a challenging example of one that does, see Joel Anderson, "A Social Conception of Personal Autonomy: Volitional Identity, Strong Evaluation, and Intersubjective Accountability" (Ph.D. diss., Northwestern University, 1996).

32. An exception must be noted for moral autonomy. Moral autonomy relies on moral understanding, which, in turn, depends crucially on taking account of others, their wants, needs, values, commitments, and so on. Taking account of others morally, however, is not a pejorative sort of "accountability" to them. Because moral autonomy is about being able to recognize on one's own how to treat *others,* those others are owed an account of one's moral perspective and reflections.

33. For black and white perspectives on whether the American dream is accessible to African Americans, see Jennifer Hochschild, *Facing Up to the American*

Dream: Race, Class, and the Soul of the Nation (Princeton, N.J.: Princeton University Press, 1995).

34. Margaret Walker calls this model of autonomy the "career self"; see Margaret Walker, *Moral Understandings: A Feminist Study in Ethics* (New York: Routledge, 1998), chap. 6.

35. This sometimes seems to be the message of Code's "Perversion of Autonomy."

36. Michael J. Sandel, *Democracy's Discontent: America in Search of a Public Philosophy* (Cambridge, Mass.: Belknap Press, 1996).

37. Nancy Fraser and Linda Gordon, "A Genealogy of Dependency: Tracing a Keyword of the U.S. Welfare State," *Signs: Journal of Women in Culture and Society* 19, 2 (1994): 309–36.

38. Ibid., pp. 194–97.

39. See Iris Marion Young, "Mothers, Citizenship, and Independence: A Critique of Pure Family Values," in Iris Marion Young, *Intersecting Voices: Dilemmas of Gender, Political Philosophy, and Policy* (Princeton N.J.: Princeton University Press, 1997), pp. 114–33.

40. Ibid., pp. 200–201.

41. Many theorists have argued that it is crucial to women's well-being to have their own sources of income. This is not, in any sense, a denigration of women who lack their own sources of income. It is a view about the social conditions under which women are more able and likely to live lives that accord with their own values and in which they will thrive. See Susan Moller Okin, *Justice, Gender, and the Family* (New York: Basic Books, 1989).

42. The problems with welfare cutbacks have to be argued in terms of the nature and impact of those programs themselves and the values that the cuts actually embody.

43. Cf. Abraham Maslow, *Motivation and Personality*, 2nd ed. (New York: Harper & Row, 1970); Carl Rogers, *Carl Rogers on Personal Power: Inner Strength and Its Revolutionary Impact* (London: Constable, 1978); and a discussion by Jean Grimshaw, *Philosophy and Feminist Thinking* (Minneapolis: University of Minnesota Press, 1986), chap. 5.

44. Whether or not my survival takes priority over my moral autonomy is a very different question, and I do not discuss it here.

45. Rawls, *Theory of Justice*; Raz, *Morality of Freedom*. For a discussion critical of the liberal emphasis on autonomy, see John Kekes, *Against Liberalism* (Ithaca, N.Y.: Cornell University Press, 1997).

46. Audre Lorde, "The Master's Tools Will Never Dismantle the Master's House," *Sister Outsider* (Freedom, Calif.: Crossing Press, 1984), pp. 110–13.

47. Niccolo Machiavelli, *The Prince*, reprinted in *Modern Moral and Political Philosophy*, ed. Robert C. Cummins and Thomas D. Christiano (London: Mayfield, 1999), pp. 25–28.

Chapter 3

1. Of course, the actor could not be thinking this thought or else the yielding of control would be intended for a reason and would thereby reflect the actor's intentions, and not really be nonautonomous after all.

2. I expand the ideas of this section in chapter 5.

3. John Stuart Mill, *On Liberty,* ed. Elizabeth Rapaport (Indianapolis: Hackett, 1978).

4. I argue in chapter 5 and elsewhere that autonomy as a tool or means of social criticism does not inherently have untoward side effects.

5. Henry David Thoreau, "On Civil Disobedience," in *Social and Political Philosophy: Readings from Plato to Gandhi,* ed. John Somerville and Ronald E. Santoni (Garden City, N.Y.: Anchor Books, 1963), pp. 282–301; quote is from p. 287.

6. Jerome Schneewind, *The Invention of Autonomy: A History of Modern Moral Philosophy* (Cambridge: Cambridge University Press, 1998).

7. Philip Pettit defends a form of republicanism that centers on the notion of freedom from domination; see Philip Pettit, *Republicanism: A Theory of Freedom and Government* (Oxford: Clarendon Press, 1997).

8. One might, of course, think the wants and values of others were morally superior to one's own and submit to those others for that reason; but such submissiveness would be at least partly voluntary based on one's own convictions and therefore would not constitute true subordination.

9. Of course, this framework is itself open to critical assessment. Someone with an autonomous perspective might take up the challenge. I do not do so because I do not regard the individualized aspects of this framework as a problem, so long as we also emphasize the social dimensions of moral competence.

10. This point is one of the general themes of Margaret Walker, *Moral Understandings: A Feminist Study in Ethics* (New York: Routledge, 1998).

11. See Leslie Pickering Francis, "Decisionmaking at the End of Life: Patients with Alzheimer's or Other Dementias," *Georgia Law Review* 35, no. 2 (winter 2001), esp. pp. 542–46.

12. See the citations at the beginning of chapter 4.

13. There is an enlarged sense of "need" in which we all need all these things to end. Here, however, I use the term "need" in a sense more narrowly attached to direct self-interest.

14. The importance of communal ties to social movements is brought out in Sara M. Evans and Harry C. Boyte, *Free Spaces: The Sources of Democratic Change in America* (New York: Harper & Row, 1986).

15. Claudia Card has made this point in colloquium presentations and private correspondence.

16. Sometimes a person wants to act or to be treated in ways that would undermine her autonomy. Respecting and abiding by her actual preferences on those sorts of occasions would diminish her future autonomy. This poses a dilemma for content-neutral accounts of autonomy. In chapters 7 and 9, I discuss examples of this sort of situation dealing with domestic violence and minority cultural traditions, respectively. In both cases, my recommendation is to try as far as possible to respect and abide by women's autonomy-undermining preferences unless this approach threatens serious harm to the woman herself or to third parties.

17. For a helpful discussion of this principle, see Jeremy Waldron, *Liberal Rights: Collected Papers 1981–1991* (Cambridge: Cambridge University Press, 1993), chap. 2.

18. The obvious source on this topic is John Rawls, *Political Liberalism* (New York: Columbia University Press, 1996).

19. I discuss this in more detail in chapter 8.

20. Most liberal theorists presume an adult population when discussing legitimacy, but rarely say so explicitly. I explicitly make the assumption here.

Chapter 4

1. Sharon Bishop Hill, "Self-determination and Autonomy," in *Today's Moral Problems*, 3rd ed., ed. Richard Wasserstrom (New York: Macmillan, 1985), pp. 55–70. Cf. Jean Grimshaw, "Autonomy and Identity in Feminist Thinking," in *Feminist Perspectives in Philosophy*, ed. Morwenna Griffiths and Margaret Whitford (Bloomington: Indiana University Press, 1988), pp. 90–108.

2. Evelyn Fox Keller, *Reflections on Gender and Science* (New Haven, Conn.: Yale University Press, 1985); Sarah Hoagland, *Lesbian Ethics: Toward New Value* (Palo Alto, Calif.: Institute for Lesbian Studies, 1988); Jennifer Nedelsky, "Reconceiving Autonomy: Sources, Thoughts, and Possibilities," *Yale Journal of Law and Feminism* 1 (1989): 7–36, Lorraine Code, "Second Persons," in Lorraine Code, *What Can She Know? Feminist Theory and the Construction of Knowledge* (Ithaca, N.Y.: Cornell University Press, 1991), pp. 71–109; Seyla Benhabib, "The Generalized and the Concrete Other: The Kohlberg-Gilligan Controversy and Moral Theory," in Seyla Benhabib, *Situating the Self: Gender, Community and Postmodernism in Contemporary Ethics* (New York: Routledge, 1992), pp. 148–77.

3. Diana T. Meyers, *Self, Society, and Personal Choice* (New York: Columbia University Press, 1989), Lynn Arnault, "The Radical Future of a Classic Moral Theory," in *Gender/Body/Knowledge: Feminist Reconstructions of Being and Knowing*, ed. Alison Jaggar and Susan R. Bordo (New Brunswick: Rutgers University Press, 1989), pp. 188–206; Code, *What Can She Know?*; Trudy Govier, "Self-Trust, Autonomy, and Self-Esteem," *Hypatia* 8 (winter 1993): 99–120; Johanna Meehan, "Autonomy, Recognition and Respect: Habermas, Benjamin and Honneth," *Constellations* 1 (1994): 270–85; and Patricia Huntington, "Toward a Dialectical Concept of Autonomy," *Philosophy and Social Criticism* 21 (1995): 37–55.

4. Judith Butler, *Gender Trouble: Feminism and the Subversion of Identity* (New York: Routledge, 1990).

5. Grimshaw, "Autonomy and Identity."

6. Code, "Second Persons."

7. Keller, *Gender and Science*; Benhabib, "The Generalized and the Concrete Other"; Hoagland, *Lesbian Ethics*; Nedelsky, "Reconceiving Autonomy"; Code, "Second Persons."

8. Alison Jaggar, *Feminist Politics and Human Nature* (Totowa, N.J.: Rowman & Allanheld, 1983); Code, "Second Persons"; and Nedelsky, "Reconceiving Autonomy."

9. Carol Gilligan, *In a Different Voice: Psychological Theory and Women's Development* (Cambridge, Mass.: Harvard University Press, 1982), chap. 1.

10. Jean Baker Miller, *Toward a New Psychology of Women* (Boston: Beacon Press, 1976).

11. Nancy Chodorow, *The Reproduction of Mothering: Psychoanalysis and the Sociology of Gender* (Berkeley: University of California Press, 1978); Nancy Chodorow, "Gender, Relation, and Difference in Psychoanalytic Perspective," in *The Future of Difference*, ed. Hester Eisenstein and Alice Jardine (New Brunswick, N.J.: Rutgers University Press, 1985), pp. 3–19; Gilligan, *In a Different Voice*; and

cf. Jessica Benjamin, "The Bonds of Love: Rational Violence and Erotic Domination," in *The Future of Difference*, ed. Eisenstein and Jardine, pp. 41–70.

12. Chodorow, "Gender, Relation, and Difference."

13. Gilligan, *Different Voice*, p. 18.

14. Ibid., p. 48.

15. Hoagland, *Lesbian Ethics*, pp. 144–47.

16. Keller, *Gender and Science*, pp. 97–99.

17. Ibid., pp. 112–13.

18. Nedelsky, "Reconceiving Autonomy," pp. 7–11.

19. Ibid., pp. 12–15.

20. Ibid., p. 21.

21. Ibid., pp. 33–34.

22. Ibid., pp. 35–36.

23. Code, "Second Persons," pp. 73–74.

24. Ibid., pp. 77–78.

25. Ibid., pp. 78–79.

26. Ibid., p. 80.

27. Ibid., pp. 82–85; cf. Annette Baier, "Cartesian Persons," in Annette Baier, *Postures of the Mind: Essays on Mind and Morals* (Minneapolis: University of Minnesota Press, 1985), p. 84.

28. Code, "Second Persons," pp. 87–94.

29. Ibid., p. 108.

30. Benhabib, "The Generalized and the Concrete Other," pp. 155–57.

31. Thomas Hobbes, "Philosophical Rudiments Concerning Government and Society," in *The English Works of Thomas Hobbes*, ed. W. Molesworth (Darmstadt: Wissenschaftliche Buchgesellschaft, 1966), p. 109.

32. John Rawls, *A Theory of Justice* (Cambridge, Mass.: Harvard University Press, 1971), p. 128. More recently, Rawls has stated his view in a different way: those who choose principles of justice behind the veil of ignorance are indeed to regard themselves as persons who have what Rawls terms "nonpolitical" moral commitments, including commitments and attachments to other persons. When choosing principles of justice, however, a person is not to *appeal* to her nonpolitical moral commitments as reasons for the choice of any particular principles of justice, since those moral commitments might reflect social or historical advantages that could bias her choice of principles of justice in favor of her particular social location; John Rawls, *Political Liberalism* (New York: Columbia University Press, 1996), pp. 22–35.

33. Thomas Hobbes, *Leviathan*, ed. Michael Oakeshott (New York: Collier Macmillan, 1962), p. 100.

34. Benhabib, "The Generalized and the Concrete Other," p. 155.

35. Ibid., p. 157.

36. Thanks to Claudia Card for suggesting that feminist and mainstream conceptions of autonomy can be thought of as "converging" on the same view.

Some mainstream philosophers deny that the traditional notion of autonomy, even in its rigorous Kantian formulation, ever really excluded or ignored the importance of interpersonal relationships; J. B. Schneewind, "The Use of Autonomy in Ethical Theory," in *Reconstructing Individualism: Autonomy, Individuality, and the Self in Western Theory*, ed. Thomas C. Heller, Morton Sosna, and David E. Wellbery (Stanford, Calif.: Stanford University Press, 1986), pp. 64–75; Thomas

E. Hill Jr., "The Importance of Autonomy," in Thomas E. Hill Jr., *Autonomy and Self-Respect* (Cambridge: Cambridge University Press, 1987), pp. 43–51.

37. Dworkin, *Theory and Practice,* p. 8.

38. Ibid., p. 12.

39. Ibid., pp. 21–23.

40. Ibid., p. 15.

41. Ibid., p. 23.

42. Ibid., pp. 30–31.

43. Ibid., p. 36.

44. Thomas E. Hill Jr., "Importance," pp. 49–50.

45. Lawrence Haworth, *Autonomy: An Essay in Philosophical Psychology and Ethics* (New Haven, Conn.: Yale University Press, 1986), pp. 201–202.

46. Joel Feinberg, "Autonomy," in *The Inner Citadel: Essays on Individual Autonomy,* ed. John Christman (New York: Oxford University Press, 1989), pp. 31–43; reprinted from Joel Feinberg, *Harm to Self* (New York: Oxford University Press, 1986).

47. Ibid., p. 33.

48. Ibid., p. 45.

49. S. I. Benn, "Individuality, Autonomy, and Community," in *Community as a Social Ideal,* ed. Eugene Kamenka (New York: St. Martin's Press, 1982), pp. 43–44.

50. Ibid., p. 50.

51. Ibid., pp. 57–61.

52. S. I. Benn, "Freedom, Autonomy, and the Concept of a Person," *Proceedings of the Aristotelian Society* 76 (12 January 1976): 125–26.

53. Ibid., p. 126.

54. Ibid., p. 128.

55. Ibid., pp. 129–30.

56. R. S. Peters, "Freedom and the Development of the Free Man," in *Educational Judgments: Papers in the Philosophy of Education,* ed. James F. Doyle (London: Routledge & Kegan Paul, 1973), pp. 129–30. As the title of the essay indicates, this essay did not use gender-neutral language. Like other writings of its time, the essay contributed to the tendency to think of (certain) males as the paradigm exemplars of ideals such as autonomy. My point in the text still stands, however. The essay does show awareness of the social conditions needed for the emergence of autonomy competency, even in male exemplars of it.

57. Ibid., pp. 134–35.

58. In addition to the works cited earlier, recent feminist work concerning a relational or intersubjective conception of autonomy includes: Meyers, *Self, Society;* Meehan, "Autonomy, Recognition, and Respect"; Huntington, "Toward a Dialectical Concept"; and John Christman, "Feminism and Autonomy," in *Nagging Questions: Feminist Ethics and Everyday Life,* ed. Dana Bushnell (Lanham, Md.: Rowman & Littlefield, 1995), pp. 17–39. Recent work that is not specifically feminist (though also not antifeminist) includes Marina A. L. Oshana, "Personal Autonomy and Society," *Journal of Social Philosophy* 29 (spring 1998): 81–102; and Joel Anderson, "A Social Conception of Personal Autonomy: Volitional Identity, Strong Evaluation, and Intersubjective Accountability" (Ph.D. dissertation, Northwestern University, 1996). The four concerns that I present in this section are partly drawn from these sources.

59. Harry G. Frankfurt, *The Importance of What We Care About* (Cambridge: Cambridge University Press, 1988); and Harry G. Frankfurt, *Necessity, Volition, and Love* (Cambridge: Cambridge University Press, 1999).

60. Feinberg, "Autonomy," p. 33.

61. Ibid., p. 31.

62. Benn, "Freedom," pp. 129–30; Dworkin, *Theory and Practice*, pp. 23–30; Feinberg, "Autonomy," pp. 38–39.

63. For an argument that substantively neutral accounts of autonomy are inadequate, see Oshana, "Personal Autonomy," and my chapter 1. Note that Dworkin (*Theory and Practice*, p. 29) does admit to believing that there are *contingent* connections between autonomy and the sort of substantive independence that involves a reluctance to accept authority, tradition, and custom uncritically. (I am grateful to Joel Anderson for bringing this point to my attention.)

64. Meyers, *Self, Society*, pp. 141–71.

65. Hoagland, *Lesbian Ethics*.

66. Sara Ruddick, *Maternal Thinking: Toward a Politics of Peace* (New York: Ballantine Books, 1989).

67. Oshana, "Personal Autonomy," p. 97.

68. Nedelsky, "Reconceiving Autonomy," p. 36; italics mine.

69. Charles Taylor, "Atomism," in Charles Taylor, *Philosophy and the Human Sciences*, Vol. 2 of *Philosophical Papers* (Cambridge: Cambridge University Press, 1985); reprinted from *Powers, Possessions, and Freedoms*, ed. Alkis Kontos (Toronto: University of Toronto Press, 1979).

70. Jürgen Habermas, "Individuation through Socialization: On George Herbert Mead's Theory of Subjectivity," in Jürgen Habermas, *Postmetaphysical Thinking: Philosophical Essays*, trans. William Mark Hohengarten (Cambridge: MIT Press, 1992).

71. Anderson, "Social Conception," esp. chaps. 1 and 7.

72. Oshana, "Personal Autonomy," pp. 94–95.

73. Although I myself reject this view, I believe it calls for more discussion.

Chapter 5

1. Yann le Pichon, *Gauguin: Life, Art, Inspiration* (New York: Harry N. Abrams, 1987), p. 26.

2. Bernard Williams's discussion of moral luck deploys the hypothetical biography of an artist whose life resembles that of the historic Gauguin; see Bernard Williams, "Moral Luck," in *Moral Luck* (Cambridge: Cambridge University Press, 1981), p. 37. See my discussion of Williams on the Gauguin-like example in my *What Are Friends For?: Feminist Perspectives on Personal Relationships and Moral Theory* (Ithaca, N.Y.: Cornell University Press, 1993), pp. 163–70.

3. Gauguin's art did not sell well during his lifetime, and he struggled and starved. Autonomous pursuits do not necessarily bring material comfort. Nevertheless, Gauguin's struggles to paint reinforce the seemingly heroic nature of his autonomous quest to dedicate himself to art. The hardships imposed on his abandoned family have not lessened that aura.

4. See the germinal work on this topic by Carol Gilligan, *In a Different Voice* (Cambridge, Mass.: Harvard University Press, 1982); and Nel Noddings, *Caring: A Feminine Approach to Ethics & Moral Education* (Berkeley: University of California Press, 1984).

5. See Susan Faludi's discussion of the popularization of research results alleging that women's chances of marrying fall precipitously after age forty: *Backlash: The Undeclared War against American Women* (New York: Crown Publishers, 1991), chap. 1. Faludi argues persuasively that the conclusions were misrepresented in mass media. My point is a different one: such research results would not have received such media coverage if it hadn't been for the presumption that people, including women, would want to know about such things.

6. See Gilligan, *Different Voice*, chap. 1.

7. See, for example, Helen Longino, *Science as Social Knowledge* (Princeton, N.J.: Princeton University Press, 1990).

8. Morwenna Griffiths explores the importance of narratives in the cultural understanding of autonomy in her *Feminisms and the Self: The Web of Identity* (London: Routledge, 1995).

9. Susan Brison, "Surviving Sexual Violence," *Journal of Social Philosophy* 24 (spring 1993): 5–22.

10. Patricia Hill Collins, *Black Feminist Thought: Knowledge, Consciousness, and the Politics of Empowerment* (New York: Routledge, 1991), esp. chaps. 4 and 5.

11. Minnie Bruce Pratt, "Identity: Skin Blood Heart," in *Yours in Struggle: Three Feminist Perspectives on Anti-Semitism and Racism*, ed. Elly Bulkin, Minnie Bruce Pratt, and Barbara Smith (Brooklyn, N.Y.: Long Haul Press, 1984), pp. 9–63.

12. Sara Ruddick, *Maternal Thinking: Toward a Politics of Peace* (New York: Ballantine Books, 1989).

13. The chancellor at a university near my own, for example, was recently fired by his university's governing board. The faculty members who supported him thought the problem was, as one of them put it, that the chancellor was "too autonomous, too independent." Faculty supporters described the governing board as wanting a "team player" instead. (See Susan C. Thomson and Kim Bell, "Mizzou Chancellor Wants Buyout," *St. Louis Post-Dispatch*, 14 June 1996, p. C7.) Note that the figure of a "team player" is a historically *masculine* metaphor for a cooperative social agent. The differences between women's and men's paradigm images of social cooperation deserve some study.

14. Michael J. Sandel, *Liberalism and the Limits of Justice* (Cambridge: Cambridge University Press, 1982); and Alasdair MacIntyre, *After Virtue,* 2nd ed. (South Bend, Ind.: University of Notre Dame Press, 1984).

15. Loren E. Lomasky, *Persons, Rights, and the Moral Community* (New York: Oxford University Press, 1987), p. 249. On the now-common content-neutral approach to autonomy, a view that I share, no particular choices are intrinsic to autonomy. An autonomous person might embrace traditional relationships, reject traditional relationships, welcome the Red Guards, or abhor the Red Guards. What matters is how she arrived at her political views and whether those views reflect her own considered convictions. Lomasky construes autonomy as a failing only of those who make political choices he rejects, but this is just as mistaken as assuming that autonomy is a virtue only of those who make what one considers to be the right political choices.

16. Genevieve Lloyd, *The Man of Reason: "Male" and "Female" in Western Philosophy* (Minneapolis: University of Minnesota Press, 1984). See also Lorraine Code, *Rhetorical Spaces: Essays on Gendered Locations* (New York: Routledge, 1995), esp. chap. 10, "Critiques of Pure Reason."

17. Feminist sources include Code, *Rhetorical Spaces;* and Alison M. Jaggar, "Love and Knowledge: Emotion in Feminist Epistemology," in *Gender/Body/ Knowledge,* ed. Alison M. Jaggar and Susan R. Bordo (New Brunswick, N.J.: Rutgers University Press, 1989), pp. 145–71.

Nonfeminist sources include Allan Gibbard, *Wise Choices, Apt Feelings: A Theory of Normative Judgment* (Cambridge, Mass.: Harvard University Press, 1990).

18. A different approach would be to argue that the stereotypic association of women with emotion was always groundless, and that women are as able as men to exercise a narrowly cognitive mode of reason. See Louise M. Antony and Charlotte Witt, eds., *A Mind of One's Own: Feminist Essays on Reason and Objectivity* (Boulder, Colo.: Westview Press, 1993), esp. the essays by Margaret Atherton and Louise Antony. See the discussion of these essays by Code, *Rhetorical Spaces,* pp. 217–223.

19. See Susan Golombok and Robyn Fivush, *Gender Development* (Cambridge: Cambridge University Press, 1994), pp. 7–8.

20. Ibid., p. 18. A social or relational account of autonomy, such as that presented in this chapter, is one that construes social relationships as necessary for autonomy but not sufficient for it. There is nothing about social interconnection as such that entails, causes, or suggests autonomy.

21. Diana T. Meyers, *Self, Society, and Personal Choice* (New York: Columbia University Press, 1989), esp. part 3.

22. This point is, of course, not universal throughout Western cultures. Men of oppressed groups, such as racial minorities, may not have had significantly greater opportunities than the women of their own groups to act and live autonomously.

23. Many feminists have charged the traditional philosophical ideal of autonomy with excessive individualism; see, for example, Lorraine Code, "Second Persons," in Lorraine Code, *What Can She Know?: Feminist Theory and the Construction of Knowledge* (Ithaca, N.Y.: Cornell University Press, 1991), pp. 76–79.

24. See, for example, Evelyn Fox Keller, *Reflections on Gender and Science* (New Haven, Conn.: Yale University Press, 1985); Nancy Chodorow, *The Reproduction of Mothering: Psychoanalysis and the Sociology of Gender* (Berkeley: University of California Press, 1978); and Jessica Benjamin, *The Bonds of Love: Psychoanalysis, Feminism, and the Problem of Domination* (New York: Pantheon, 1988).

25. Annette Baier, "Cartesian Persons," in Annette Baier, *Postures of the Mind: Essays on Mind and Morals* (Minneapolis: University of Minnesota Press, 1985). See also the discussion of this notion in Code, "Second Persons."

26. One prominent philosopher who neglects socialization, and, indeed, social relationships generally, in his account of autonomy is Harry G. Frankfurt; cf. Harry G. Frankfurt, *The Importance of What We Care About* (Cambridge: Cambridge University Press, 1988); and Harry G. Frankfurt, *Necessity, Volition, and Love* (Cambridge: Cambridge University Press, 1999).

27. See the discussion of both of these points by John Christman, "Feminism and Autonomy," in *"Nagging" Questions: Feminist Ethics in Everyday Life,* ed. Dana E. Bushnell (Lanham, Md.: Rowman & Littlefield, 1995), pp. 17–39.

28. Gerald Dworkin provides one example of a content-neutral account of autonomy; see his *The Theory and Practice of Autonomy* (Cambridge: Cambridge University Press, 1988), p. 18, 21–33.

29. See Marina Oshana, "Personal Autonomy and Society," pp. 81–102.

30. Feminist theorists who have developed this view include Keller, *Reflections;* Jennifer Nedelsky, "Reconceiving Autonomy: Sources, Thoughts, and Possibilities," *Yale Journal of Law and Feminism* 1 (spring 1989): 7–36; Meyers, *Self, Society;* and Code, "Second Persons."

Mainstream theorists who have developed this view include Joseph Raz, *The Morality of Freedom* (Oxford: Clarendon Press, 1986); Dworkin, *Theory and Practice;* and Joel Feinberg, "Autonomy," in *The Inner Citadel*, ed. John Christman (New York: Oxford University Press, 1989), pp. 27–53.

For a discussion of the convergence of these two groups around a social conception of autonomy, see Christman, "Feminism and Autonomy," and chapter 4 here.

Some mainstream philosophers deny that the traditional notion of autonomy, even in its rigorous Kantian formulation, ever really excluded or ignored the importance of interpersonal relationships; see J. B. Schneewind, "The Use of Autonomy in Ethical Theory," in *Reconstructing Individualism: Autonomy, Individuality, and the Self in Western Theory*, ed. Thomas C. Heller, Morton Sosna, and David E. Wellbery (Stanford, Calif.: Stanford University Press, 1986); and Thomas E. Hill Jr., "The Importance of Autonomy," in *Autonomy and Self-Respect* (Cambridge: Cambridge University Press, 1991).

31. See, for example, Sandel, *Liberalism,* p. 19.

32. Richard Rorty, *Contingency, Irony, and Solidarity* (Cambridge: Cambridge University Press, 1989).

33. Gerald Dworkin notes the impossibility of creating our own moral principles. Such a requirement "denies our *history*. . . . We . . . are deeply influenced by parents, siblings, peers, culture, class, climate, schools, accident, genes, and the accumulated history of the species. It makes no more sense to suppose we invent the moral law for ourselves than to suppose that we invent the language we speak for ourselves"; *Theory and Practice*, p. 36.

34. Ibid., p. 21.

35. If abusive relationships persist for long periods of time, it is usually because the abused partner has, or thinks she has, no other viable options or because she sacrifices her own well-being to that of her abuser. For a survey of the reasons why longtime battered women finally seek court orders of protection against abusive male partners, see Karla Fischer and Mary Rose, "When 'Enough Is Enough': Battered Women's Decision Making around Court Orders of Protection," *Crime & Delinquency* 41 (October 1995): 414–29. For a detailed discussion of the situation of abused women who remain with their abusive partners, see chapter 7.

36. I do not endorse this maxim; I merely cite it as an example of the strategies that people use to keep disagreements from disrupting social relationships.

37. See Susan J. Brison's discussion of the difficulties that arose in her relationships with family, friends, and others after she was violently raped; "Surviving Sexual Violence."

38. As Dworkin notes, "Those who practice in their daily life a critical reflection on their own value structure will tend to be suspicious of modes of thought that rely on the uncritical acceptance of authority, tradition, and custom"; *Theory and Practice*, p. 29.

39. For further discussion of this theme, see my *What Are Friends For? Feminist Perspectives on Personal Relationships and Moral Theory* (Ithaca, N.Y.: Cornell University Press, 1993), chap. 9.

40. See Alison MacKinnon, *Love and Freedom: Professional Women and the Reshaping of Personal Life* (Cambridge: Cambridge University Press, 1997), on

the hurdles faced by women in Australia at the end of the nineteenth and beginning of the twentieth century who sought higher education and careers outside the home.

41. There are many feminist discussions of problems that women face in social relationships; see, for example, Susan Moller Okin, *Justice, Gender, and the Family* (New York: Basic Books, 1989).

42. See Audre Lorde, "The Master's Tools Will Never Dismantle the Master's House," *Sister Outsider* (Freedom, Calif.: Crossing Press, 1984), pp. 110–113.

43. On this topic, see the essays in Martha Nussbaum and Jonathan Glover, eds., *Women, Culture and Development: A Study of Human Capabilities* (Oxford: Clarendon Press, 1995).

44. See the essays in Penny Weiss and Marilyn Friedman, eds., *Feminism and Community* (Philadelphia: Temple University Press, 1995).

45. See, for example, Robert E. Goodin, *Protecting the Vulnerable: A Reanalysis of Our Social Responsibilities* (Chicago: University of Chicago Press, 1985); Neera Kapur Badhwar, ed., *Friendship: A Philosophical Reader* (Ithaca, N.Y.: Cornell University Press, 1993); and Joan C. Tronto, *Moral Boundaries: A Political Argument for an Ethic of Care* (New York: Routledge, 1994).

46. Should we devalue autonomy for individuals, perhaps recasting it as an ideal for groups only? The notion of group autonomy is extremely important, especially for oppressed groups; see, for example, Laurence Mordekhai Thomas, *Vessels of Evil: American Slavery and the Holocaust* (Philadelphia: Temple University Press, 1993), 182–89. Group autonomy, however, does not necessarily help individuals when they face oppressive conditions in isolation. Group autonomy complements but does not replace individual autonomy.

In addition, group autonomy promotes its own risk of social disruption in the relationships between groups. The possible advantages as well as the possible costs of autonomy's socially disruptive potential simply reappear at a more encompassing level of social integration.

47. I am grateful to Natalie Stoljar and Catriona Mackenzie for helpful editorial suggestions on an earlier draft of this chapter.

Chapter 6

1. Willard Gaylin, *Rediscovering Love* (New York: Viking Penguin, 1986); quoted in Alan Soble, "Union, Autonomy, and Concern," in *Love Analyzed*, ed. Roger E. Lamb (Boulder, Colo.: Westview, 1997), p. 71.

2. Gaylin, *Rediscovering Love*, pp. 20–21, 100, 103.

3. Funk & Wagnalls *Standard Dictionary of the English Language*, International Edition (Chicago: Encyclopaedia Britannica, 1965), pp. 754–55.

4. Roger Scruton, *Sexual Desire* (New York: Free Press, 1986), pp. 231, 241.

5. Robert Solomon, "The Virtue of (Erotic) Love," in *The Philosophy of (Erotic) Love*, ed. Robert C. Solomon and Kathleen M. Higgins (Lawrence: University Press of Kansas, 1991), p. 511.

6. Robert Nozick, *The Examined Life* (New York: Simon & Schuster, 1989), p. 70.

7. Neil Delaney, "Romantic Love and Loving Commitment: Articulating a Modern Ideal," *American Philosophical Quarterly* 33 (October 1996): 340. The other two interests are to be loved for attributes of certain sorts and to have this love foster and promote a certain type of commitment by the loved one.

8. Nozick, *The Examined Life*, pp. 71–72.

9. Solomon, "Virtue," p. 514.

10. Richard Schmitt, *Beyond Separateness: The Social Nature of Human Beings—Their Autonomy, Knowledge, and Power* (Boulder, Colo.: Westview, 1995), p. 113.

11. Delaney, "Romantic Love," pp. 341–42. Delaney actually talks about "sovereign states" forming a "republican nation."

12. Soble, "Union," pp. 68, 77–92.

13. Nozick, for example, puts the point this way, *Examined Life*, pp. 70–71.

14. Delaney, "Romantic Love," p. 342.

15. Sandra Lee Bartky, *Femininity and Domination: Studies in the Phenomenology of Oppression* (New York: Routledge, 1990), pp. 111–13. This tendency, in Bartky's estimation, raises moral problems for the lover who, in an asymmetric love relationship, provides substantially more care than she receives. I deal with these issues below.

16. Delaney, "Romantic Love," p. 347.

17. Nozick, *Examined Life*, p. 72.

18. Ibid., p. 71

19. Ibid., p. 72.

20. Solomon, "Virtue," p. 511.

21. Nozick, *Examined Life*, p. 86.

22. Scruton, *Sexual Desire*, p. 239.

23. Delaney, "Romantic Love," pp. 343–44. Delaney separates this feature of romantic love from that of merged identity, but it seems to me that it constitutes an element of merged identity. This feature invokes the Aristotelian idea that the best sorts of intimate relationships involve character building as a joint project. They bring out and promote the best in us through the approval and encouragement of those whose attitudes we value because we love and respect them.

24. Bartky, *Femininity*, p. 111.

25. See William Blackstone, *Commentaries on the Laws of England*, 15th ed. (1756; reprint, Oxfordshire: Professional Books, 1982), Vol. 1, pp. 442–45. See the discussion of this view in Deborah L. Rhode, *Justice and Gender* (Cambridge, Mass.: Harvard University Press, 1989), p. 10.

26. In lesbian or gay relationships, power imbalances may well occur, of course, but they do not arise simply from the gender identities of the parties.

27. Simone de Beauvoir, *The Second Sex*, trans. and ed. H. M. Parshley (New York: Alfred A. Knopf, 1952; New York: Vintage Books, 1989), pp. 643, 650, 653 (page citations are to the reprint edition).

28. Shulamith Firestone, *The Dialectic of Sex: The Case for Feminist Revolution* (Toronto: Bantam Books, 1970), p. 127.

29. Jessica Benjamin, *The Bonds of Love: Psychoanalysis, Feminism, and the Problem of Domination* (New York: Pantheon Books, 1988), p. 7.

30. Nozick, *Examined Life*, pp. 73–74.

31. Soble, "Union," pp. 74, 77.

32. Scruton, *Sexual Desire*, p. 240.

33. Francesca Cancian, *Love in America: Gender and Self-Development* (Cambridge: Cambridge University Press, 1987), p. 24.

34. Most philosophers would merely qualify the point by insisting that equality, mutuality, and reciprocity should govern a love relationship overall and not as mathematical obsessions.

35. Several philosophers have explored these possibilities. See, for example, Mike W. Martin, *Love's Virtues* (Lawrence: University Press of Kansas, 1996); and Keith Lehrer, *Self-Trust: A Study of Reason, Knowledge, and Autonomy* (Oxford: Clarendon Press, 1997), esp. chap. 5.

36. Cancian, *Love in America*, p. 45.

37. Ibid., p. 42.

38. Ibid., pp. 39–41.

39. Michael Gordon, "From Unfortunate Necessity to a Cult of Mutual Orgasm: Sex in American Marital Education Literature, 1830–1940," in *The Sociology of Sex*, rev. ed., ed. J. Henslin and E. Sagarin (New York: Schocken, 1978), pp. 59–84; cited by Cancian, *Love in America*, p. 48.

40. Lionel S. Lewis and Dennis Brisset, "Sex as Work: A Study of Avocational Counseling," *Social Problems* 15 (1967): 8–18; cited in Cancian, *Love in America*, p. 175 n. 70.

41. Cancian, *Love in America*, pp. 44–45.

42. Ibid., p. 39.

43. In *Habits of the Heart*, Robert Bellah and his associates attribute this view to certain groups of Christian fundamentalists. See Robert Bellah, Richard Madsen, William M. Sullivan, Ann Swidler, and Steven M. Tipton, *Habits of the Heart: Individualism and Commitment in American Life* (New York: Harper & Row, 1985), pp. 93–97.

44. Ibid., p. 94.

45. For this discussion, I omit all considerations arising from the presence of children or other dependents whom lovers may have brought into their household. The creation or inclusion of new dependents changes the situation entirely. My text pertains to childless couples.

46. Cancian, *Love in America*, pp. 33, 36.

47. Ibid., p. 46.

48. See Bartky's argument against the idea that the movement of *power* from a woman to a man in a heterosexual relationship is a zero-sum game: *Femininity*, pp. 107–108. On her view, there is a net loss of power in such transactions; women are more *dis*empowered than men are empowered by them.

49. Martha Nussbaum, "Objectification," *Philosophy and Public Affairs* 24 (fall 1995): 290.

50. Theorists whose writings suggest this view include Carol Gilligan, *In a Different Voice* (Cambridge, Mass.: Harvard University Press, 1982); and Nel Noddings, *Caring: A Feminine Approach to Ethics & Moral Education* (Berkeley: University of California Press, 1984). See the discussion of this view in Alison Weir, *Sacrificial Logics: Feminist Theory and the Critique of Identity* (New York: Routledge, 1996), esp. chap. 2.

51. See Carol Gilligan, *Different Voice*; and the review of literature on these topics by Cancian, *Love in America*, pp. 73–75.

52. Beauvoir, *Second Sex*, pp. 653–58.

53. Ann Ferguson, *Blood at the Root: Motherhood, Sexuality, and Male Dominance* (London: Pandora, 1989).

Chapter 7

1. Some social theorists worry that terms such as "abused woman" and "battered woman" suggest the women in question are the problem; they are marred by

the identity of being "abused" or "battered." I share this worry, but to avoid unnecessary complexity tangential to this chapter, I retain the common usage.

2. Susan L. Miller and Charles F. Wellford, "Patterns and Correlates of Interpersonal Violence," in *Violence Between Intimate Partners: Patterns, Causes, and Effects*, ed. Albert P. Cardarelli (Boston: Allyn and Bacon, 1997), p. 17. The fraction of this abuse of women that was inflicted by other women was negligible.

3. This contemporary cliché is of course the main title of Christopher Lasch's *Haven in a Heartless World: The Family Beseiged* (New York: Basic Books, 1977).

4. See, for example, Susan Schechter and Lisa T. Gray, "A Framework for Understanding and Empowering Battered Women," in *Abuse and Victimization across the Life Span*, ed. Martha B. Straus (Baltimore: Johns Hopkins University Press, 1988), p. 241.

In one Massachusetts study of women who sought court restraining orders against their intimate male partners, it was found that the majority of incidents alleged by the women constituted clear-cut criminal offenses, in most cases assault and battery; see James Ptacek, "The Tactics and Strategies of Men Who Batter: Testimony from Women Seeking Restraining Orders," in *Violence Between Intimate Partners: Patterns, Causes, and Effects*, ed. Albert P. Cardarelli (Boston: Allyn and Bacon, 1997), pp. 109–11.

5. See, for example, Joseph Raz, *The Morality of Freedom* (Oxford: Clarendon Press, 1986), pp. 155–56.

6. See, for example, Lenore Walker, *The Battered Woman Syndrome* (New York: Springer, 1984), p. 79; and Kathleen J. Ferraro, "Battered Women: Strategies for Survival," in *Violence between Intimate Partners*, ed. Albert P. Cardarelli (Boston: Allyn and Bacon, 1997), pp. 128–29.

7. Ferraro, "Battered Women," pp. 124–40. See also Dee L. R. Graham, Edna Rawlings, and Nelly Rimini, "Survivors of Terror: Battered Women, Hostages, and the Stockholm Syndrome," in *Feminist Perspectives on Wife Abuse*, ed. Kersti Yllö and Michele Bograd (Newbury Park, Calif: Sage, 1990), pp. 223–24.

8. This is the theme of Ann Jones and Susan Schechter, *When Love Goes Wrong: What to Do When You Can't Do Anything Right* (New York: HarperCollins, 1992). See also Martha Mahoney, "Legal Images of Battered Women: Redefining the Issue of Separation," *Michigan Law Review* 90, 1 (October 1991), esp. pp. 53–71.

9. Angela Browne, "Violence in Marriage: Until Death Do Us Part?" in *Violence Between Intimate Partners*, ed. Albert P. Cardarelli (Boston: Allyn and Bacon, 1997), pp. 57–58. Unfortunately for women, our culture values controlling tendencies in men, including control exercised in intimate relationships. A man's jealousy and possessiveness, for example, are often regarded as endearing signs that he loves a woman deeply. Browne, by contrast, emphasizes the "potential for violence" latent in such culturally sanctioned behavior.

10. More than twelve hundred battered women's shelters, for example, were created around the country between 1975 and 1995 as places of refuge for women and their children who are endangered by domestic violence (Albert P. Cardarelli, "Violence and Intimacy: An Overview," in *Violence Between Intimate Partners*, ed. Cardarelli [Boston: Allyn and Bacon, 1997], p. 7). I discuss recent legal innovations later in this chapter.

11. See, for example, Nancy A. Crowell and Ann W. Burgess, eds., *Understanding Violence Against Women* (Washington, D.C.: National Academy Press, 1996), 130–33.

12. "Empowerment" is the key word in the treatment of abused women; see, for example, M. A. Dutton, *Empowering and Healing the Battered Woman: A Model for Assessment and Intervention* (New York: Springer, 1992).

13. See, for example, B. Pressman, "Wife-Abused Couples: The Need for Comprehensive Theoretical Perspectives and Integrated Treatment Models," *Journal of Feminist Family Therapy* 1 (1989): 23–43.

14. Cf. Kathleen Ferraro, "Battered Women," p. 124; Elizabeth Schneider, "Particularity and Generality: Challenges of Feminist Theory and Practice in Work on Woman-Abuse," *New York University Law Review* 67 (June 1992): 558; and Ann Jones, *Next Time She'll Be Dead: Battering & How to Stop It* (Boston: Beacon Press, 1994), chap. 5.

15. To be sure, the question does reveal ignorance on the part of the questioner. Recent decades have witnessed an explosion of knowledge about women's lives. Anyone at all familiar with this literature already has some idea about why some women stay in abusive relationships.

16. This approach certainly does not mean we should give up on rehabilitating abusive men. Unfortunately, however, as I noted earlier, the rehabilitation project is going slowly. Something else has to be done in the meantime in order to diminish the level of intimate partner abuse of women in the immediate future.

17. See, for example, Paula Caplan, *The Myth of Female Masochism* (New York: Dutton, 1985); and Edward W. Gondolf with Ellen R. Fisher, *Battered Women as Survivors: An Alternative to Treating Learned Helplessness* (New York: Macmillan, 1988), chap. 2.

18. Lenore Walker, *The Battered Woman* (New York: Harper Collins, 1979); and Walker, *Battered Woman Syndrome*.

19. Gondolf and Fisher, *Battered Women as Survivors*, chap. 2 and passim. For example, Gondolf and Fisher classify some batterers as "sociopaths." The typical counseling techniques used for abusers, however, are simply ineffective with sociopaths (pp. 65–66). Yet, women often remain in abusive relationships because the abuser has gone into counseling.

20. According to some studies, women in households with incomes under $10,000 have the highest rates of intimate partner abuse. These women often have less than a full high school education and no employment experience. Their abusive partners may be their only means of financial support. See, for example, Angela M. Moore, "Intimate Violence: Does Socioeconomic Status Matter?" in *Violence Between Intimate Partners,* ed. Albert P. Cardarelli (Boston: Allyn and Bacon, 1997), pp. 94, 96.

21. Browne, "Violence in Marriage," p. 68. The man may not be able to carry out such a threat, especially if there is a legal record of his abusiveness, but the woman may not be legally informed enough to know this.

22. Mahoney, "Legal Images of Battered Women," p. 87. Abusive relationships in which the abuser batters a woman who tries to leave are, in Mahoney's view, a kind of captivity. She compares the women who endure such relationships to hostages and prisoners of war.

23. Browne, "Violence in Marriage," pp. 67–68.

24. Ptacek, "Tactics and Strategies," pp. 113–14.

25. Kathleen J. Ferraro and John M. Johnson, "How Women Experience Battering: The Process of Victimization," *Social Problems* 30, 3 (February 1983): 328–29.

26. Ibid.

27. In the view of Gerald Dworkin, it must be the product of reflection that was not coerced or manipulated; Gerald Dworkin, *The Theory and Practice of Autonomy* (Cambridge: Cambridge University Press, 1988), chap. 1. On John Christman's view, the reflection must also include accepting the history by which the underlying desire was formed; see his "Autonomy and Personal History," *Canadian Journal of Philosophy* 21, 1 (March 1991): 1–24.

28. Cheryl Hanna, "No Right to Choose: Mandated Victim Participation in Domestic Violence Prosecutions," *Harvard Law Review* 109, 8 (June 1996): 1859. In general, police were already permitted to arrest someone on probable cause who had committed a felony.

The results of the Minneapolis study have been challenged by subsequent studies that did not fully replicate its findings. The general view now seems to be that arrest has a qualified deterrent effect. Cf. Donald G. Dutton, *The Domestic Assault of Women: Psychological and Criminal Justice Perspectives* (Vancouver: University of British Columbia Press, 1995), chap. 8.

29. Hanna, "No Right to Choose," p. 1861.

30. Wayne R. LaFave and Austin W. Scott Jr., *Criminal Law*, 2nd ed. (St. Paul, Minn.: West Publishing., 1986), p. 13.

31. Ibid., p. 14.

32. Hanna, "No Right to Choose," p. 1862.

33. Ibid., pp. 1867, 1892. Moderate no-drop policies do not force the participation of uncooperative victims. Instead, counseling and support services are made available to uncooperative victims, and they are *encouraged* to continue the legal process. If, after this support, an abused woman still refuses to cooperate, and the evidence apart from her testimony would not be likely to gain a conviction, the prosecutor following a moderate no-drop policy will usually drop the charges (Hanna, "No Right to Choose," pp. 1862-63). The stringent no-drop policies with their mandated victim participation are the ones that have generated the most controversy, so these are what I will focus on in the remainder of the discussion.

34. Hanna, "No Right to Choose," pp. 1864–65; p. 1865 n. 71; p. 1887 nn. 169, 170.

35. This assumption is crucial for the discussion that follows. If the assumption is not empirically warranted, the argument below would need substantial revision. For a brief summary of some of the evidence, see Crowell and Burgess, *Understanding Violence Against Women*, pp. 114–24; and Rosemary Chalk and Patricia A. King, eds., *Violence in Families: Assessing Prevention and Treatment Programs* (Washington, D.C.: National Academy Press, 1998), pp. 174–81.

36. Hanna, "No Right to Choose," p. 1884.

37. Ibid., p. 1876.

38. Ibid., p. 1866.

39. Ibid., pp. 1891–92.

40. See, for example, Elizabeth A. Stanko, "Fear of Crime and the Myth of the Safe Home: A Feminist Critique of Criminology," in *Feminist Perspectives on Wife Abuse*, ed. Kersti Yllö and Michele Bograd (Newbury Park, Calif.: Sage, 1990), pp. 75–88.

41. LaFave and Scott, *Criminal Law*, pp. 10, 13.

42. Hanna, "No Right to Choose," p. 1890; italics mine.

43. Ibid., p. 1891.

44. See Ruth Gavison, "Feminism and the Public/Private Distinction," *Stanford Law Review* 45 (1992): 37.

45. See Laura Stein, "Living with the Risk of Backfire: A Response to the Feminist Critique of Privacy and Equality," *Minnesota Law Review* 77 (1993): 1173.

46. The literature concerning "paternalism" contains many examples of this viewpoint. Paternalism is typically defined in terms of manipulative or coercive interference with the choices or actions of competent adults for their own good but without their consent. Antipaternalistic philosophers challenge manipulative and coercive attempts to change someone's mind or behavior, but they defend the use of rational persuasion. See, for example, Bernard Gert and Charles M. Culver, "Paternalistic Behavior," *Philosophy and Public Affairs* 6, 1 (1976): 45–57; Donald VanDeVeer, *Paternalistic Intervention* (Princeton, N.J.: Princeton University Press, 1986); and the various essays in Rolf Sartorius, ed., *Paternalism* (Minneapolis: University of Minnesota Press, 1983). The classic statement of this view is of course that of John Stuart Mill, *On Liberty* (Indianapolis: Hackett, 1978).

47. See, for example, Elizabeth Register, "Feminism and Recovering from Battering: Working with the Individual Woman," in *Battering and Family Therapy: A Feminist Perspective*, ed. Marsali Hansen and Michèle Harway (Newbury Park, Calif.: Sage, 1993), p. 99.

48. Cf. Paul M. Hughes, "Paternalism, Battered Women, and the Law," *Journal of Social Philosophy* 30, 1 (spring 1999): 18–28, for different arguments in support of the same conclusion that I reach here.

49. See, for example, Dworkin's comments on whether the concept of autonomy applies primarily to individual choices or primarily to whole lives; *Theory and Practice*, pp. 15–16.

50. John Kultgen, who defends rational persuasion, argues that someone who intervenes paternalistically (or "parentalistically," to use Kultgen's improved terminology) in another's life should do so only when she has good reason to think her own judgment about the circumstances of the subject's life is better than almost anyone else's, better even than that of the recipient of care; John Kultgen, *Autonomy and Intervention: Parentalism in the Caring Life* (New York: Oxford University Press, 1995), pp. 81–83.

51. Register, "Feminism and Recovering," p. 99.

52. A caregiving friend or relative is even more likely to know this about an abused woman. The present discussion, however, is restricted to the consideration of professional caregivers.

53. This point is made, for example, by Lenore Walker, *Abused Women and Survivor Therapy: A Practical Guide for the Psychotherapist* (Washington, D.C.: American Psychological Association, 1994), 303–11; and Mary P. Koss et al., *No Safe Haven: Male Violence against Women at Home, at Work, and in the Community* (Washington, D.C.: American Psychological Association, 1994), p. 98.

54. Walker, *Abused Women and Survivor Therapy*, pp. 402–407.

55. Koss et. al., *No Safe Haven*, p. 95.

56. As Alison Jaggar argued in comments on an earlier version of this chapter when it was presented at the Pacific Division American Philosophical Meetings in March 1999, caregiving professionals would tend to hold the balance of power in relationships with their abused clients, and this power would give them a big advantage in rational discussion.

57. On the low self-esteem of abused women, see, for example, Elizabeth A. Waites, *Trauma and Survival: Post-Traumatic and Dissociative Disorders in Women* (New York: W. W. Norton, 1993), pp. 104–106.

58. Mill, *On Liberty*, pp. 32–33.

59. Kultgen is rare among contemporary defenders of the rational persuasion model in recognizing that rational arguments may not be welcome to all persons; Kultgen, *Autonomy and Intervention,* p. 71.

60. Marsali Hansen, "Feminism and Family Therapy: A Review of Feminist Critiques of Approaches to Family Violence," in *Battering and Family Therapy,* ed. Marsali Hansen and Michèle Harway (Newbury Park, Calif.: Sage, 1993), pp. 76–77.

61. A skillful caregiver might, for example, be able to stimulate someone's rational consideration of her choices without appearing overtly to criticize those choices and without undermining her self-confidence. A skillful caregiver, that is, might be able to find a middle ground between outright and obvious rational persuasion, on the one hand, and uncritical support, on the other. Let us, however, put the possibility of intermediate alternatives aside for the present. I am interested in how to compare rational persuasion to uncritical support for cases in which no intermediate alternatives are available.

62. The use of the term "survivors" is advocated, for example, by Gondolf and Fisher, *Battered Women as Survivors,* esp. chap. 2.

63. Caregivers, however, are not immune to those effects, as witness the frequent exhortations in therapeutic literature for caregivers and therapists to understand how the setbacks and frustrations of caregiving may impinge on their own attitudes; see, for example, Register, "Feminism and Recovering," pp. 101–103.

64. Kultgen, *Autonomy and Intervention,* p. 90.

65. Of course, an abused woman's abusive relationship is itself a major coercive condition in her life, something that affects most of her decision making. Content-neutral autonomy would not be an easy achievement under such conditions. For the sake of discussion, however, I am going to suppose that her choices about whether to remain in the relationship can be made somehow independently of the coercion that characterizes the relationship. Remember that we are dealing in the last part of this chapter, by hypothesis, with women who may safely leave their abusive relationships and whose decisions to remain are based not on threats by their abusers, but rather on their own commitments, such as those to "higher loyalties" or a "salvation ethic."

66. As Waites puts it, "glib approaches to choice, such as those that . . . exhort [the abused woman] simply to leave an abusive context, are likely to be ineffective and, in some instances, to contribute to revictimization"; *Trauma and Survival,* p. 88.

Chapter 8

1. John Rawls, *Political Liberalism* (New York: Columbia University Press, 1993, 1996), p. 216. In this chapter, all references to *Political Liberalism* are to the 1996 edition.

2. The exact wording varies with different passages. See, for example, *Political Liberalism,* p. 217, where Rawls states that political power is justifiable "only when it is exercised in accordance with a constitution the essentials of which all citizens may reasonably be expected to endorse in the light of principles and ideals acceptable to them as reasonable and rational. This is the liberal principle of legitimacy."

3. See, for example, Thomas Scanlon, "Contractualism and Utilitarianism," in *Utilitarianism and Beyond,* ed. Amartya Sen and Bernard Williams (Cambridge:

Cambridge University Press, 1982); and Thomas Nagel, *Equality and Partiality* (New York: Oxford University Press, 1991).

4. Rawls, *Political Liberalism*, p. 258.
5. Ibid., p. 51.
6. Ibid., p. 49 n. 1, pp. 49–51.
7. Ibid., pp. 54–58.
8. Ibid., pp. 53–54.
9. Ibid., p. 52.
10. Ibid., p. 74.
11. Ibid., p. 72.
12. Jeremy Waldron, *Liberal Rights: Collected Papers* 1981–1991 (Cambridge: Cambridge University Press, 1993), pp. 36–37; emphasis added.
13. Ibid., p. 44.
14. Nagel, *Equality and Partiality*, pp. 8, 33.
15. Joseph Raz argues that consent to a political authority is binding only in case the authority is independently justifiable on certain specified sorts of grounds; see Joseph Raz, *The Morality of Freedom* (Oxford: Oxford University Press, 1986), pp. 88–94.
16. Nagel, *Equality and Partiality*, p. 8.
17. John Rawls, *A Theory of Justice* (Cambridge, Mass.: Harvard University Press, 1971).
18. This issue, however, reveals a difference between the legitimacy of a government's exercise of its coercive power and a citizen's obligation to obey that government. Waldron argues that, even though it makes the coercive action of government more legitimate, hypothetical consent does not increase the degree of someone's obligation to obey the dictates of her government (*Liberal Rights*, pp. 49–50). Hobbes recognized this distinction between legitimacy and obligation when arguing that the state might rightfully attempt to execute someone who, at the same time, had no obligation to submit to this treatment and could, furthermore, rightfully attempt to escape. (See Thomas Hobbes, *Leviathan*, ed. Michael Oakeshott [New York: Collier Books, 1962], p. 164. For Waldron's reference to this passage, although to a different edition of *Leviathan*, see *Liberal Rights*, p. 50.)
19. Waldron, *Liberal Rights*, p. 49.
20. Ibid., pp. 41–42.
21. Ibid., p. 55.
22. Ibid., p. 56.
23. According to Leif Wenar, Catholic doctrine is premised on this view; see Leif Wenar, "*Political Liberalism*: An Internal Critique," *Ethics* 106 (October 1995): 32–62, esp. pp. 42–48.
24. Rush Limbaugh, *The Way Things Ought to Be* (New York: Pocket Star Books, 1993), esp. chap. 25, "Religion and America: They Do Go Together." Strictly speaking, Limbaugh's view is not unreasonable in Rawls's sense. Limbaugh believes that "America was founded as a Judeo-Christian country" (p. 278), and like Rawls, Limbaugh bases his politics on traditional values. The difference between them lies in what they believe the basic values of that tradition to be.
25. Waldron, *Liberal Rights*, p. 57.
26. Rawls, *Political Liberalism*, pp. 63–64.
27. Ibid., p. 64 n. 19.
28. Ibid., p. 61.

29. This potential, as we all know, is often unrealized in practice.

30. Susan Golombok and Robyn Fivush, *Gender Development* (Cambridge: Cambridge University Press, 1994), pp. 7, 18. Golombok and Fivush refer here to the Bem Sex Role Inventory; see S. Bem, "The Measurement of Psychological Androgyny," *Journal of Consulting and Clinical Psychology*. 42 (1974): 155–62.

31. For Rawls, rationality is self-interested, instrumental rationality. It involves finding means to one's ends and adjusting one's ends in light of still broader aims and goals for one's life. There might well be people who think that women are incapable of doing this, or less capable of doing it than men. Once again, that view is not a part of Rawls's theory as such, so the only question is whether the stereotype of women will lead to widespread misapplication of Rawls's conception of rationality when applied to women. Even this may not be a problem. Although the stereotypes of agency and instrumentality are applied to men more often than to women, women are still thought to be capable of finding the means to the ends that *they* are supposed to seek, namely, promoting social relationships and expressing emotion.

It is true that women have been traditionally characterized as irrational. In the end, I can ignore this stereotype, however, since all the interesting philosophical problems for Rawls's political liberalism turn on his notion of reasonableness.

32. On this point, see the discussion by Carole Pateman, "'The Disorder of Women': Women, Love, and the Sense of Justice," *Ethics* 91 (1980): 20–34.

33. G. W. F. Hegel, *The Phenomenology of Mind,* trans. J. B. Baillie, intro. by George Lichtheim (New York: Harper Torchbooks, 1967), p. 496.

34. See Mike Royko, *Boss: Richard J. Daley of Chicago* (New York: New American Library, 1971).

35. Genevieve Lloyd, *The Man of Reason: "Male" and "Female" in Western Philosophy* (Minneapolis: University of Minnesota, 1984).

36. This would be reminiscent of the persistent anthropological idea that, in hunter-gatherer societies, men are the hunters and women are the gatherers, an idea that persists despite recent evidence showing that women's frequent capture of small game contributed more to the protein needs of such societies than did men's occasional capture of big game.

37. See the discussion of this issue by Waldron, *Liberal Rights,* pp. 283–92.

38. Rawls, Political Liberalism, p. 19.

39. Susan Moller Okin, "Political Liberalism, Justice, and Gender," *Ethics* 105 (October 1994): 31–32.

40. Rawls, *Political Liberalism,* pp. 196, 210.

41. Discussions of *Political Liberalism* sometimes use the example of right-wing religious fundamentalism as a test case for political liberalism; see, for example, Okin, "Political Liberalism, Justice, and Gender;" and Michael Huemer, "Rawls's Problem of Stability," *Social Theory and Practice* 22 (fall 1996): 375–95.

42. Samuel Scheffler, "The Appeal of Political Liberalism," *Ethics* 105 (October 1994): 20.

43. Some of my opponents on women's issues may not hold such elaborate theories and may simply be hypocrites who mask with high-sounding rationales what they themselves secretly recognize to be the subordination of women. I do not suppose, however, that all my opponents are hypocrites. On my view, there are people who believe sincerely in the inferiority of women or in the "equal" value of those female roles that involve subordination. These sincere disputes exemplify the sort of pluralism that Rawls attempts to surmount—unsuccessfully, I believe.

44. Rawls, *Political Liberalism*, pp. 195–211.

45. Ibid., p. 61.

46. Ibid., p. 258; also cited in note 4 above.

Chapter 9

1. Cf. Will Kymlicka, *Multicultural Citizenship: A Liberal Theory of Minority Rights* (Oxford: Clarendon Press, 1995). For discussion of this issue, see the essays in Will Kymlicka, ed., *The Rights of Minority Cultures* (Oxford: Oxford University Press, 1995).

2. Susan Moller Okin, "Is Multiculturalism Bad for Women?" in Susan Moller Okin with Respondents, *Is Multiculturalism Bad for Women?* ed. Joshua Cohen, Matthew Howard, and Martha C. Nussbaum (Princeton, N.J.: Princeton University Press, 1999), p. 13.

3. Ibid., pp. 13 and 17; italics mine.

4. Ayelet Shachar, "Should Church and State Be Joined at the Altar? Women's Rights and the Multicultural Dilemma," in *Citizenship in Diverse Societies*, ed. Will Kymlicka and Wayne Norman (Oxford: Oxford University Press, 2000), pp. 204–205.

5. Ibid., p. 205.

6. Okin, "Multiculturalism," pp. 18–19.

7. Ibid. pp. 22–23.

8. Susan Moller Okin, "Reply," in *Is Multiculturalism Bad for Women?* ed. Joshua Cohen, Matthew Howard and Martha C. Nussbaum (Princeton, N.J.: Princeton University Press, 1999), p. 119.

9. Ibid., p. 20; italics mine.

10. Katha Pollitt, "Whose Culture?" in *Is Multiculturalism Bad for Women?* ed. Joshua Cohen, Matthew Howard, and Martha C. Nussbaum (Princeton, N.J.: Princeton University Press, 1999), p. 29.

11. Jeffrey Reiman, *Critical Moral Liberalism: Theory and Practice* (Lanham, Md: Rowman & Littlefield, 1997), pp. 36–37, 42–44, and 49–51.

12. Uma Narayan, "Essence of Culture and a Sense of History: A Feminist Critique of Cultural Essentialism," *Hypatia* 13 (spring 1998): 97.

13. As is well known, such rights have been unevenly enforced within liberal systems; for a discussion of the inadequate judicial response to abused women, see chapter 7.

14. The concepts may also be found in cultural traditions that are not Western; see Uma Narayan, *Dislocating Cultures: Identities, Traditions, and Third World Feminism* (New York: Routledge, 1997), chap. 1.

15. John Stuart Mill, *On Liberty*, ed. Elizabeth Rapaport (Indianapolis: Hackett, 1978), pp. 9, 73.

16. Kymlicka, *Multicultural Citizenship*, p. 170.

17. Whether the frequency of migration to liberal societies tells us that liberal political systems are more preferred as such to alternative political systems by global migrants is a question I leave open in this context. It may be that the primary lure of liberal political systems is their great wealth. Without additional evidence that the wealth was produced or acquired justly, both domestically and internationally, great wealth alone is no sign that a political system is morally healthy.

18. Kymlicka, *Multicultural Citizenship*, pp. 163–70.

19. Leila Ahmed, *Women and Gender in Islam: Historical Roots of a Modern Debate* (New Haven, Conn: Yale University Press, 1992), p. 244; the quotation is from Anouar Majid, "The Politics of Feminism in Islam," *Signs* 23, 2 (winter 1998): 340. The authors make this defense for women living in Islamic countries, but the same sort of argument could be made as readily for women in cultural minorities residing in liberal democracies.

20. Bhikhu Parekh, "A Varied Moral World," in *Is Multiculturalism Bad for Women?* ed. Joshua Cohen, Matthew Howard, and Martha C. Nussbaum (Princeton, N.J.: Princeton University Press, 1999), pp. 71, 73.

21. Sandra D. Lane and Robert A. Rubinstein, "Judging the Other: Responding to Traditional Female Genital Surgeries," *Hastings Center Report* (May–June 1996), p. 35.

22. Ibid., p. 36.

23. Martha Nussbaum, *Women and Human Development: The Capabilities Approach* (Cambridge: Cambridge University Press, 2000), p. 146.

24. Katherine P. Ewing, "Can Psychoanalytic Theory Explain the Pakistani Woman? Intrapsychic Autonomy and Interpersonal Engagement in the Extended Family," *Ethos* 19 (1991), 131–60.

25. Sawitri Saharso, "Female Autonomy and Cultural Imperative: Two Hearts Beating Together," in *Citizenship in Diverse Societies,* ed. Will Kymlicka and Wayne Norman (Oxford: Oxford University Press, 2000), pp. 235–36.

26. Jeremy Waldron, *Liberal Rights: Collected Papers 1981–1991* (Cambridge: Cambridge University Press, 1993), pp. 44, 50.

27. Kymlicka, *Multicultural Citizenship,* chap. 8, esp. p. 152.

28. Parekh, "A Varied Moral World," esp. pp. 71–74.

29. Azizah Y. al-Hibri, "Is Western Patriarchal Feminism Good for Third World/Minority Women?" in *Is Multiculturalism Good for Women?* ed. Joshua Cohen, Matthew Howard, and Martha C. Nussbaum (Princeton, N.J.: Princeton University Press, 1999), pp. 41–42.

30. Bonnie Honig, "'My Culture Made Me Do It'," in *Is Multiculturalism Bad for Women?* ed. Joshua Cohen, Matthew Howard, and Martha C. Nussbaum (Princeton, N.J.: Princeton University Press, 1999), pp. 38–39.

31. Abdullahi An-Na'im, "Promises We Should All Keep in Common Cause," in *Is Multiculturalism Bad for Women?* ed. Joshua Cohen, Matthew Howard, and Martha C. Nussbaum (Princeton, N.J.: Princeton University Press, 1999), p. 61.

32. Homi Bhabha, "Liberalism's Sacred Cow," in *Is Multiculturalism Bad for Women?* ed. Joshua Cohen, Matthew Howard, and Martha C. Nussbaum (Princeton, N.J.: Princeton University Press, 1999), p. 82.

33. Ofelia Schutte, "Cultural Alterity: Cross-Cultural Communication and Feminist Theory in North-South Contexts," in *Decentering the Center: Philosophy for a Multicultural, Postcolonial, and Feminist World,* ed. Uma Narayan and Sandra Harding (Bloomington: Indiana University Press, 2000), p. 59.

34. Bhabha, "Liberalism's Sacred Cow," p. 83.

35. Ibid.

36. An-Na'im, "Promises We Should All Keep," p. 59.

37. French law differs in this respect, requiring public school students to wear uniforms; hence the controversy over whether Muslim girls could wear head scarves in French public schools.

38. Bhabha, "Liberalism's Sacred Cow," p. 80.

39. An-Na'im, "Promises We Should All Keep," pp. 60–61.

40. Al-Hibri, "Western Patriarchal Feminism," p. 46.

41. Jerome Schneewind, *The Invention of Autonomy: A History of Modern Moral Philosophy* (Cambridge: Cambridge University Press, 1998), pp. 4–9 and passim. See chapter 3 for my discussion of Schneewind's account.

42. Okin, "Is Multiculturalism Bad for Women?" p. 21.

43. See, for example, Patricia Rice, "Southern Baptists Call for Wives to Be Submissive," *St. Louis Post-Dispatch,* 10 June 1998, pp. A1, 9.

44. Martha Nussbaum explores the potential conflicts between the state's interests in promoting the capabilities of children and parents' interests in, and rights in, socializing their children to participate in their own (the parents') religious and cultural traditions. Conflicts arise in Nussbaum's framework in case the religious and cultural traditions prevent or suppress the development of valuable capabilities in children. Nussbaum resolves the conflict by, for example, giving great weight to the state's interest in educating its children, although allowing for variable ad hoc limitations to this interest arising from parents' rights and interests in raising their children as they choose; cf. Martha Nussbaum, *Women and Human Development: The Capabilities Approach* (Cambridge: Cambridge University Press, 2000), pp. 230–35.

References

Ahmed, Leila. *Women and Gender in Islam: Historical Roots of a Modern Debate*. New Haven, Conn.: Yale University Press, 1992.

al-Hibri, Azizah Y. "Is Western Patriarchal Feminism Good for Third World/Minority Women?" In *Is Multiculturalism Good for Women?* by Susan Moller Okin with respondents. Edited by Joshua Cohen, Matthew Howard, and Martha Nussbaum, 41–46. Princeton, N.J.: Princeton University Press, 1999.

Anderson, Joel. "A Social Conception of Personal Autonomy: Volitional Identities, Strong Evaluation, and Intersubjective Accountability." Ph.D. diss. Northwestern University, 1996.

An-Na'im, Abdullahi. "Promises We Should All Keep in Common Cause." In *Is Multiculturalism Bad for Women?* by Susan Moller Okin with respondents. Edited by Joshua Cohen, Matthew Howard, and Martha Nussbaum, 59–64. Princeton, N.J.: Princeton University Press, 1999.

Antony, Louise M., and Charlotte Witt, eds. *A Mind of One's Own: Feminist Essays on Reason and Objectivity*. Boulder Colo: Westview Press, 1993.

Arendt, Hannah. *Eichmann in Jerusalem: A Report on the Banality of Evil*. New York: Viking Press, 1964.

Arnault, Lynn. "The Radical Future of a Classic Moral Theory." In *Gender/Body/Knowledge: Feminist Reconstructions of Being and Knowing*. Edited by Alison Jaggar and Susan P. Bordo, 188–206. New Brunswick, N.J.: Rutgers University Press, 1989.

Badhwar, Neera Kapur, ed. *Friendship: A Philosophical Reader*. Ithaca, N.Y.: Cornell University Press, 1993.

Baier, Annette. "Cartesian Persons." In *Postures of the Mind: Essays on Mind and Morals*. Minneapolis: University of Minnesota Press, 1985.

Bartky, Sandra Lee. *Femininity and Domination: Studies in the Phenomenology of Oppression*. New York: Routledge, 1990.

Bellah, Robert, Richard Madsen, William M. Sullivan, Ann Swidler, and Steven M. Tipton. *Habits of the Heart: Individualism and Commitment in American Life*. New York: Harper & Row, 1985.

Bem, S. "The Measurement of Psychological Androgyny." *Journal of Consulting and Clinical Psychology* 42 (1974): 155–62.

231

Benhabib, Seyla. "The Generalized and the Concrete Other: The Kohlberg Gilligan Controversy and Moral Theory. In *Situating the Self: Gender, Community and Postmodernism in Contemporary Ethics*, 148–77. New York: Routledge, 1992.

Benjamin, Jessica. *The Bonds of Love: Psychoanalysis, Feminism, and the Problem of Domination.* New York: Pantheon Books, 1988.

———. "The Bonds of Love: Rational Violence and Erotic Domination." In *The Future of Difference*, edited by Hester Eisenstein and Alice Jardine, 41–70. New Brunswick, N.J.: Rutgers University Press, 1985.

Benn, S. I. "Freedom, Autonomy and the Concept of a Person." *Proceedings of the Aristotelian Society* 76 (12 January 1976), 109–30.

———. "Individuality, Autonomy, and Community." In *Community as a Social Ideal*, edited by Eugene Kamenka, 43–62. New York: St. Martin's Press, 1982.

Benson, Paul. "Autonomy and Oppressive Socialization." *Social Theory and Practice* 17 (1991): 385–408.

———. "Feminist Second Thoughts about Free Agency." *Hypatia* 3 (1990): 47–64.

Bhabha, Homi. "Liberalism's Sacred Cow." In *Is Multiculturalism Bad for Women?* by Susan Moller Okin with respondents, 78–84. Edited by Joshua Cohen, Matthew Howard, and Martha C. Nussbaum. Princeton, N.J.: Princeton University Press, 1999.

Blackstone, William. *Commentaries on the Laws of England.* (1756. 15th ed., Oxfordshire: Professional Books, 1982.

Brison, Susan. "Surviving Sexual Violence." *Journal of Social Philosophy* 24 (spring 1993): 5–22.

Browne, Angela. "Violence in Marriage: Until Death Do Us Part?" In *Violence Between Intimate Partners*. edited by Albert P. Cardarelli. Boston: Allyn and Bacon, 1997, 48–69.

Buss, Sarah. "Autonomy Reconsidered." *Midwest Studies in Philosophy* 19 (1994): 95–121.

Butler, Judith. *Gender Trouble: Feminism and the Subversion of Identity.* New York: Routledge, 1990.

Cancian, Francesca. *Love in America: Gender and Self-Development.* Cambridge: Cambridge University Press, 1987.

Caplan, Paula. *The Myth of Female Masochism.* New York: Dutton, 1985.

Card, Claudia. "Complicity and Gray Zones." Unpublished manuscript, 1999.

Cardarelli, Albert P. "Violence and Intimacy: An Overview." In *Violence Between Intimate Partners*, edited by Albert P. Cardarelli, 1–9. Boston: Allyn and Bacon, 1997.

———, ed. *Violence Between Intimate Partners.* Boston: Allyn and Bacon, 1997.

Chalk, Rosemary, and Patricia A. King, eds. *Violence in Families: Assessing Prevention and Treatment Programs.* Washington, D.C.: National Academy Press, 1998.

Chodorow, Nancy. "Gender, Relation, and Difference in Psychoanalytic Perspective." In *The Future of Difference*, edited by Hester Eisenstein and Alice Jardine, 3–19. New Brunswick N.J.:Rutgers University Press, 1985.

———. *The Reproduction of Mothering: Psychoanalysis and the Sociology of Gender.* Berkeley: University of California Press, 1978.

Christman, John. "Autonomy and Personal History." *Canadian Journal of Philosophy* 21 (March 1991): 1–24.

———. "Feminism and Autonomy." In *Nagging Questions: Feminist Ethics and Everyday Life*, edited by Dana Bushnell, 17–39. Lanham, Md.: Rowman & Littlefield, 1995.

———. ed. *The Inner Citadel: Essays on Individual Autonomy*. New York: Oxford University Press, 1989.

Code, Lorraine. "The Perversion of Autonomy and the Subjection of Women: Discourses of Social Advocacy at Century's End." In *Relational Autonomy: Feminist Perspectives on Autonomy, Agency, and the Social Self*, edited by Catriona Mackenzie and Natalie Stoljar, 181–209. New York: Oxford University Press, 2000.

———. *Rhetorical Spaces: Essays on Gendered Locations*. New York: Routledge, 1995.

———. *What Can She Know? Feminist Theory and the Construction of Knowledge*. Ithaca, N.Y.: Cornell University Press, 1991.

Collins, Patricia Hill. *Black Feminist Thought: Knowledge, Consciousness, and the Politics of Empowerment*. New York: Routledge, 1991.

Crowell, Nancy A., and Ann W. Burgess, eds. *Understanding Violence Against Women*. Washington, D.C.: National Academy Press, 1996.

de Beauvoir, Simone. *The Second Sex*. Translated and edited by H. M. Parshley. New York: Vintage Books, 1989.

Delaney, Neil. "Romantic Love and Loving Commitment: Articulating a Modern Ideal." *American Philosophical Quarterly* 33 (October 1996): 339–56.

Dennett, Daniel C. *Consciousness Explained*. Boston: Little, Brown, 1991.

Dutton, Donald G. *The Domestic Assault of Women: Psychological and Criminal Justice Perspectives*. Vancouver: University of British Columbia Press, 1995.

Dutton, M. A. *Empowering and Healing the Battered Woman: A Model for Assessment and Intervention*. New York: Springer, 1992.

Dworkin, Gerald. *The Theory and Practice of Autonomy*. Cambridge: Cambridge University Press, 1988.

Elster, Jon. "Sour Grapes—Utilitarianism and the Genesis of Wants." In *The Inner Citadel: Essays on Individual Autonomy*, edited by John Christman, 170–88. New York: Oxford University Press, 1989.

Evans, Sara M., and Harry C. Boyte. *Free Spaces: The Sources of Democratic Change in America*. New York: Harper & Row, 1986.

Ewing, Katherine P. "Can Psychoanalytic Theory Explain the Pakistani Woman? Intrapsychic Autonomy and Interpersonal Engagement in the Extended Family." *Ethos* 19 (1991): 131–60.

Faludi, Susan. *Backlash: The Undeclared War against American Women*. New York: Crown Publishers, 1991.

Feinberg, Joel. "Autonomy." In *The Inner Citadel: Essays on Individual Autonomy*, edited by John Christman, 31–43. New York: Oxford University Press, 1989.

Ferguson, Ann. *Blood at the Root: Motherhood, Sexuality, and Male Dominance*. London: Pandora, 1989.

Ferraro, Kathleen J. "Battered Women: Strategies for Survival." In *Violence Between Intimate Partners*, edited by Albert P. Cardarelli, 124–40. Boston: Allyn and Bacon, 1997.

Ferraro, Kathleen J., and John M. Johnson. "How Women Experience Battering: The Process of Victimization." *Social Problems* 30, 3 (February 1983): 325–39.

Firestone, Shulamith. *The Dialectic of Sex: The Case for Feminist Revolution.* Toronto: Bantam Books, 1970.

Fischer, Karla, and Mary Rose. "When 'Enough Is Enough': Battered Women's Decision Making around Court Orders of Protection." *Crime & Delinquency* 41 (October 1995): 414–29.

Francis, Leslie Pickering. "Decisionmaking at the End of Life: Patients with Alzheimer's or Other Dementias." *Georgia Law Review* 35, 2 (winter 2001): 539–92.

Frankfurt, Harry G., "Freedom of the Will and the Concept of a Person." *Journal of Philosophy* 68 (1971): 5–20.

———. *The Importance of What We Care About: Philosophical Essays.* Cambridge: Cambridge University Press, 1988.

———. *Necessity, Volition, and Love.* Cambridge: Cambridge University Press, 1999.

Fraser, Nancy, and Linda Gordon. "A Genealogy of Dependency: Tracing a Keyword of the U.S. Welfare State." *Signs: Journal of Women in Culture and Society* 19, 2 (1994): 309–36.

Friedman, Marilyn. "Autonomy and the Split-Level Self." *Southern Journal of Philosophy* 24, 1 (1986): 19–35.

———. *What Are Friends For? Feminist Perspectives on Personal Relationships and Moral Theory.* Ithaca, N.Y.: Cornell University Press, 1993.

Gavison, Ruth. "Feminism and the Public/Private Distinction." *Stanford Law Review* 45 (1992): 1–45.

Gaylin, Willard. *Rediscovering Love.* New York: Viking Penguin, 1986.

Gert, Bernard, and Charles M. Culver. "Paternalistic Behavior." *Philosophy and Public Affairs* 6, 1 (1976): 45–57.

Gibbard, Allan. *Wise Choices, Apt Feelings: A Theory of Normative Judgment.* Cambridge, Mass.: Harvard University Press, 1990.

Gilligan, Carol. *In a Different Voice: Psychological Theory and Women's Development.* Cambridge: Mass.: Harvard University Press, 1982.

Golombok, Susan, and Robyn Fivush. *Gender Development.* Cambridge: Cambridge University Press, 1994.

Gondolf, Edward W., with Ellen R. Fisher. *Battered Women as Survivors: An Alternative to Treating Learned Helplessness.* New York: Macmillan, 1988.

Goodin, Robert E. *Protecting the Vulnerable: A Reanalysis of Our Social Responsibilities.* Chicago: University of Chicago Press, 1985.

Gordon, Michael. "From Unfortunate Necessity to a Cult of Mutual Orgasm: Sex in American Marital Education Literature, 1830–1940." In *The Sociology of Sex,* edited by J. Henslin and E. Sagarin, 59–84. Revised ed. New York: Schocken, 1978.

Govier, Trudy. "Self-Trust, Autonomy, and Self-Esteem," *Hypatia* 8 (winter 1993): pp. 99–120.

Graham, Dee L. R., Edna Rawlings, and Nelly Rimini. "Survivors of Terror: Battered Women, Hostages, and the Stockholm Syndrome." In *Feminist Perspectives on Wife Abuse,* edited by Kersti Yllö and Michele Bograd, 217–35. Newbury Park, Calif.: Sage, 1990.

Griffiths, Morwenna. *Feminisms and the Self: The Web of Identity.* London: Routledge, 1995.

Grimshaw, Jean. "Autonomy and Identity in Feminist Thinking." In *Feminist Perspectives in Philosophy*, edited by Morwenna Griffiths and Margaret Whitford, 90–108. Bloomington: Indiana University Press, 1988.

———. *Philosophy and Feminist Thinking*. Minneapolis: University of Minnesota Press, 1986.

Habermas, Jürgen. "Individuation through Socialization: On George Herbert Mead's Theory of Subjectivity." In *Postmetaphysical Thinking: Philosophical Essays*, translated by William Mark Hohengarten. Cambridge: MIT Press, 1992.

Hanna, Cheryl. "No Right to Choose: Mandated Victim Participation in Domestic Violence Prosecutions." *Harvard Law Review*, 109, 8 (June 1996): 1849–1910.

Hansen, Marsali. "Feminism and Family Therapy: A Review of Feminist Critiques of Approaches to Family Violence." In *Battering and Family Therapy*, edited by Marsali Hansen and Michèle Harway, 69–81. Newbury Park, Calif.: Sage 1993.

Hansen, Marsali, and Michèle Harway. *Battering and Family Therapy*. Newbury Park, Calif.: Sage, 1993.

Haworth, Lawrence. *Autonomy: An Essay in Philosophical Psychology and Ethics*. New Haven, Conn.: Yale University Press, 1986.

Hegel, G. W. F. *The Phenomenology of Mind*. Translated by J. B. Baillie, with an introduction by George Lichtheim. New York: Harper Torchbooks, 1967.

Helm, Bennett W. "Freedom of the Heart." *Pacific Philosophical Quarterly* 77 (1996): 71–87.

———. "Integration and Fragmentation of the Self." *Southern Journal of Philosophy* 34 (1996): 43–63.

Hill, Sharon Bishop. "Self-determination and Autonomy." In *Today's Moral Problems*. 3rd ed. Edited by Richard Wasserstrom, 55–70. New York: Macmillan, 1985.

Hill, Thomas E., Jr. *Autonomy and Self-Respect*. Cambridge: Cambridge University Press, 1987.

Hoagland, Sarah. *Lesbian Ethics: Toward New Value*. Palo Alto, Calif.: Institute for Lesbian Studies, 1988.

Hobbes, Thomas. *Leviathan*. Edited by Michael Oakeshott. New York: Collier Macmillan, 1962.

———. "Philosophical Rudiments Concerning Government and Society." In *The English Works of Thomas Hobbes*, edited by W. Molesworth. Darmstadt: Wissenschaftliche Buchgesellschaft, 1966.

Hochschild, Jennifer. *Facing Up to the American Dream: Race, Class, and the Soul of the Nation*. Princeton, N.J.: Princeton University Press, 1995.

Honig, Bonnie. "'My Culture Made Me Do It'." In *Is Multiculturalism Bad for Women?* by Susan Moller Okin with respondents. Edited by Joshua Cohen, Matthew Howard, and Martha Nussbaum, 35–40. Princeton, N.J.: Princeton University Press, 1999.

Honneth, Axel. "Decentered Autonomy: The Subject after the Fall." Translated by John Farrell. In *The Fragmented World of the Social*, edited by Charles W. Wright, 261–71. Albany: SUNY Press, 1995.

Huemer, Michael. "Rawls's Problem of Stability." *Social Theory and Practice* 22 (fall 1996): 375–95.

Hughes, Paul M. "Paternalism, Battered Women, and the Law," *Journal of Social Philosophy* 30, 1 (spring 1999): 18–28.

Huntington, Patricia. "Toward a Dialectical Concept of Autonomy." *Philosophy and Social Criticism* 21 (1995): 37–55.

Hursthouse, Rosalind. "Arational Action." *Journal of Philosophy* 88, 2 (February 1991): 57–68.

Jaggar, Alison M. "Love and Knowledge: Emotion in Feminist Epistemology." In *Gender/Body/Knowledge*, edited by Alison M. Jaggar and Susan R. Bordo, 145–71. New Brunswick, N.J.: Rutgers University Press, 1989.

———. *Feminist Politics and Human Nature*. Totowa, N.J.: Rowman & Allanheld, 1983.

Jaggar, Alison M., and Susan R. Bordo, eds. *Gender/Body/Knowledge*. New Brunswick, N.J.: Rutgers University Press, 1989.

Jones, Ann. *Next Time She'll Be Dead: Battering & How to Stop It*. Boston: Beacon Press, 1994.

Jones, Ann, and Susan Schechter. *When Love Goes Wrong: What to Do When You Can't Do Anything Right*. New York: HarperCollins, 1992.

Kekes, John, 1997. *Against Liberalism*. Ithaca, N.Y.: Cornell University Press.

Keller, Evelyn Fox. *Reflections on Gender and Science*. New Haven, Conn.: Yale University Press, 1985.

Koss, Mary P. Lisa A. Goodman, Angela Browne, Louise F. Fitzgerald, Gwendolyn Purgear Keita, and Nancy Felipe Russo. *No Safe Haven: Male Violence against Women at Home, at Work, and in the Community*. Washington, D.C.: American Psychological Association, 1994.

Kristinsson, Sigurdur. "The Limits of Neutrality: Toward a Weekly Substantive Account of Autonomy." *Canadian Journal of Philosophy* 30, 2 (June 2000): 257–86.

Kultgen, John. *Autonomy and Intervention: Parentalism in the Caring Life*. New York: Oxford University Press, 1995.

Kymlicka, Will. *Multicultural Citizenship: A Liberal Theory of Minority Rights*. Oxford: Clarendon Press, 1995.

———, ed. *The Rights of Minority Cultures*. Oxford: Oxford University Press, 1995.

Kymlicka, Will, and Wayne Norman, eds. *Citizenship in Diverse Societies*. Oxford: Oxford University Press, 2000.

LaFave, Wayne R., and Austin W. Scott Jr. *Criminal Law*. 2nd ed. St. Paul, Minn.: West Publishing, 1986.

Lane, Sandra D., and Robert A. Rubinstein. "Judging the Other: Responding to Traditional Female Genital Surgeries." *Hastings Center Report* 26 (May–June 1996): 31–40.

Lasch, Christopher. *Haven in a Heartless World: The Family Besieged*. New York: Basic Books, 1977.

Lehrer, Keith. *Self-Trust: A Study of Reason, Knowledge, and Autonomy*. Oxford: Clarendon Press, 1997.

le Pichon, Yann. *Gauguin: Life, Art, Inspiration*. New York: Harry N. Abrams, 1987.

Lewis, Lionel S., and Dennis Brisset. "Sex as Work: A Study of Avocational Counseling." *Social Problems* 15 (1967): 8–18.

Limbaugh, Rush. *The Way Things Ought to Be*. New York: Pocket Star Books, 1993.

Lloyd, Genevieve. *The Man of Reason: "Male" and "Female" in Western Philosophy*. Minneapolis: University of Minnesota Press, 1984.

Lomasky, Loren E. *Persons, Rights, and the Moral Community*. New York: Oxford University Press, 1987.

Longino, Helen. *Science as Social Knowledge*. Princeton, N.J.: Princeton University Press, 1990.

Lorde, Audre. "The Master's Tools Will Never Dismantle the Master's House." *Sister Outsider*. Freedom, Calif.: Crossing Press, 1984.

Lukes, Steven. "The Meanings of Individualism." In *Figures on the Horizon*, edited by Jerrold Siegal, 1–22. Rochester, N.Y.: University of Rochester Press, 1993.

Machiavelli, Niccolo. *The Prince*. Reprinted in *Modern Moral and Political Philosophy*, edited by Robert C. Cummins and Thomas D. Christiano, 5–40. London: Mayfield, 1999.

MacIntyre, Alasdair. *After Virtue*. 2nd ed. South Bend, Ind.: University of Notre Dame Press, 1984.

Mackenzie, Catriona. "Imagining Oneself Otherwise." In *Relational Autonomy: Feminist Perspectives on Autonomy, Agency, and the Social Self*, edited by Catriona Mackenzie and Natalie Stoljar, 124–50. New York: Oxford University Press, 2000.

Mackenzie, Catriona, and Natalie Stoljar, eds. *Relational Autonomy: Feminist Perspectives on Autonomy, Agency, and the Social Self*. New York: Oxford University Press, 2000.

MacKinnon, Alison. *Love and Freedom: Professional Women and the Reshaping of Personal Life*. Cambridge: Cambridge University Press, 1997.

Mahoney, Martha. "Legal Images of Battered Women: Redefining the Issue of Separation," *Michigan Law Review* 90, 1 (October 1991): 1–94.

Majid, Anouar. "The Politics of Feminism in Islam," *Signs* 23, 2 (winter 1998): 321–61.

Martin, Mike W. *Love's Virtues*. Lawrence: University Press of Kansas, 1996.

Maslow, Abraham. *Motivation and Personality*. 2nd ed. New York: Harper & Row, 1970.

Meehan, Johanna. "Autonomy, Recognition and Respect: Habermas, Benjamin and Honneth." *Constellations* 1 (1994): 270–85.

Meyers, Diana Tietjens, ed. *Feminists Rethink the Self*. Boulder, Colo.: Westview, 1997.

———. *Self, Society, and Personal Choice*. New York: Columbia University Press, 1989.

Mill, John Stuart. *On Liberty*. Edited by Elizabeth Rapaport. Indianapolis: Hackett, 1978.

Miller, Jean Baker. *Toward a New Psychology of Women*. Boston: Beacon Press, 1976.

Miller, Susan L., and Charles F. Wellford. "Patterns and Correlates of Interpersonal Violence." In *Violence Between Intimate Partners*, edited by Albert P. Cardarelli, 16–28. Boston: Allyn and Bacon, 1997.

Moore, Angela M. "Intimate Violence: Does Socioeconomic Status Matter?" In *Violence Between Intimate Partners*, edited by Albert P. Cardarelli, 91–100. Boston: Allyn and Bacon, 1997.

Nagel, Thomas. *Equality and Partiality*. New York: Oxford University Press, 1991.

Narayan, Uma. *Dislocating Cultures: Identities, Traditions, and Third World Feminism*. New York: Routledge, 1997.

———. "Essence of Culture and a Sense of History: A Feminist Critique of Cultural Essentialism." *Hypatia* 13 (spring 1998): 86–106.

Nedelsky, Jennifer. "Reconceiving Autonomy: Sources, Thoughts, and Possibilities." *Yale Journal of Law and Feminism* 1 (spring 1989): 7–36.

Noddings, Nel. *Caring: A Feminine Approach to Ethics & Moral Education*. Berkeley: University of California Press, 1984.

Nozick, Robert. *The Examined Life*. New York: Simon & Schuster, 1989.

Nussbaum, Martha. "Objectification." *Philosophy and Public Affairs* 24 (fall 1995): 249–91.

———. *Women and Human Development: The Capabilities Approach*. Cambridge: Cambridge University Press, 2000.

Nussbaum, Martha, and Jonathan Glover, eds. *Women, Culture and Development: A Study of Human Capabilities*. Oxford: Clarendon Press, 1995.

Okin, Susan Moller. *Justice, Gender, and the Family*. New York: Basic Books, 1989.

———. "*Political Liberalism*, Justice, and Gender." *Ethics* 105 (October 1994): 23–43.

Okin, Susan Moller, with Respondents. *Is Multiculturalism Bad for Women?* Edited by Joshua Cohen, Matthew Howard, and Martha C. Nussbaum. Princeton, N.J.: Princeton University Press, 1999.

Oshana, Marina A. L. "Personal Autonomy and Society." *Journal of Social Philosophy* 29 (spring 1998): 81–102.

Parekh, Bhikhu. "A Varied Moral World." In *Is Multiculturalism Bad for Women?* by Susan Moller Okin and respondents. Edited by Joshua Cohen, Matthew Howard, and Martha C. Nussbaum, 69–75. Princeton, N.J.: Princeton University Press, 1999.

Pateman, Carole. "'The Disorder of Women': Women, Love, and the Sense of Justice." *Ethics* 91 (1980): 20–34.

Peters, R. S. "Freedom and the Development of the Free Man." In *Educational Judgments: Papers in the Philosophy of Education*. Edited by James F. Doyle, 119–42. London: Routledge & Kegan Paul, 1973.

Pettit, Philip. *Republicanism: A Theory of Freedom and Government*. Oxford: Clarendon Press, 1997.

Pollitt, Katha. "Whose Culture?" In *Is Multiculturalism Bad for Women?* by Susan Moller Okin and respondents. Edited by Joshua Cohen, Matthew Howard, and Martha C. Nussbaum 27–30. Princeton, N.J.: Princeton University Press.

Pratt, Minnie Bruce. "Identity: Skin Blood Heart." In *Yours in Struggle: Three Feminist Perspectives on Anti-Semitism and Racism*, edited by Elly Bulkin, Minnie Bruce Pratt, and Barbara Smith, 9–63. Brooklyn, N.Y.: Long Haul Press, 1984.

Pressman, B. "Wife-Abused Couples: The Need for Comprehensive Theoretical Perspectives and Integrated Treatment Models." *Journal of Feminist Family Therapy* 1 (1989): 23–43.

Ptacek, James. "The Tactics and Strategies of Men Who Batter: Testimony from Women Seeking Restraining Orders." In *Violence Between Intimate Partners*, edited by Albert P. Cardarelli, 104–23. Boston: Allyn and Bacon, 1997.

Rawls, John. *Political Liberalism*. New York: Columbia University Press, 1993, 1996.

———. *A Theory of Justice*. Cambridge, Mass.: Harvard University Press, 1971.

Raz, Joseph. *Engaging Reason: On the Theory of Value and Action*. Oxford: Oxford University Press, 1999.

———. *The Morality of Freedom*. Oxford: Clarendon Press, 1986.

Register, Elizabeth. "Feminism and Recovering from Battering: Working with the Individual Woman." In *Battering and Family Therapy*, edited by Marsali Hansen and Michèle Harway, 93–104. Newbury Park, Calif.: Sage, 1993.

Reiman, Jeffrey. *Critical Moral Liberalism: Theory and Practice*. Lanham, Md.: Rowman & Littlefield, 1997.

Rhode, Deborah L. *Justice and Gender*. Cambridge, Mass.: Harvard University Press, 1989.

Rice, Patricia. "Southern Baptists Call for Wives to Be Submissive." *St. Louis Post-Dispatch*, 10 June 1998, A1, 9.

Rogers, Carl. *Carl Rogers on Personal Power: Inner Strength and Its Revolutionary Impact*. London: Constable, 1978.

Rorty, Richard. *Contingency, Irony, and Solidarity*. Cambridge: Cambridge University Press, 1989.

Ross, Lee, and Richard E. Nisbett. *The Person and the Situation: Perspectives of Social Psychology*. Philadelphia: Temple University Press, 1991.

Royko, Mike. *Boss: Richard J. Daley of Chicago*. New York: New American Library, 1971.

Ruddick, Sara. *Maternal Thinking: Toward a Politics of Peace*. New York: Ballantine Books, 1989.

Saharso, Sawitri. "Female Autonomy and Cultural Imperative: Two Hearts Beating Together." In *Citizenship in Diverse Societies*, edited by Will Kymlicka and Wayne Norman, 224–42. Oxford: Oxford University Press, 2000.

Sandel, Michael J. *Democracy's Discontent: America in Search of a Public Philosophy*. Cambridge, Mass.: Belknap Press, 1996.

———. *Liberalism and the Limits of Justice*. Cambridge: Cambridge University Press, 1982.

Sartorius, Rolf, ed. *Paternalism*. Minneapolis: University of Minnesota Press, 1983.

Scanlon, Thomas. "Contractualism and Utilitarianism." In *Utilitarianism and Beyond*, edited by Amartya Sen and Bernard Williams, 103–28. Cambridge: Cambridge University Press, 1982.

Schechter, Susan, and Lisa T. Gray. "A Framework for Understanding and Empowering Battered Women." In *Abuse and Victimization across the Life Span*, edited by Martha B. Straus, 240–53. Baltimore: Johns Hopkins University Press, 1988.

Scheffler, Samuel. "The Appeal of Political Liberalism." *Ethics* 105 (October 1994): 4–22.

Schmitt, Richard. *Beyond Separateness: The Social Nature of Human Beings— Their Autonomy, Knowledge, and Power*. Boulder, Colo.: Westview, 1995.

Schneewind, Jerome. *The Invention of Autonomy: A History of Modern Moral Philosophy*. Cambridge: Cambridge University Press, 1998.

———. "The Use of Autonomy in Ethical Theory." In *Reconstructing Individualism: Autonomy, Individuality, and the Self in Western Theory*, edited by Thomas C. Heller, Morton Sosna, and David E. Wellbery, 64–75. Stanford, Calif.: Stanford University Press, 1986.

Schneider, Elizabeth. "Particularity and Generality: Challenges of Feminist Theory and Practice in Work on Woman-Abuse," *New York University Law Review* 67 (June 1992): 520–68.

Schutte, Ofelia. "Cultural Alterity: Cross-Cultural Communication and Feminist Theory in North-South Contexts." In *Decentering the Center: Philosophy for a Multicultural, Postcolonial, and Feminist World*, edited by Uma Narayan and Sandra Harding, 47–66. Bloomington: Indiana University Press, 2000.

Scruton, Roger. *Sexual Desire*. New York: Free Press, 1986.

Shachar, Ayelet. "Should Church and State Be Joined at the Altar? Women's Rights and the Multicultural Dilemma." In *Citizenship in Diverse Societies*, edited by Will Kymlicka and Wayne Norman, 199–223. Oxford: Oxford University Press, 2000.

Soble, Alan. "Union, Autonomy, and Concern." In *Love Analyzed*, edited by Roger E. Lamb, 65–92. Boulder, Colo.: Westview, 1997.

Solomon, Robert C. "The Virtue of (Erotic) Love." In *The Philosophy of (Erotic) Love*, edited by Robert C. Solomon and Kathleen M. Higgins, 492–518. Lawrence: University Press of Kansas, 1991.

Stanko, Elizabeth A. "Fear of Crime and the Myth of the Safe Home: A Feminist Critique of Criminology." In *Feminist Perspectives on Wife Abuse* edited by Kersti Yllö, and Michele Bogard, 75–88. Newbury Park, Calif.: Sage, 1990.

Stein, Laura W. "Living with the Risk of Backfire: A Response to the Feminist Critique of Privacy and Equality." *Minnesota Law Review* 77 (1993): 1153–91.

Stoljar, Natalie. "Autonomy and the Feminist Intuition," in *Relational Autonomy: Feminist Perspectives on Autonomy, Agency, and the Social Self*, edited by Catriona Mackenzie and Natalie Stoljar, 94–111. New York: Oxford University Press, 2000.

Taylor, Charles. "Atomism." In *Philosophy and the Human Sciences*, Vol. 2 of *Philosophical Papers*. Cambridge: Cambridge University Press, 1985.

———. "Responsibility for Self." In *The Identities of Persons*, edited by Amelie Oksenberg Rorty, 281–99. Berkeley: University of California Press, 1976.

———. "What Is Human Agency?" In *Human Agency and Language*, Vol. 1 of *Philosophical Papers*. New York: Cambridge University Press, 1985.

Thomas, Laurence Mordekhai. *Vessels of Evil: American Slavery and the Holocaust*. Philadelphia: Temple University Press, 1993.

Thomson, Susan C., and Kim Bell. "Mizzou Chancellor Wants Buyout." *St. Louis Post-Dispatch,* 14 June 1996, C7.

Thoreau, Henry David. "On Civil Disobedience." In *Social and Political Philosophy: Readings from Plato to Gandhi*, edited by John Somerville and Ronald E. Santoni, 282–301. Garden City, N.Y.: Anchor Books, 1963.

Tronto, Joan C. *Moral Boundaries: A Political Argument for an Ethic of Care*. New York: Routledge, 1994.

VanDe Veer, Donald. *Paternalistic Intervention*. Princeton, N.J.: Princeton University Press, 1986.

Waites, Elizabeth A. *Trauma and Survival: Post-Traumatic and Dissociative Disorders in Women*. New York: W. W. Norton, 1993.

Waldron, Jeremy. *Liberal Rights: Collected Papers 1981–1991*. Cambridge: Cambridge University Press, 1993.

Walker, Lenore. *Abused Women and Survivor Therapy: A Practical Guide for the Psychotherapist*. Washington, D.C.: American Psychological Association, 1994.

———. *The Battered Woman*. New York: HarperCollins, 1979.

———. *The Battered Woman Syndrome*. New York: Springer, 1984.

Walker, Margaret. *Moral Understandings: A Feminist Study in Ethics*. New York: Routledge, 1998.

Weir, Alison. *Sacrificial Logics: Feminist Theory and the Critique of Identity*. New York: Routledge, 1996.

Weiss, Penny, and Marilyn Friedman, eds. *Feminism and Community*. Philadelphia: Temple University Press, 1995.

Wenar, Leif. "*Political Liberalism*: An Internal Critique." *Ethics* 106 (October 1995): 32–62.

Williams, Bernard. *Moral Luck*. Cambridge: Cambridge University Press, 1981.

Ylló, Kersti, and Michele Bograd, eds. *Feminist Perspectives on Wife Abuse*. Newbury Park, Calif.: Sage, 1990.

Young, Iris Marion. "Mothers, Citizenship, and Independence: A Critique of Pure Family Values." In *Intersecting Voices: Dilemmas of Gender, Political Philosophy and Policy*. Princeton, N.J.: Princeton University Press, 1997.

Index